THE FILMS OF JAMES CAGNEY

THE FILMS OF

OTHER BOOKS BY HOMER DICKENS

THE FILMS OF MARLENE DIETRICH
THE FILMS OF GARY COOPER
THE FILMS OF KATHARINE HEPBURN

THE CITADEL PRESS   SECAUCUS, NEW JERSEY

JAMES CAGNEY

by Homer Dickens

ACKNOWLEDGMENTS

For valued assistance above and beyond the call of duty the author wishes to thank the following for giving freely of their knowledge, time and experience to make this book possible:

MARJORIE ARONSON	NORMAN MILLER
BOB BOARD	MARK RICCI
JOHN COCCHI	MARION SHAHINIAN
PHILIP KENDAL	GEORGE SHAHINIAN
AL KILGORE	ALEXANDER SOMA
LEONARD MALTIN	MICHAEL SPARKS
GORDON MATHEWS	LOU VALENTINO
DOUG MCCLELLAND	JERRY VERMILYE
DION MCGREGOR	JAMES WATTERS

DOUGLAS WHITNEY

The entire staff of the Theatre and Film Department of the New York Public Library at Lincoln Center; The British Museum's Newspaper Division (London); United Press International (L.A. and N.Y.C.); and the motion picture studios that produced the films of James Cagney.

FOR
D O N   A N D   J E N N Y
so far and yet so near
WITH LOVE

CONTENTS

The Anti-Hero 1
Rogues Gallery 31

FILMOGRAPHY

THE SHORTER FILMS 39
SINNER'S HOLIDAY 41
DOORWAY TO HELL 43
OTHER MEN'S WOMEN 45
THE MILLIONAIRE 47
THE PUBLIC ENEMY 49
SMART MONEY 54
BLONDE CRAZY 56
TAXI! 58
THE CROWD ROARS 61
WINNER TAKE ALL 64
HARD TO HANDLE 67
PICTURE SNATCHER 70
THE MAYOR OF HELL 73
FOOTLIGHT PARADE 76
LADY KILLER 80
JIMMY THE GENT 83
HE WAS HER MAN 86
HERE COMES THE NAVY 89
THE ST. LOUIS KID 92
DEVIL DOGS OF THE AIR 95
G-MEN 98
THE IRISH IN US 102
A MIDSUMMER NIGHT'S DREAM 105
FRISCO KID 111
CEILING ZERO 115
GREAT GUY 118
SOMETHING TO SING ABOUT 121
BOY MEETS GIRL 125
ANGELS WITH DIRTY FACES 129

THE OKLAHOMA KID 134
EACH DAWN I DIE 138
THE ROARING TWENTIES 143
THE FIGHTING 69TH 147
TORRID ZONE 151
CITY FOR CONQUEST 154
THE STRAWBERRY BLONDE 158
THE BRIDE CAME C.O.D. 162
CAPTAINS OF THE CLOUDS 165
YANKEE DOODLE DANDY 168
JOHNNY COME LATELY 176
BLOOD ON THE SUN 179
13 RUE MADELEINE 182
THE TIME OF YOUR LIFE 185
WHITE HEAT 188
THE WEST POINT STORY 191
KISS TOMORROW GOODBYE 194
COME FILL THE CUP 196
STARLIFT 199
WHAT PRICE GLORY? 201
A LION IS IN THE STREETS 204
RUN FOR COVER 207
LOVE ME OR LEAVE ME 210
MISTER ROBERTS 214
THE SEVEN LITTLE FOYS 217
TRIBUTE TO A BAD MAN 219
THESE WILDER YEARS 222
MAN OF A THOUSAND FACES 224
SHORT CUT TO HELL 229
NEVER STEAL ANYTHING SMALL 231
SHAKE HANDS WITH THE DEVIL 234
THE GALLANT HOURS 237
ONE, TWO, THREE 241

A Theatre Chronicle 245

THE ANTI-HERO

A BRIEF BIOGRAPHY

With the release of *The Public Enemy*, in 1931, a new brand of screen idol emerged: the *anti-hero*. When James Cagney squashed a half-grapefruit into the whining face of Mae Clarke, gasps were heard in movie houses around the world. The Cagney style of woman-mauling (like that of his great contemporary, Edward G. Robinson) brought cheers from men, but, at first, disapproval from women, whose taste inexorably ruled the screen.

Through that simple, yet forceful, gesture with the grapefruit, the impudent, red-haired young actor be-

came an overnight sensation; he was the screen's most dynamic actor. He treated most things with contempt, including women, but there was enough charm in his grin to reach the last row in the balcony. Thus, a "new realism" was born out of Depression-ridden America, and audiences soon relished every move Cagney made as he rebelled against a society he not only did not help create, but felt compelled to challenge.

Cagney represented the perfect portrait of the American urban man and boy—in all his complexities—whose life was so insecure in the Thirties. This was

1

apparent in his every gesture: his walk, his nervous fists, his abrupt silences and his steadily mounting rage. Not surprisingly, his fast-talking, finger-jabbing traits became trademarks, and mimics had a field day. The fact that he conveyed every emotion with his entire body, not just his face or voice, added immeasurably to his persuasiveness. Moviegoers were fascinated by him.

His early training as a hoofer stood him in good stead, for only an actor who had previously been a dancer could possibly have moved with the economy and easy balance with which Cagney managed his bantam physique.

Warners was quick to latch onto his explosive, engaging and candid personality. "He's Irish, but good-natured," touted an early Warners press release. All of his action-packed scripts were tailored to his personality, a neat blend of cocky conceit and cool charm —a mixture that spelled dynamite at the box office. Cagney was quick to note that the receipts of his pictures warranted fatter paychecks for him. Thus began a relentless battle with the brothers Warner for bigger salaries and more liberal contracts. During the filming of *The Public Enemy* he made $450 a week. By 1941, he was earning an annual salary of $362,500.

However, it is a credit to Cagney's innate intelligence that he was not condemned to continue playing only gangster roles, because of his rightness in the role of Tom Powers in *The Public Enemy*, until he was diluted and weakened "in type" as so many in Hollywood had been before and have been since.

As early as 1932, critic Lincoln Kirstein summed up the Cagney appeal: "Cagney has an inspired sense of timing, an arrogant style, a pride in the control of his body and a conviction and lack of self-consciousness that is unique in the deserts of the American screen. . . . No one expresses more clearly in terms of pictorial action the delights of violence, the overtones of a semiconscious sadism, the tendency toward destruction, toward anarchy, which is the base of American sex-appeal."

Cagney was not in any sense an actor who was dependent upon an occasional brilliant director or a chance excellent script. Nor was he one who benefitted solely from the editor's craft. He was, and always remained, an original.

Few actors could afford to destroy their own charm in the creation of a role, as Cagney never hesitated to do. In *Devil Dogs of the Air* he was an insufferable braggart; in *The Fighting 69th*, a coward; in *The Crowd Roars*, an overbearing racing driver; in *Love*

Me or Leave Me, continually cruel to Doris Day. Granted, by the final reel, he had usually vindicated himself, but he either had to die or to reform to accomplish this.

But as hard and tough as he was on the screen, he was modest and retiring off: "My biggest concern is that doing a rough-and-tumble scene I might hurt someone accidentally." Jimmy Cagney does not believe that development of a characterization necessitates what is known as "living the role." "Far from it," he once told a reporter. "All I try to do is to realize the man I'm playing fully, then put as much into my acting as I know how. To do it, I draw upon all that I've ever known, heard, seen or remember."

When asked about star quality, he replied: "Star quality is difficult to define. I'd say it is an awareness of technique—a skill which prevents anything coming between the actor and his audience. . . . The technique is built up from many things. But it starts with observation."

Reviewing his sixty-odd films, one wonders why Warners never presented him with a workable script of James T. Farrell's *Studs Lonigan*, the symbol of Irish-American youth. It would have made the perfect Cagney vehicle.

James Francis Cagney, Jr., was born on July 17, 1899 (although studio biographies early in his career altered that to read 1904, and it stuck), above his father's saloon at the corner of Avenue D and Eighth Street on New York City's lower East Side. At that time, and for many years thereafter, this section was known as the "gas house district," on the southern border of the notorious "Hell's Kitchen."

He was the second of five children born to James Francis Cagney and Carolyn Nelson Cagney. Mr. Cagney's family was descended from the O'Caignes of County Leitrim and his mother was half-Irish, half-Norwegian.

His father was a good man, but too easy-going. More often than not, he drank more than his customers did. When Jimmy was but a year old, the Cagney clan moved uptown to First Avenue, between 79th and 80th streets. Seven years later, they moved to 96th Street, between Third and Lexington avenues, the northern tip of the Yorkville section. Says Cagney, "That always sticks in my memory as a street of stark tragedy, somehow. It seems, as I look back, that there was always crepe hanging on a door or two somewhere on the block. There was always the clanging of an ambulance bell. Patrol wagons came often. . . ."

The neighborhood was hardly luxurious; in fact, it

James Francis Cagney, Jr., at one

Self-confidence at ten

At the beach with younger brother Bill

A member of the Yorkville Nut Club

As a clerk at Wanamaker's

As second chorus "girl" from left in vaudeville act

was a lower middle-class working family district. The Cagney's neighbors included Germans, Italians, Hungarians, Irish and Jews. By his teens, Jimmy could speak fluent Yiddish (a talent that crept into several of his films, viz., his humorous contretemps with the Jewish man in *Taxi!*).

All of the Cagney boys had after-school jobs, but Jimmy, who functioned better, even at an early age, when he took on more work, sometimes held as many as three jobs simultaneously. Recalling this period of his life, he once said: "During one vacation, I wrapped bundles for Wanamaker's department store during the day. At night I was a switchboard operator and attendant [and sort of general bouncer] at a pool hall. On Sunday, my day off, I sold tickets for the Hudson River Day Line. It was good for me. I feel sorry for the kid who has too cushy a time of it. Suddenly he has to come face-to-face with the realities of life without any papa or mama to do his thinking for him."

At fourteen, he was a copy boy for the *New York Sun*. Whether Jimmy was on the block or in the school yard the familiar cry "Y'wanna fight?" greeted his ears. Typically, he would answer "Sure!" and the fight was on. Soon this bantamweight was highly respected throughout the Yorkville section.

Jimmy, at seventeen, was a bellhop in the Friars' Club while attending high school during the day. His ambition, at this juncture, was to become an artist. His mother encouraged him in this endeavor. He then got a job as custodian in a branch of the New York Public Library at 67th Street and First Avenue. "Custodian is certainly a title," he once said. "My job was to gather in the books, wheel them round, and put them in their proper places on the shelves."

He graduated from Stuyvesant High School and got a job as a junior architect. The pay was good and, as Jimmy later put it, "We needed every penny." But his wise mother, Carrie, persuaded him to continue his education and work in the evenings. So he entered Columbia University for a course in Fine Arts, meanwhile working as a waiter in a restaurant. Within two weeks, Jimmy managed to get his brother Harry a job as a waiter and later Eddie. Then fourteen-year-old Bill, the youngest Cagney boy, got into the act. One day, when the cashier became ill, Jimmy, in his usual enterprising manner, suggested a fine woman of reliable character to take care of the cash. Before he could get his mother the job, the cashier recovered and returned to work. The manager soon discovered that the four boys were brothers, and they were fired *en masse*.

Along with his brothers Harry and Edward, Jimmy was sent to the Lenox Hill Settlement House to take a course in public speaking. From time to time, the Settlement staged little plays in which the boys and girls of the neighborhood took part. Harry got a small part in a Chinese pantomime, while brother Jimmy worked as a painter of the backdrop. However, to aid the family's financial situation, Harry took a job during his after-school hours and, reluctantly, had to withdraw from the Chinese pantomime. Jimmy took over the part at his suggestion. He wasn't crazy about the idea, for he was the catcher for the Yorkville Nut Club, a boys' team in the neighborhood. But to help the boys put their show on, he agreed.

Jimmy found his first theatrical experience as stimulating as it was interesting. He then joined the Society because he liked the gang there more than his friends on the baseball team, which had occupied much of his spare time up to that point. Other spare time had been devoted to taking part in several amateur boxing elimination contests (in his mid-teens) resulting in the status of runner-up for the New York State lightweight title.

The next Settlement production had Jimmy in another Oriental role, this time as an emperor in a Japanese musical comedy called *What, for Why?* Later, in an Italian harlequinade, especially written by a member of the Society, he appeared as Pagliaccio.

Finally Jimmy got his first leading role in Lord Dunsany's one-act play *The Lost Silk Hat*. At about that time, the Dramatic Society of Hunter College, a well-known girls' school (which has since become co-ed), used guest actors from the Lenox Hill Settlement Society for the male parts. In a period costume melodrama, *The Two Orphans*, he played the part of Picard, a young butler.

In the fall of 1918, a Spanish influenza epidemic swept the Eastern seaboard and Jimmy's father died, at forty-two. Shortly thereafter, his sister Jeanne was born. At this point, Jimmy was in his sixth month of study at Columbia, but withdrew in order to help with family expenses. By the following year, he was back wrapping bundles at Wanamaker's. To keep his acting itch satisfied, he appeared in a two-act verse drama entitled *The Faun* and captured the audience's attention as he bounded over the stage in a costume made, rather skimpily, of goat skin.

He became friendly with a Wanamaker salesman, formerly a vaudeville actor, who told Jimmy about a show that was then on the boards of Keith's 86th Street Theatre. It seemed that the management needed a re-

Mr. and Mrs. James Cagney in Hollywood

placement for a boy who had just left the cast.

Cagney auditioned and was accepted for an engagement with this vaudeville show, called *Every Sailor*, a wartime revue that was still popular with audiences. However, he was horrified to learn that he was to play a comic female impersonator along with seven other boys. He almost refused, but in 1919 a weekly salary of $25 was too good to pass up. There were eight fellows dressed as girls trying to woo the sailor in the act. Jimmy was one of the *girls!*

On "his" opening night, Mrs. Cagney, still the indomitable guardian of the clan, arrived with family and friends galore to cheer Jimmy on. Once he made his appearance, they all sat stunned until Carrie firmly passed the word to "Applaud!" He remained with this well-paying act for eight weeks.

In the summer of 1920, Jimmy went to an open-call audition for a new Broadway musical entitled *Pitter Patter*. Said Cagney later: "I didn't know the highland fling from a sailor's hornpipe and I couldn't even sing 'Sweet Adeline' but I needed that job. Fifty applicants assembled. I watched the fellow's feet next to me and did what he did." His ingenuity certainly paid off, for

he was hired as a chorus boy for *Pitter Patter* at $35 a week. In twelve weeks he was given a specialty in the show and added $15 to his weekly salary as a dresser for William Kent, the star, and later performed similar services for Ernest Truex, who replaced Kent. Jimmy also got the opportunity of understudying these gentlemen after a brief time, but, alas, neither missed a performance.

Pitter Patter, adapted from the farce *Caught in the Rain* by William Collier and Grant Stewart, boasted a book by Will M. Hough and music and lyrics by William B. Friedlander. It opened at the Longacre Theatre on September 29, 1920, and was a hit. When the play toured, Cagney was not only Truex's dresser, but took on still another job, worth $10 more a week, caring for the baggage. Obviously, the busier he was, the better he liked it.

Also in that male chorus line was young Allen Jenkins, who later appeared as Jimmy's sidekick in many a Warners film. On the distaff side of the chorus line was a petite young Iowa girl named Frances Willard (Billie) Vernon. One evening Billie was waiting for a date that didn't show up and the doorman asked Jimmy: "Why don't you take her to dinner?"

"I'd like to," he replied, "but I haven't the money."

"I'll take *you*," Billie said.

When *Pitter Patter* closed in 1921, he and Billie were married. They set out in the vaudeville circuits, either together (as "Vernon and Nye") or separately. Said Cagney: "My wife was much better known than I was; her name meant something, mine didn't. The name of Nye was a rearrangement of the last syllable of my name." So, for the next few years, they hit what must have been every tank town in the United States, the route Jimmy later referred to as "the Cagney circuit." As a beginner, he had to do the circuits until he became known.

A few years before, a certain round-faced actor wrote and produced an act called *Dot's My Boy*, which concerned a Jewish boy acting on the stage under an Irish name. The man who had been playing the part was now too old, and Cagney got the job. The actor-writer-producer was Hugh Herbert. The revamped act met with success everywhere.

After he left Herbert, Jimmy toured with the Jaffe Troupe, headed by Ada Jaffe, the mother of Sam Jaffe. During this time, Billie became a member of a "sister" act playing towns along the same route traveled by her husband. Her "sister" was Wynne Gibson, who later became a star at Paramount.

Finally, Jimmy and Billie got an opportunity to

At the Ambassador Hotel with Mr. and Mrs. William
Cagney (Boots Mallory), Mrs. James
Cagney, Sr., and Jeanne Cagney

appear in the same act when the Shuberts packaged a
complete unit of shows to tour the States. Cagney and
the "sister" act were incorporated into *Lew Fields'
Ritz Girls* of 1922.

After two more years of solid trouping, the Cagneys
landed in Los Angeles, where they visited Billie's
mother, who had never met her son-in-law. Jimmy had
no thoughts about breaking into the movies until Billie
and he discussed the possibilities of settling down in
that area. He needed a job, but knew no one in Hollywood. Therefore, he tried vaudeville, which he did
know. He and a partner, Harry Gribbon, opened an
act in San Pedro, but it flopped and the newly formed
team soon parted.

He even tried teaching dance, but this proved unsuccessful at that time, because the few students that
applied knew more than he did. "That finished me as
a dancing-school boss for some years!" he said.

Jimmy and Billie then went to Chicago, and managed
to exist doing a variety of odd jobs when they were
not appearing as Vernon and Nye in an act called
"Out-of-Town Papers." He finally got into a big vaudeville act, in which he did a dramatic sketch with Victor
Kilian, who later left the act to appear in Eugene
O'Neill's *Desire Under the Elms.*

Not long afterward, Kilian got in touch with Jimmy

to tell him that the juvenile lead was about to leave
his company. He urged Jimmy to audition for the part,
and advised, "Give it everything you've got."

Jimmy auditioned for the stage manager, who did
not consider him the right type for the O'Neill drama,
but, because of his carrot-red hair and 5-foot 8-inch
frame, did think him ideal for a part in a play the
same producers were planning to produce in the fall.
Thinking that this was a polite brush-off ("Don't call
us, we'll call you"), he returned to vaudeville.

But in the fall of 1925, he was summoned to read
for, and eventually got a part in, Maxwell Anderson's
Outside Looking In, a dramatization of Jim Tully's
hobo yarn *Beggars of Life.* Jimmy was Little Red and
Charles Bickford was dynamic as Oklahoma Red. He
was given $150 a week, but, shortly after the opening,
he signed a "run-of-the-play" contract at $200 a week.

Critic Burns Mantle noted: "If you are interested
in mean, noble, cruel and witty vagabonds, there is
a chance . . . to see one of them in *Outside Looking In.*
Mr. Charles A. Bickford, as Oklahoma Red, imper-
sonates a frontier Villon, and he does it so well that
you can renew your waning faith in the art of histrionics. He and Mr. James Cagney, as his adversary,
Little Red, do the most honest acting now to be seen
in New York. I believe that Mr. Barrymore's effective
performance of Hamlet would be a mere feat of elo-
cution if compared to the characterizations of either
Mr. Bickford or Mr. Cagney, both of whom are unknown."

When *Outside Looking In* closed, Jimmy was invited
to join the Theatre Guild, which then boasted Edward
G. Robinson as one of their stars, but he refused when
he learned that the salary wouldn't match the prestige.

One of the biggest successes then in New York was
Broadway, the Philip Dunning-George Abbott gangster melodrama, with Lee Tracy in the leading role. Jed
Harris, the producer, and the playwrights were about
to cast the London company when Cagney's name came
up. Dunning had seen the Maxwell Anderson play and
had been impressed with Cagney's work as Little Red.
Thus, Jimmy was offered the leading role of Roy Lane,
the hoofer, in the London company. It was quite
sudden, and too good to be true. Two weeks of intensive rehearsals followed and the company was about
to sail for London, with a show every bit as good as
the New York group, when the producers, suddenly
thinking Cagney was not right in the part, fired him.

They had given a great dress rehearsal and the Cagneys had even given a farewell party before sailing
(their trunks were already aboard the ship) when they

6

were told the bad news. The one thing that saved the day was Cagney's "run-of-the-play" contract. If he had wanted to enforce it, he could have collected his weekly paycheck during the complete London run, although he wouldn't have been able to work elsewhere during that time. However, Jed Harris offered him an alternative in the matter: he could understudy Lee Tracy. Jimmy accepted, and, in time, he replaced Roy R. Lloyd in the part of Mike.

Once Cagney's London company contract expired, he went into rehearsals of *Women Go On Forever*, starring Mary Boland and directed by John Cromwell. Everyone had high hopes for Daniel N. Rubin's bleak drama, but, as Cagney later said: "Mary Boland, who starred, had decided to abandon comic roles and return to serious dramas. On opening night, Mary's first word was 'hummph!' and the audience broke up. That was the end of that play. We ran for eighteen weeks, but it wasn't the play we started with."

During the run of *Women Go On Forever*, Jimmy decided, now that he was an expert hoofer, to open a tap-dancing school. It was christened the Cagné School of the Dance and was strictly for hoofers, *i.e.*, professional dancers. Its base was in Elizabeth, New Jersey, where rents were decidedly cheaper, and Billie ran it most of the time, with Jimmy devoting whatever time he could to it in his spare hours.

It proved to be a somewhat lucrative venture, but, more importantly, it gave Cagney a chance to stage the dances, as well as dance and act in, *The Grand Street Follies of 1928*, subtitled "A Topical Revue of the Season." It was a sparkling show with the young cast taking pot-shots at theatre notables like Ina Claire and Ethel Barrymore, and successful plays of the day like *Dracula*. While some parts dragged, critics were enthusiastic about Dorothy Sands' impersonation of Mae West and Paula Trueman's take-off on Helen Hayes. Jimmy followed up this engagement with stock in Cleveland and in Stockbridge, Massachusetts.

His next Broadway assignment was in *The Grand Street Follies of 1929*. Jimmy acted and danced, but the dances were staged by Dave Gould. He was funny in a sketch called "The A.B.C. of Traffic" as a dancing cop and as a harlequin in "I Need You So."

George Kelly's *Maggie the Magnificent* then offered him the role of Elwood. Also in the cast was a pert, sassy blonde actress named Joan Blondell. They soon became fast friends. While most of the critics agreed that this play was second-rate Kelly, Robert Littell, writing in the *New York World*, stated: "The direction and acting of this humdrum tragi-comedy did not add

to its virtues. Except for the tantalizingly brief appearance of Joan Blondell, a sympathetic young lover by Frank Rowan, and the perfect gas-house lingo of James Cagney, the acting was, to say the least, hard and graceless."

It opened on October 22, 1929, and had a deservedly short life. George Kelly liked Cagney, and from his experience in this play Jimmy learned much about timing and technique. One evening before the curtain went up during the brief run, Jimmy told Joan that a Hollywood talent scout was out front, but he apparently was not sufficiently impressed to make an offer.

However, Blondell and Cagney were to meet again, in a few months time, in a play called *Penny Arcade* by Marie Baumer, which William Keighley and W. P. Tanner were producing with Keighley directing. This time, they both gained personal notices. It opened on March 10, 1930. Arthur Ruhl, in the *New York Herald Tribune* noted: "James Cagney was . . . all there as the good-for-nothing son. Joan Blondell was just right as the flip assistant to the long-suffering photographer." The *Times* critic thought: "Some capable actors have been summoned to the task of impersonating these various characters. The play contains an excellent performance by James Cagney as the weakling." They were hits, but the play was a failure—it closed three weeks later.

Al Jolson, then at the height of his career, bought the screen rights to *Penny Arcade* and re-sold them to Warner Bros. with the stipulation that Cagney and

Keeping in shape

Blondell repeat their roles in the screen version. Jimmy was hired at $400 a week with a three-week guarantee, plus train fare to and from the Coast. However, before filming began, Warners wanted to test Jimmy for photographic effects, costume, make-up, lighting and so forth. He was not only nervous in this new medium, he also found it difficult adhering to the chalked floor directions given him by the test director. When the scene began, it was apparent that Cagney could not be confined to a certain area and a new scene, allowing maximum freedom of movement, was selected.

Penny Arcade, re-titled *Sinner's Holiday*, was a real quickie under John G. Adolfi's direction. Grant Withers, Evalyn Knapp and Lucille La Verne were assigned the top roles. Cagney's depiction of the cowardly son who tries to frame an innocent man with a crime he committed was a telling piece of work and convinced Warners that they should utilize his talents.

He was immediately put in, in support of Lew Ayres, *Doorway to Hell*, one of the best of the early gangster pictures. The Cagney screen image was beginning to take hold. As Steve Mileway, Ayres' righthand man, Jimmy gave a memorable performance.

His third film assignment was again with Joan Blondell, but they were unhappily pushed into the background in a love triangle between Grant Withers, Mary Astor and Regis Toomey called *The Steel Highway*. By the time that this William A. Wellman melodrama was released, its title had been changed to *Other Men's Women*, which made little sense.

Jimmy almost got the lead in *The Front Page*. Director Lewis Milestone, who had been impressed with him in *Sinner's Holiday* and *Doorway to Hell*, once told an interviewer: "I originally wanted Jimmy Cagney to play Hildy Johnson. Zanuck agreed, but Howard Hughes wouldn't accept him—he considered Cagney 'a little runt'; this was before Cagney had made his mark in *Public Enemy*." Milestone later got even with Hughes when he informed the millionaire playboy that Jean Harlow, whose contract Hughes owned, had no talent and he better sell her contract to MGM for $60,000, which he later did.

George Arliss, one of the few stars on the Warner payroll with cast selection and approval, had noticed Jimmy's work and thought he would be ideal as the bold insurance salesman in his film *The Millionaire*, based on the story "Idle Hands" by Earl Derr Biggers. Arliss, who had a keen eye for talent, was not wrong. Jimmy benefited greatly from his brief (one-scene) bit in this picture. Further evidence of Arliss' instinctive sense about performers was Bette Davis, whom he

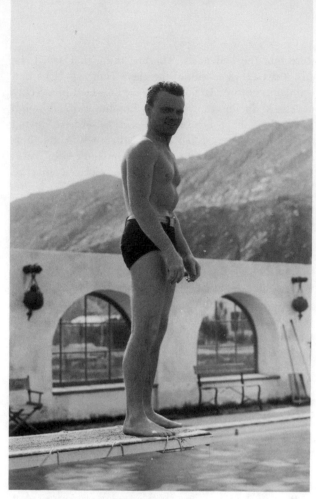

Enjoying his pool

had also helped that same year in *The Man Who Played God*. He played an important part in both these players' careers.

Arriving in Hollywood about the same time as Cagney were two ex-Chicago newspaper reporters, Kubec Glasmon and John Bright, with a story of the Chicago underworld they hoped to peddle to one of the Hollywood studios. Their saga, *Beer and Blood*, concerned two hoodlums of the Prohibition era who eventually met violent ends. Edward Woods had the lead and Cagney, who had worked previously for director Wellman in *Other Men's Women*, was selected as his sidekick, Matt Doyle.

Said director Wellman years later: "We hire a guy named Eddie Woods to play the lead. We get a relatively unknown guy named Jimmy Cagney who has a tough little way, and he is playing the second part. I didn't see the rushes for three days because I was working late and said, 'Aw, to hell with them. I'll see them over the weekend.' When I looked at the rushes I said

At 1934 Film Star's Frolic with Jimmy Durante, Eddie Cantor, Ann Harding, Adolphe Menjou, and Robert Woolsey

[to head of production Darryl F. Zanuck], 'Look, there is a horrible mistake. We have the wrong guy in here. Cagney should be the lead.' Zanuck said, 'Well, you know who Eddie Woods is, don't you?' And I said, 'No, I don't. Who is he?' 'He's engaged to marry Louella Parsons' daughter.' I said, 'Well, for Christ's sake, are you going to let some newspaperwoman run your business?' He said, 'Change them.' We changed them, and Cagney became a big star.' "

By the time it was released, this film not only had a new star, it also had a new title: *The Public Enemy*. It was the first film of the gangster genre that gave a background to the criminals, in effect shifting the blame for their lawlessness onto society.

The Public Enemy was generally well conceived, although most critics found it too similar to other current fare. The direction had pace and potency, style and substance, and it was agreed that the acting was first-rate. Besides Cagney and Woods, the cast included Jean Harlow (just prior to her association with Metro-Goldwyn-Mayer), who gave poor readings at the beginning but by the end had gained in stature. Mae Clarke as Kitty was in only two scenes, but won the distinction of being the recipient of the half-grapefruit Cagney wielded at the breakfast table, possibly the most memorable movie scene of the thirties. Joan Blon-

dell, Donald Cook, Leslie Fenton and Beryl Mercer rounded out the cast.

After two films with William Wellman, Cagney was cast as Nick the hard-as-nails chauffeur in the director's next film, *Night Nurse*, starring Barbara Stanwyck. However, Warners withdrew him from this assignment when the "rushes" of *The Public Enemy* had been screened. Seeing his potential, they began looking around for a bigger part for this young dynamo. He was replaced by Clark Gable, on loan from MGM, while Mildred Harris, cast the same time as Jimmy, was replaced by Charlotte Merriam.

The team of Kubec Glasmon and John Bright wrote Cagney's next four pictures. While *The Public Enemy* was being edited, he was assigned to *Smart Money* with Edward G. Robinson. Warners wasted no time in teaming this dynamic duo in the same flick, to capitalize on *Little Caesar* and *The Public Enemy*. Like these two films, *Smart Money* made money for the studio.

In *Larceny Lane*, subsequently entitled *Blonde Crazy*, Jimmy got his first star billing. As Bert Harris, an opportunistic young con man with a gift of gab, he was first-rate in a series of misadventures. His support included Joan Blondell, Noel Francis, Louis Calhern and another young actor on the rise, Raymond Milland.

9

At the Cocoanut Grove with Alice Faye, Phil Regan, Pat O'Brien and Billie

At Jack Oakie's *Gone With the Wind* party with Dick Powell, Joan Blondell and Billie

Again, Cagney's vitality and enormous energy uplifted all the action director Roy Del Ruth injected into the film.

With *Blonde Crazy* in the can, Cagney—who was still making the same $450 a week—staged his first walk-out and departed for New York. The studio executives were up in arms, but little did they realize the effect that Cagney would have on other actors in the industry from then on. His last three films had surpassed anything his studio had envisioned, but they hadn't made him a new offer. After three months, on October 13, 1931, Cagney and Jack L. Warner signed a new five-year contract, effective November 1st, at $1,000 a week, with an option at $1,400.

The first film under this new agreement was *The Blind Spot*, which became *Taxi, Please*, which became *Taxi!* His leading lady, bettering that average, changed *four* times: Joan Blondell was replaced by Dorothy Mackaill, who was replaced by Nancy Carroll, who was—finally—replaced by Loretta Young. This time Warners used Cagney's explosive personality on the side of good in a rough-and-ready action story concerning independent cabbies caught up in a ,full-fledged union war. Jimmy displayed his usual strength and chip-on-the-shoulder attitude throughout, while Miss Young was convincing as his young wife. Dorothy Burgess and David Landau were standouts as a pair of underworld lovers. A strange fact came to light when work began on this film: Cagney had never learned to drive. The studio insisted that he learn in order to handle scenes with the cabs.

The gangster-racketeer cycle was coming to an abrupt end, because pressure groups were complaining that movies like *The Public Enemy* and *Little Caesar* glamorized these types, so Warners quickly put Jimmy's pugnacious charm to use elsewhere. His next role was a hot-tempered racing driver in Howard Hawks' *The Crowd Roars*. The director's attention to the smallest details of this dangerous sport and his passion for accurate atmosphere made this film more than just a routine programmer. Cagney's co-stars were Ann Dvorak, Joan Blondell, Eric Linden and Frank McHugh.

With cronies Russell Gleason, James Gleason, Stuart Irwin, Robert Armstrong and Boris Karloff

The rat pack (old and dear friends): Spencer Tracy, Pat O'Brien, Frank McHugh and Lynn Overman

For the role of Jim Kane in *Winner Take All*, Cagney trained in Palm Springs for three weeks under the tutelage of Harvey Perry, a former bantam and flyweight boxer who also played a role in the film. Roy Del Ruth directed, with fine results. Cagney played a young fighter who gets involved with a society girl, played with spunk by Virginia Bruce.

Jimmy then asked Warners for another raise, basing his demand on the premise that "a player should be in a position to demand what he is worth so long as

11

he is worth it. When his box-office value drops, his earnings should be lopped off accordingly." He further pointed out that the last few pictures he had just completed were cheaply made but were very profitable for the studio.

So he left for New York again, telling the press that if Warners didn't meet his demands for a substantial increase, he would quit the business and become a doctor. Warners suspended him, and during the next five months at least one major studio offered to buy his contract for $150,000, but was refused.

Said Cagney: "I feel that I have given the best years of my life working for inadequate compensation. My employers can't see my way so I'm through. I have dispensed with my home here and next week I'm leaving for a tour of America and Europe. While abroad, I'll very probably accept vaudeville offers.

"Luck gave me my break, I received honors, but I could not obey the studio code, so after my return to America I'll write a book called *Luck, Honor and Obey*. I hope you'll like it. After that I'm turning seriously to the study of medicine."

During this lay-off period, Warners gave the leading role in *Blessed Event*, a play they had especially purchased for Cagney, to Lee Tracy. He was, reportedly, also being considered, along with Spencer Tracy and Paul Muni, for the leading role in *I Am a Fugitive From a Chain Gang*. Muni got it and made film history with his vivid performance. It was also rumored that Cagney would return to Broadway in Albert Bein's *Little Ol' Boy*, but this did not materialize. More pressure came when Mary Pickford announced that she wanted Jimmy for her leading man in a waterfront story, *Shanty Town*.

The wage dispute was finally settled, in September 1932, between Cagney and Darryl F. Zanuck and Jack L. Warner, with Frank Capra as the arbitrator assigned by the Academy of Motion Picture Arts and Sciences. Jimmy was now to make $3,000 weekly, with increases at stated intervals, to go up to $4,500 by 1935.

When Cagney returned to work on October 15, 1932, it was announced that he would make *Bad Boy* with Carole Lombard, on loan from Paramount, as his co-star. Negotiations fell through regarding Lombard, who had just completed a loan-out at Columbia called *Virtue* with Pat O'Brien and Mayo Methot and was being recalled by her studio. Meanwhile, work began on the Houston Branch story, now entitled *The Inside*. Mervyn LeRoy was assigned the directorial chores, and Mary Brian and Ruth Donnelly were key supports. In this flick, Cagney played a no-holds-barred press agent

who got into plenty of trouble. By the completion, the title had undergone two more changes. First to *Hard to Hold* and finally to *Hard to Handle* (as apt a title for Cagney as *Bad Boy*). LeRoy directed in his usual frenzied style, with strong emphasis on humor.

The "hard to handle" star went immediately into *Picture Snatcher* for director Lloyd Bacon, and, with his usual gusto, played an ex-con who becomes a photographer for a scandal sheet. Patricia Ellis was the heroine, but critical nods, and audience approval, went to Alice White and Ralph Bellamy, along with Cagney. Bacon's direction was crisp, and he kept the pace moving along in this action-packed yarn.

Archie Mayo, who had directed Cagney's second film, *Doorway to Hell*, was now given the assignment of directing star Jimmy in an opus called *Reform School*. This was a strong melodrama in which Cagney smashed the evil administration of a boy's reformatory and established a self-rule system. This time he was a mobster who did a good turn for boys behind bars. The release title was *The Mayor of Hell* and his co-star was Madge Evans. Dudley Digges, in a major supporting role, gave a memorable performance as the reform school's evil boss. It was later re-made by Warners, with some modifications, as *Crime School*, with Humphrey Bogart.

Spending his leisure hours aboard his yacht
Martha

At radio broadcast of "Revlon Revue" with
Gertrude Lawrence

With Jack L. Warner

In April 1933, Cagney was reportedly to play the role of Biff Grimes in Henry Duffy's West Coast stage production of *One Sunday Afternoon*, which he ultimately did much later as *The Strawberry Blonde*.

Although Jimmy actually danced for the first time on the screen in *Taxi!*, *Footlight Parade* finally gave him the opportunity to strut his stuff as a song-and-dance man who produces live prologues for movie theatres. Lloyd Bacon and Busby Berkeley shared the director's chair—Bacon concentrating on the over-all storyline, while Berkeley worked out his intricate musical numbers. Cagney and Ruby Keeler were memorable in the "Shanghai Lil" number, where one can glimpse, ever so briefly, young John Garfield (in close-up) as a sailor behind a table during the fight scene.

The huge cast also included Dick Powell, Joan Blondell, Frank McHugh, Guy Kibbee, Claire Dodd and Hugh Herbert. This was one of the best of Warner's super-duper musical extravaganzas and has withstood countless revivals. *Footlight Parade* remains one of Cagney's favorite films. After the success of *Footlight Parade* Warners planned to re-team him with Ruby Keeler in *Stage Struck*, but the part eventually went to Pat O'Brien.

In the delightful farce *Lady Killer*, Cagney went to being a racketeer who, while trying to escape his underworld associations, accidentally becomes a movie star. The film took many pot-shots at Hollywood customs and mores. The gal to take all those Cagney knocks was, again, Mae Clarke. This time, however, she didn't rate a grapefruit in the kisser, although she *was* dragged around by the hair. The dependable Warners stock company supplied the necessary support, with winning results.

Next on Cagney's agenda was a slick, fast-paced farce that went through three titles. *The Heir Chaser* became *Always a-Gent* became *Jimmy the Gent*, but, whatever the title, this was a breezy, fun-packed and nimbly played comedy, with Jimmy as an "heir-chaser" who provides heirs to heirless fortunes. In this film he tries to win back a competitor's top assistant, whom he loves, in the bargain. Bette Davis, wasted on such rompings, was nonetheless fun, and she delivered her lines with her accustomed polish ("You're the greatest chiseler since Michelangelo"). Alan Dinehart was in top form, as were Mayo Methot and Alice White. Allen Jenkins provided more laughs.

It was during this time that William Cagney entered films as an actor, appearing in such movies as *Palooka* for Reliance Pictures and *Ace of Aces*. It is strange to notice that, in Paramount's *Stolen Harmony* (1935),

Bill emulated Jimmy's "dance of death" from *The Public Enemy* at the climax when he was shot in the gutter. Bill married Boots Mallory and later became an agent and then a producer.

Cagney's next film was his seventh and last film with Joan Blondell, and it was certainly one of their strangest. Originally entitled *Without Honor*, the film features Jimmy as an ex-con fleeing the law who runs across a prostitute on the way to marry a Portuguese fisherman (Victor Jory). Lloyd Bacon directed this without his usual dash. The public saw it as *He Was Her Man*. It was not popular and, because Blondell was cast as a prostitute, it has not made the television circuits yet.

Warners followed this grisly tale with a rip-snorting naval yarn called *Here Comes the Navy*, which began the eight-picture association of Cagney with Pat O'Brien. Lloyd Bacon was in his element here and directed with verve, so the action never flagged. The humor was goodnatured and raucous, while the training and life of the peace-time sailor had genuine appeal. One change had come about, however. The powerful Legion of Decency had come into full effect and this was Cagney's first film after its production code took the industry by storm. In order not to offend this pressure group, producers bent to their will. As a consequence, Jimmy didn't smack Dorothy Tree in this film, he merely glared at her.

It was announced that Cagney's next picture would be *Goin' to Town* with Gene Markey and Kathryn Scola scripting, but Paramount's Mae West beat 'em to it. *The Patent Leather Kid*, the Richard Barthelmess-Molly O'Day silent was being considered for Cagney and Ginger Rogers. Jimmy, also, was to join Margaret Lindsay in *Gentlemen Are Born*, but Dick Powell and Josephine Hutchinson replaced them and the title became *Happiness Ahead*.

While director Frank Lloyd was filming portions of *Mutiny on the Bounty* for MGM at Catalina Island, Cagney reportedly pulled up along side in his yacht, *Martha*, and asked, "Any chance of a job, Mr. Lloyd? I'm laid off for a couple of weeks" Lloyd's cameramen were fixing reflectors and preparing a deck shot on that particular day, and Jimmy was welcomed aboard. He was given a uniform of the King's Navy and worked alongside the other men during the day's shooting. Whether his "bit" was used in the finished film is anybody's guess. It is interesting to note that Frank Lloyd would direct Jimmy ten years later in *Blood on the Sun*.

Cagney was also slated to do *King of the Ritz* and

14

At a charity function with Fredric March, Joan Crawford and conductor Leopold Stokowski

then something called *Boulder Dam*, which was changed to *Backfire*, but these projects did not pan out.

Cagney made the headlines in 1935, when Ella Winter, divorced wife of writer Lincoln Steffens, tried to implicate him in a "Red plot," saying that she had the actor's money for the cause. There was something about an asserted contribution by Cagney to Miss Winter for strike relief in Imperial Valley labor trouble, but the rap never stuck.

Cagney's pictures were getting better budgets, but, while Warners were beginning to spend a little money on his pictures, they still contained much of the same old ingredients. *The St. Louis Kid*, directed by Ray Enright, was full of action and accentuated one of the problems of the day—the milk war between dairy farmers and truckers. Patricia Ellis was back as Jimmy's leading lady, and Allen Jenkins was again on hand to supply the laughs.

Devil Dogs of the Air did for the Marine Flying Corps what *Here Comes the Navy* did for the Navy.

Lloyd Bacon was assigned to direct and Pat O'Brien was Jimmy's co-star. Margaret Lindsay was the girl they fought over. Again, there were loads of thrills and romance and action, highlighted by some fine special effects.

At about this time, Cagney hoped to set up a theatrical troupe to do Irish plays in cities of less than 100,000 population. Others interested in this project were Pat O'Brien, Robert Montgomery and William Gargan. The first play they were considering was J. M. Synge's famous play of Irish life, *The Playboy of the Western World*. Said Cagney: "I have a cast fairly well lined up in my mind. The next thing is to see if we can arrange it. I'd like to tour this country, then take the play to Ireland and England. We might even make a film of it later, either abroad or here." Nothing ever came of this plan, however.

In a switch, Warners put Jimmy on the side of the law in their salute to the newly-formed Federal Bureau of Investigation. William Keighley, who had directed

15

At a "March of Dimes" broadcast with Humphrey Bogart, Jim and Marian Jordan (Fibber McGee and Molly) and Bob Hope

Cagney on the stage in *Penny Arcade* (and was dialogue director for *Picture Snatcher* and *Footlight Parade*), directed *G-Men* in an exciting fashion. In its semi-documentary approach, illustrating the training a new "government-man" gets, the film was at its best.

Cagney played a young lawyer who witnessed his friend's death and joined the FBI to "get the guys who did it." Margaret Lindsay, Ann Dvorak and Lloyd Nolan headed a large cast. This film proved extremely popular and was nationally revived on the Bureau's twenty-fifth anniversary in 1949, with a special added prologue, with David Brian.

Bacon, O'Brien and Cagney teamed up again for a trifle called *The Irish in Us*, which gave its best moments to supporting actors like Mary Gordon and Frank McHugh. Young Olivia de Havilland was pitted between Messrs. Cagney and O'Brien.

The world of Shakespeare then claimed his talents. The renowned European producer-director Max Reinhardt announced plans to film *A Midsummer Night's Dream* with William Dieterle, who had the motion picture experience Reinhardt lacked, as co-director. Warners pulled out all the stops and ordered the biggest sets, the wildest costumes, the jazziest special effects, and fitted an all-star cast into them.

The result looked more Reinhardt-Warner Bros. than Shakespeare. Of the large cast, possibly the best performances were turned in by Joe E. Brown, as Flute the bellows-mender, Mickey Rooney as a marvelous Puck and Cagney as Bottom the weaver. Cagney's rendition of his part was not totally satisfying, since he became too cutesy in the play-within-the-play sequences; otherwise, his characterization was one of imagination and invention.

Said Jimmy: "I'm reasonably certain if the dramatist were alive today, movie producers would have asked Mr. Shakespeare to write in a scene in which I did physical violence to someone, for producers seem convinced that the public does not care for me if I don't deliver at least one punch per picture." The big glossy production of *A Midsummer Night's Dream* pleased Warner Bros., if not the directors, but the critics were about equally divided. The public, in the main, did not go for it at all. It never recouped its money at the box office.

This was followed up with another costumer, *Frisco Kid*, in which Cagney was a seaman who became the terror of the notorious Barbary Coast. Again, action, handled astutely by Lloyd Bacon, was the primary quality. Margaret Lindsay, Donald Woods and Lily Damita headed the cast.

Ceiling Zero, from Frank Wead's popular Broadway play, provided Jimmy with one of his best films of the thirties. He played hot-shot pilot Dizzy Davis, while Pat O'Brien was Jake Lee. It was a tense melodrama, directed with style by Howard Hawks, who had previously directed Cagney in *The Crowd Roars*. Even though he was pretty much of a heel throughout, Jimmy proved he had guts—and a streak of heroism—by the final fadeout.

The Robert Montgomerys and the James Cagneys at the world premiere of Warners' *Yankee Doodle Dandy*

After the completion of *Ceiling Zero*, he was offered another routine actioner for which his name and personality alone would generate returns at the box office. It was called *Over the Wall*, and he was to play Alabama Pitts, the ex-convict whose fight to become a professional baseball player had been written by Warden Lewis E. Lawes of Sing Sing Prison. (Dick Foran later did this "B" attraction.) Jimmy refused and walked out; Warners wanted him to do five pictures a year, he said, while his contract specified only four.

At the peak of his popularity, Cagney spoke out against over-exposure in his profession. "It doesn't make any difference how competent an actor you may be, if the public doesn't want to see you anymore, you're all washed up." He went to court with this as his premise. He won.

His demands, which were not met, included fewer vehicles a year, more vitality and purpose in them, and not just a display of muscle. Once the decision of the legal battle was his (thus freeing him to work elsewhere, if he chose to do so), he shocked the movie industry by signing with Grand National, a newly-formed independent company.

Jimmy's walk-out hit Warners right where it hurt—the box office. By 1936, he had reached the "top ten money-makers" list and, since 1934, none of his pictures had grossed under $1,000,000. The studio had just purchased William Wister Haines' *Slim* especially for him as another Cagney-O'Brien actioner. Henry Fonda was later given the part.

In March of 1936, he began working on *Great Guy*, his twenty-sixth film. John G. Blystone directed and, once again, Cagney was teamed with Mae Clarke. The film's obviously small budget and non-Warner gloss showed, but Jimmy was good in it and the critics and public responded.

His second film for Grand National was Victor Schertzinger's *Something to Sing About*, which gave him another opportunity to sing and dance—his first musical film since *Footlight Parade*. It was not very good, despite Cagney's vital performance, and the production creaked from lack of funds to produce it properly. This time the critics booed and the public did likewise.

The deal with Grand National called for two pictures a year. He had completed two and was about to start filming *Angels With Dirty Faces*, which G.N. had purchased for $30,000 from Rowland Brown. While this was being readied for production, it was rumored that Samuel Goldwyn wanted his services for something called *Murder in Massachusetts*, which later was supposed to be called *Shake Hands With Murder*. Either way, it didn't come out.

At this time Warners had purchased a number of properties for Cagney in hopes of getting him back on their payroll: *Invisible Stripes* for Cagney and John Garfield; *The House Across the Bay* for Cagney and Marlene Dietrich; *John Dillinger, Outlaw* for Bogart in the title role and Cagney as Melvin Purvis; *They Died With Their Boots On*; *Dust Be My Destiny*; *High Sierra*; *Three Cheers for the Irish*; and *Mama Raviola* which John Garfield finally did as *East of the River*.

A drama about the Texas oil fields called *Dynamite* was bought up as a Cagney vehicle. Other sources thought that Cagney might return to the stage, in George S. Kaufman's production of *Of Mice and Men*; Warners, in a burst of good will, offered to buy the screen rights especially for him besides offering him the musical *On Your Toes*, which they were preparing for Ginger Rogers, but was eventually done by Vera Zorina. He would have been terrific in that Rodgers and Hart musical and might just have done it, except for the fact that Warner Bros. finally decided to withdraw its appeal to the California Supreme Court, filed after Cagney's victory in a lower court abrogated his contract.

Warners drew up a superb contract that Cagney could not afford to turn down. All his years of struggling for actor's rights paid off: $150,000 per picture against 10% of the gross! This contract was in full force until it expired with the completion of *Yankee Doodle Dandy*, five years later.

The studio had acquired the film rights to Bella and Sam Spewack's farce *Boy Meets Girl* for Marion Davies, but the star insisted on many script alterations with which they refused to comply. So it was decided to give this nutty script, about two daffy scenarists, the Cagney-O'Brien treatment, with Marie Wilson essaying the part meant for Miss Davies. Jimmy was not ideally cast, but his spunk and drive put the frantic antics into high gear and one could tell he was having the time of his life.

When he returned to Warners, Grand National decided to drop plans to film Rowland Brown's *Angels with Dirty Faces*, and rights automatically reverted to the author, who in turn sold them to Warners.

For his role in *Angels*, Cagney adapted various mannerisms from boyhood friends. "One of my friends was a boy who had a trick way of handling his body while talking. He held his elbows against his sides as he spoke, poking his fingers to make his point. Another fellow talked while hitching up his trousers, combining the movement with a nervous twitching of the neck and shoulders."

All of these mannerisms went toward etching a complete characterization of Rocky Sullivan, the criminal whose boyhood friend, Pat O'Brien, was a local parish priest. Humphrey Bogart appeared as a crooked lawyer and George Bancroft was Cagney's former partner who crossed him. Ann Sheridan was a girl from his past he had nearly forgotten. The Dead End Kids were there in force, emulating their hero to the hilt.

Jimmy received his first Academy Award nomination for this super-charged portrayal and won the New York Film Critics' award as Best Actor of 1938. Michael Curtiz directed with a firm hand, achieving striking results, and the production values were superb, especially Sol Polito's photography and Max Steiner's musical score. The Securities and Exchange Commission revealed that Cagney led Warners' stars in 1938 ($234,000), while Kay Francis was a close second ($224,000).

Cagney then went West for the first time, in *The Oklahoma Kid*, as a man who takes the law into his own hands to track down his father's killer. Rosemary Lane was the heroine, while Bogart played the heavy in this most enjoyable Western. James Wong Howe's impressive camera work helped immeasurably.

Each Dawn I Die, a fine prison drama, followed, with George Raft as Cagney's co-star. These two originally met in vaudeville, and it was Cagney who got Raft a bit part of a dancing contest contestant in *Taxi!* back in 1932. Now they were sharing the bill. William Keighley, who had directed the successful *G-Men*, handled his assignment with flair.

Warren Duff, scenarist of *Frisco Kid*, *Angels With Dirty Faces* and *Each Dawn I Die*, had this to say about him: "Cagney is the perfect writer's actor. Every writer enjoys writing for an actor who will not just speak the lines but will bring the character to life. Cagney's almost intuitive understanding of the character he plays, plus his intelligent approach to creating it, guarantees the role's interpretation. This, of course, is gratifying to the writer."

In May of 1939, Warners announced, with a certain pride, that Paul Muni would do *The Life of Beethoven* and Cagney would do *The Story of John Paul Jones*. Neither project materialized.

Producer Mark Hellinger next concocted a newsreel-like semi-documentary melodrama of the prohibition era entitled *The Roaring Twenties*. Cagney played a character based loosely on New York mobster Larry Fay. All of the Warner production values were in evidence, resulting in one of the best films of its kind. Raoul Walsh directed with a punch and the supporting cast was top-notch: Humphrey Bogart, Priscilla Lane, Gladys George and Frank McHugh.

When 1939's top wage earners were announced, the list included two actors: Gary Cooper (first) and Cagney (sixth—with $368,333.)

William Keighley again served as a Cagney director in the popular World War I saga *The Fighting 69th.* Pat O'Brien played Father Duffy and George Brent was "Wild Bill" Donovan, while Jeffrey Lynn played well in the role of poet Joyce Kilmer. Cagney played Jerry Plunkett, a fictitious character who took the audience from training camp show-off to battlefield coward to a hero's death. This was Jimmy's only all-male-cast film (a part had been written in for Priscilla Lane, but it was removed from the shooting script.) Cagney gave a fine performance in a repulsive part. The photography of Tony Gaudio was especially good.

Like many stars in the thirties and forties, Cagney did a good deal of radio work. In 1936, he did *Is Zat So?* with his sister-in-law, Boots Mallory, for the "Lux Radio Theater." In 1939, Lux got his services for two broadcasts: *Ceiling Zero* was broadcast in February, with Ralph Bellamy and Stuart Erwin; and Pat O'Brien and Gloria Dickson joined Jimmy in May for *Angels With Dirty Faces.* He also joined Gertrude Lawrence on the "Revlon Revue" broadcast over the Blue Network (later ABC).

In 1940, Cagney did *Johnny Got His Gun* on Arch Oboler's program. An adaptation of Dalton Trumbo's stirring novel about an armless, legless, faceless veteran who shouts his anti-war message to the world, it touched the toughest heart, and the broadcast caused a sensation. (It was finally filmed in 1971 with Timothy Bottoms in Cagney's part.)

Torrid Zone, his next movie, brought the Cagney-O'Brien combo to an end. It was their eighth picture. The usual fireworks between these men sparked the air, but the "Oomph" girl herself, Ann Sheridan, came off with the winning hand. Helen Vinson came in second, as a married lady with a hankering for Jimmy. The brittle dialogue of Jerry Wald and Richard Macaulay provided many a laugh, but their script was routine stuff.

A New York story was next on Cagney's agenda. *City for Conquest,* directed by Anatol Litvak in true lyric style, reunited him with Ann Sheridan. Arthur Kennedy was splendid as his sensitive younger brother. The supporting cast included Donald Crisp, Anthony Quinn, Frank Craven and Elia Kazan (making his

acting film debut as Googie.) Max Steiner's musical contributions were especially fine.

Jimmy then got involved with hearings of the House Un-American Activities Committee because he had always been a soft touch for anyone in need. It seems that he donated an ambulance to the Abraham Lincoln Brigade, fighting for the Loyalists in the Spanish Civil War, and frequently contributed to various relief funds, including those for starving cotton pickers in the San Joaquin Valley and women and children caught up in the Salinas lettuce strike.

Said Cagney: "When somebody tells you a hard-luck story, you don't investigate him first, you help him first." The House Un-American Activities Committee Chairman, Martin Dies, who had been conducting the secret hearings into alleged West Coast subversive activities, cleared Cagney. Throughout this period, Cagney was supported by fifty World War I veterans who rallied to his aid under the leadership of William Wilson, past state commander of the Veterans of Foreign Wars. Also cleared of all charges were Philip Dunne, Humphrey Bogart and Fredric March.

The Cagneys adopted a son, James Jr., three years old, in December of 1940. Later, they added a girl to their family—Cathleen, called Casey.

1941 was comedy time for Jimmy. It provided a change-of-pace that would still make use of his aggressive and explosive charm. First, he did a re-make of *One Sunday Afternoon* called *The Strawberry Blonde,* with Olivia de Havilland and Rita Hayworth as the ladies in his life. Raoul Walsh brought freshness as well as charm to the quaint 1910 period, yet he blended enough robust humor to keep the interest high. Cagney's performance was astute because he was perfect for the role of Biff Grimes, whereas Gary Cooper, who essayed the same role in the 1933 Paramount film, was against "type" and less successful in the final analysis. Olivia de Havilland, who had appeared in two previous films with Jimmy, added tremendously to the success of this film by her quietly moving performance. Cagney's brother William became an Associate Producer at Warners with this film.

The Bride Came C.O.D. was his second change-of-pace film, and it brought Jimmy and Bette Davis together for the first time since *Jimmy the Gent* in 1934. It is a pity that it was another comedy instead of a drama or melodrama, like *Marked Woman,* for example; this pairing would have been sensational in the right property. *The Bride Came C.O.D.* was not that property. It was, however, pleasant enough, mainly through the bold and brassy playing of these two pros.

19

It is even more of a pity when one realizes that Warner Bros. *did* buy Henry Bellamann's 1940 novel *Kings Row* for Jimmy, Bette and Pat O'Brien. But even this illustrious trio couldn't have bettered the flawless performances in that 1942 Sam Wood production.

Despite this, and maybe because of it, both Cagney and Davis appeared on the 1941 best-paid list. Cagney (second) with $362,500 and Davis 6th. Clark Gable was in third place.

Michael Curtiz then directed Cagney in his first film in Technicolor, *Captains of the Clouds*, in which he played, in his usual competent fashion, a headstrong bush pilot who joins the Royal Canadian Air Force. The aerial photography was especially beautiful, although the story, as was typical of many of his previous vehicles, was best when it delved into the training of Canadian tyro aviators.

His next film was perhaps his finest screen contribution, and certainly one of the very best musical biographies. *Yankee Doodle Dandy* highlighted the life and times of George M. Cohan. Cohan, himself, had held off selling the rights to his life story for several years, waiting for just the right (1) studio, (2) price, and (3) star to portray him. He personally chose Cagney to play him. He also approved the casting of Walter Huston as the senior Cohan, Rosemary De Camp as his mother and Jimmy's young sister Jeanne as Cohan's sister Josie.

To aid himself in the characterization of Cohan, Cagney again patterned the hoarseness in his voice after the same boyhood friend whose mannerisms he successfully employed in *Angels With Dirty Faces*. He also decided only to adapt "mannerisms" of Cohan himself while appearing as Cohan the performer. For Cohan the man, he merely suggested those mannerisms so as not to mimic a performance.

Naturally, this became Cagney's favorite role and he later said: "I was both flattered and pleased when I was told that he had picked me to play the lead in the picture *Yankee Doodle Dandy*. . . . In addition to being a fine performer, Cohan was a fine American and a warm human being. When the picture was finished, he had to approve it for release, and, although he was far from well when he was brought into the projection room, he gave it an immediate O.K.; then made me very happy with a telegram saying: 'Thanks for a job well done.'"

Cagney is also fond of telling this story: "Once a young actor insisted on stopping George M. Cohan on the corner of Forty-fourth Street and Broadway to do an impersonation of him. When he finished, Cohan just looked at him and said: 'One of us is awful bad!'"

The world premiere in New York played to a full house representing a ticket sale of $5,750,000 in War Bonds. Jimmy was awarded his second New York Film Critics' Award as Best Actor, and won the coveted Oscar, on his second nomination, from the Academy of Motion Picture Arts and Sciences. At the annual Awards dinner, in March of 1943 at the Ambassador Hotel, Gary Cooper, the previous year's winner for another Warner production, *Sergeant York*, presented Jimmy his Oscar. Cagney, brief and to the point said, "An actor is only as good as people think he is and as bad as people think he is. I am glad so many thought I was good."

He did more radio work in 1942. Besides appearing on top variety shows and special March of Dimes programs, Jimmy did *Captains of the Clouds* on the "Cavalcade of America" program over NBC and *Yankee Doodle Dandy* for the Screen Guild Players. The proceeds from the latter broadcast went to support of the Motion Picture Relief Fund.

His deal with Warners over (after being voted one of the top ten money-making stars of 1935, 1939, 1940, 1941, 1942 and 1943), United Artists offered Cagney a unit including brother Bill as producer, with financial support and UA personnel made available to Cagney's production setup. On March 30, 1942, Cagney signed with UA for a five-picture, five-year production deal. Bankers Trust Company of New York and Security First National Bank of Los Angeles provided financing. Thus ended his twelve-year association with Warner Bros.

While his new production unit was deciding on what properties to invest in, Jimmy busied himself by entertaining troops as an Irish jig-and-clog dancer, doing as many as twelve shows a day. He was installed as President of the Screen Actors Guild on September 28, 1942, and, as such, became the chairman of the Hollywood Victory Committee in 1943, and travelled throughout the country on bond-selling tours with stars like Judy Garland and Dick Powell. In other efforts, he turned over his vast estate on Martha's Vineyard to the Army for maneuvers, offered his summer home as quarters for staff officers and let the Coast Guard utilize his yacht.

Besides these patriotic efforts, Cagney made several short subjects for all branches of the Armed Services, as well as recruiting trailers. One of the finest short subjects to come out of this period was directed by Mervyn LeRoy for the Office of War Information and released by MGM. In *You, John Jones*, Cagney portrayed an air raid warden who informs us just what would happen to his wife (Ann Sothern) and daughter

(Margaret O'Brien) if the U. S. should be conquered. It was an eight-minute short with tremendous impact.

Another short, produced for the U. S. Coast Guard by 20th Century-Fox, concerned the Spars (the Coast Guard's women's branch) and included music by Vernon Duke. Cagney co-narrated it with Ginger Rogers. Called *Battle Stations*, it was released in July of 1944.

The first property William Cagney Productions did for United Artists was based on Louis Bromfield's *McCloud's Folly*. Jimmy thought up the title *Johnny Come Lately* and, for the pivotal role of Minnie McCloud, he got the services of Grace George, one of the great ladies of the American stage. William K. Howard, a fine but generally overlooked director, handled the nostalgic period piece well. Marjorie Main,

Marjorie Lord, Hattie McDaniel and Margaret Hamilton headed a capable cast. By fighting small town corruption, Cagney helped an old lady carry on the traditions of her husband's newspaper. It was, to say the least, an unusual film for him to be associated with, for its pace was leisurely and not the zippy tour-de-force one would have expected of him. Despite generally fine reviews, the film went unappreciated.

Frank Lloyd then directed *Blood on the Sun* for Cagney-UA, in which Sylvia Sidney returned to the screen after an absence of four years. The setting was Tokyo in the 1920s, where reporter Cagney stumbles on a war plot (the famous Yamata plan). For his role in this film, a police judo instructor named Jack Halloran helped Cagney during the filming.

In January 1944, 20th Century-Fox offered him *The*

On the set of *Run for Cover* with Billie, daughter Cathleen ("Casey") and son Jimmy

A pre-circus conference with Marilyn Monroe

Life of O. Henry for producer George Jessel, but Cagney turned it down. However, in 1946, he accepted the lead in Louis de Rochemont's *13 Rue Madeleine* at Fox, which Henry Hathaway directed. It concerned a Nazi spy in the ranks of Americans working for the OSS. Cagney's job was to flush the spy out into the open. It was one of the better of the semi-documentaries produced during this period.

In 1946, Cagney paid $150,000 for a seven-year lease on William Saroyan's prize-winning play *The Time of Your Life*. Saroyan and the Theatre Guild had turned down offers of $225,000 from Warners and MGM for outright purchases. The Cagney brothers also leased, for a ten-year period, Adria Locke Langley's novel *A Lion Is in the Streets*, paying $250,000. Their agenda of properties also included Thorne Smith's *The Stray Lamb*, William Faulkner's *Two Soldiers*, Charles Marquis' *Only the Valiant* and Ernest Haycox's *Bugles in the Afternoon*.

Away from Hollywood on his farm on Martha's Vineyard

Cavorting at the Friars Club (where he once was a bellhop) with Buster Keaton, Harpo Marx and George Burns

The Time of Your Life was filmed in late 1947 and released to the public in 1948. H. C. Potter directed the fantasy with loving care. The cast also performed in much the same manner; those involved were William Bendix, Wayne Morris, Jeanne Cagney—fresh from her fine performance in O'Neill's *The Iceman Cometh* on Broadway—James Barton and Gale Page. It was not a commercial hit.

With their five-year production deal with United Artists completed, the Cagneys, Jimmy and Bill, returned to Warners. The film was *White Heat*, which brought Jimmy back to the front ranks of gangsterdom. One critic referred to his character as "a mean grin with an Oedipus complex and migraine headaches." It is interesting to note that, at this same time, Edward G. Robinson (*Key Largo*) and Clark Gable (*Any Number Can Play*) also returned to bad-guy parts, thus giving the new generation of moviegoers a sampling of what movies of the thirties had offered.

White Heat, intensely directed by Raoul Walsh, brought neurosis into the crime film with a bang. Cagney's Cody Jarrett had a mother fixation and was given to epileptic fits. This was a new kind of gangster and he played it to the hilt. His supporting cast was extremely effective: Virginia Mayo, as his unfaithful moll with a strong yen for gang member Steve Cochran; Edmond O'Brien, as an undercover man; and Margaret Wycherly as Ma, who protected him from everything, including himself. Bosley Crowther said, in part, in his *New York Times* review: "Mr. Cagney plays it with such dynamic arrogance and such beautiful laying out of detail that he gives the whole picture a high charge. His crisp and commanding Cody Jarrett is no muscle-bound stereotype. He pops with the vigor and precision of a real personality. He is cruel, merciless and sadistic. . . . He is eloquently sardonic, as when he kicks his fresh 'moll' off a chair, and he is hard, with a cold and terrible hardness, when he faces the minions of the law."

It was then his misfortune to be associated with a second-rate musical called *The West Point Story* directed without style by Roy Del Ruth. Its big-name cast (Virginia Mayo, Doris Day, Gordon MacRae and Gene Nelson) could not save it from the fate it deserved. Because of the tremendous success of *White Heat*, Warners then came up with a grisly crime melodrama called *Kiss Tomorrow Goodbye*. Violence for violence's sake got in the way of whatever storyline there was, and the supporting cast, headed by Barbara Payton, was lost in the shuffle. But, there was still Cagney to enjoy, even in moments of extreme unpleasantness.

Gordon Douglas, who had directed *Kiss Tomorrow Goodbye*, then did a much better job with a much better script. *Come Fill the Cup* was a grim story of a top newspaperman's bout with alcohol and his eventual return to normality through the kindness of an ex-boozer, well played by James Gleason. Had the producers and scenarists stayed on that track, *Come Fill the Cup* might have been a finer picture than it was. But, instead, they got sudsy in the latter half and had Cagney trying to reform his publisher's drunken nephew, who then becomes responsible for the ex-boozer's death. The best thing about this last half, however, was the first-rate acting of Gig Young, who was rewarded with an Academy Award nomination. Phyllis Thaxter and Raymond Massey were as effective as the script allowed.

Cagney then did "box-office duty" for pal Roy Del Ruth by appearing as a "guest star" in the dreary musical *Starlift*. It was a waste of time for all concerned.

At 20th Century-Fox, John Ford got Cagney for his re-make of the World War I chestnut *What Price Glory?* It was not successful for a number of reasons. First, Cagney's personality and Captain Flagg's were miles apart and, even though he injected wonderful bits of business, they proved meaningless in the realm of war comedy-drama, since the idea of *What Price Glory?*

was so very much out-of-date. Second, Ford's direction was tired and certainly uninspired, when one considers that this closely followed his marvelous Irish farce *The Quiet Man*. Third, the cheapness of the production, with its theatrical backdrops and rose-colored lighting, removed it further from the realism it deserved. The only one who can be proud of that picture is Dan Dailey—it was his best piece of acting.

Two of the three properties that Cagney owned screen rights to were sold to Warners as vehicles for other stars. *Only the Valiant* gave Gregory Peck a stalwart role, while *Bugles in the Afternoon* was filmed with Ray Milland, Helena Carter and Gertrude Michael in 1952.

Jimmy did hold on to Adria Locke Langley's *A Lion Is in the Streets*. Under Raoul Walsh's knowing hand, Cagney gave a superb delineation of a Huey Long type from the Deep South. The acting, by all concerned, was most persuasive. Barbara Hale and Jeanne Cagney were especially good, and young Anne Francis attracted attention as a girl called Flamingo. *A Lion Is in the Streets* was really quite a Cagney family affair. Not only did brother Bill produce and sister Jeanne appear in the supporting cast in what was her first character part, but brother Edward was story editor.

The following year, 1954, was a busy one for Jimmy, although the films he made were not released until 1955.

Run for Cover was an unusual Western drama which offered Cagney and young John Derek fine roles. Viveca Lindfors, a fine actress, was only utilized for the romantic interest in the script; the role did not do her justice. The horse that Jimmy rode was from his own farm. As Westerns go, *Run for Cover* was above average and boasted splendid color photography by Daniel Fapp.

Love Me or Leave Me offered him a terrific role as Martin "The Gimp" Snyder, the racketeer-promoter who later married songstress Ruth Etting. Metro-Goldwyn-Mayer gave a true accounting of these two and Miss Etting's second husband, Johnny Alderman, because they secured their permission to tell the story as it really happened. The result was a factual, gutsy and most unusual musical drama. Doris Day, giving the performance of her career, was splendid and, adding to her lustre, there were ten "standard" Etting numbers, plus two new songs beautifully arranged by Percy Faith, which she sang perfectly.

After talking over Snyder's game leg with his two doctor brothers, Cagney decided it was something Snyder had been born with, but learned to accept, thus giving a further realistic touch to his fine acting. He was nominated for an Academy Award for his portrayal. It was his third nomination.

John Ford then cast him as the Captain in the filmization of the hit play *Mister Roberts.* Henry Fonda recreated the role he played for three years on Broadway and an additional two years on the road. His effortless style of acting, brought about by much study and work, served him well in an otherwise difficult role. William Powell was Doc and Jack Lemmon played, and received an Academy Award for, the supporting role of Ensign Pulver. Jimmy was directed more for whatever humor the Captain had than the straight way he was presented on the stage. But he was, nonetheless, effective. Halfway through the filming in Hawaii, John Ford became ill (reportedly a gall bladder attack) and Mervyn LeRoy completed the picture for him.

As a favor to Bob Hope, Jimmy then "guest-starred" in the comedian's *The Seven Little Foys,* about vaudevillian Eddie Foy. Cagney appeared briefly as George M. Cohan in a Friars Club scene where they did a "spontaneous" routine atop the banquet table. This "spontaneous" routine took two weeks of intensive rehearsals.

Cagney's "favor" meant that, according to Screen Actors Guild ruling, he could, and did, appear for minimum salary. But Hope, and Paramount Studios, gave him an especially made red leather-lined horse trailer and a scroll saying "Thanks for the trailer you did for us. Here's one for you."

On February 28, 1955, James Cagney was awarded an honorary doctorate in the humanities at Rollins College, Winter Park, Florida.

As part of the gala premiere of the Ringling Bros., Barnum and Bailey circus on March 25, Cagney (as the Fourth of July) joined Milton Berle (as the Ringmaster) and lovely Marilyn Monroe (majestically riding in on a pink elephant) for the festivities. To say the least, these stars, and a number of others, caused a sensation.

His television experience has been minimal. He appeared on one of the Christopher programs and then, on June 20, 1955, he did a "live" short dramatic scene from *Mister Roberts* on the "Ed Sullivan Show." Fonda, Cagney and Jack Lemmon, from the film cast, and David Wayne and John Forsythe, of the Broadway company, participated in *Mister Roberts,* with a clip from the film itself.

Said Jack Gould in *The New York Times:* "Manifestly, it is not fair to judge Mr. Cagney's performance in the film on the basis of an excerpt, but last night he

Cagney as the Captain in *Mister Roberts* as seen through the watercolor artistry of James Cagney

certainly seemed wrong for the part of the skipper— much too bouncy and pugnacious." His third appearance was on the Bob Hope Chevy Show on NBC.

In 1956, Cagney worked exclusively for Metro-Goldwyn-Mayer. First, he did *Tribute to a Bad Man* for director Robert Wise, replacing his pal Spencer Tracy, who had been "fired" over continual disagreements with studio brass. This was a rather routine pioneer story (maybe this is what Tracy was fighting about), which introduced Greek actress Irene Pappas to the American screen as the woman in the old pioneer's life.

Barbara Stanwyck and Cagney then did a lovely story of adoption called *Somewhere I'll Find Him,* which was later retitled *These Wilder Years.* Both players expertly approached parts heavily laden with saccharine and made them work despite the script. Young Don Dubbins, fresh from his superb national tour of *Tea and Sympathy* with Deborah Kerr, was the juvenile lead in both *Tribute to a Bad Man* and *These Wilder Years.*

25

On May 24, 1956, Cagney was master of ceremonies at the White House Correspondents' Association dinner, at which President Eisenhower was in attendance. Said Ike in a brief tribute to Cagney: "No one in show business has a warmer heart or has done more for the less privileged."

In July, Columbia announced that Cagney and Jack Lemmon were signed for John Ford's *The Last Hurrah*, but by the time it was ready to be filmed, both actors were involved in other commitments. Spencer Tracy and Jeffrey Hunter were used instead.

It was Jimmy's old friend Robert Montgomery who assigned Robert Wallace to write a play that could be used to lure Cagney to television for his dramatic TV debut. Called *Soldier From the Wars Returning*, it was the story of Army sergeant George Bridgeman, who responds cynically to escorting home the body of a soldier killed in the Korean war. Directed by Perry Lafferty, it was presented on September 10, 1956, over the NBC network on "Robert Montgomery Presents."

The title was taken from an A. E. Housman poem, and Jimmy played a sergeant in the U. S. Military Escort Detachment escorting a flag-draped coffin containing a victim of a Communist mortar shell back to the boy's home town. It was, according to *Time*, "a noble-minded but often pedestrian tone poem which confused patriotism with adulation of the anonymous dead. Cagney's usual clipped, staccato style was properly subdued—especially when, at the end, he tried to work out a salvation for his hero. 'Where do you go when you die? The book says, "In my father's house there are many mansions." Where? In the sky, under the ground, or in the minds of men?'"

Since this was his first major television appearance, and, alas, his only one, it was widely reviewed. Said Jack Gould: "*Soldier From the Wars Returning* realized its exalted purpose in Mr. Cagney's movingly spoken definition of the hereafter. But, before that inspirational moment, Mr. Wallace's play fell lamentably short of its ennobling theme. . . . In the closing scene, in which he had something to say, Mr. Cagney rose to his opportunity with convincing sincerity."

Harriet Van Horne, in the *New York World-Telegram*, said: "It was a quiet play, and the sergeant's awakening perhaps lacked impact. But Mr. Cagney gave a strong, quietly understated performance that was a joy to watch. The supporting cast, headed by Audra Lindley, Muriel Kirkland and George Matthews, was top-notch."

Cagney then got one of the best parts of his career when Universal-International offered him the role of Lon Chaney in *Man of a Thousand Faces* on a "share-in-the-profits" basis. He readily accepted, and worked long and hard on his portrayal, giving added depth to Chaney the performer and Chaney the man. It was a brilliant piece of acting. His near-perfect performance should have garnered him his fourth Academy Award nomination, but somehow he was overlooked.

Dorothy Malone gave a fine account of herself as Chaney's first and troubled wife, Cleva, while Jane Greer added a touch of dignity and strength to her portrayal as the second Mrs. Chaney. Celia Lovsky, as Chaney's mother, was superb. She, too, was overlooked in the Oscar race. Hers was indeed the true meaning of a "supporting" part. Joseph Pevney directed *Man of a Thousand Faces* and saw to it that the attention to every detail regarding the movies and parts Chaney created were faithfully reproduced. The production was highlighted by a sensitively beautiful musical score by Frank Skinner.

At the 1958 Academy Award festivities with winner Susan Hayward and Kim Novak

On November 10, 1956, Cagney accepted an honorary chairmanship of the Greer School, near Millbrook, New York, a non-profit institution where boys and girls from broken homes live and receive vocational and academic training.

In 1957, Cagney accepted an offer to direct his first picture. Producer A. C. Lyles offered him a modern re-telling of *This Gun for Hire* at Paramount called *Short Cut to Hell*. The production was a low-budget affair, but the challenge was there. Jimmy met that challenge with his instinctive know-how. There are some effective touches in this little picture, and newcomers Robert Ivers and Georgann Johnson did well in their assignments under Cagney's guiding hand. In fact, he appeared on film in an especially prepared "prologue" to introduce these two young actors. He worked on a minimum-salary basis with a percentage of the profits.

Universal-International got his services again for

Never Steal Anything Small, from the 1952 play *Devil's Hornpipe* by Charles Lederer and Rouben Mamoulian. The studio originally wanted Doris Day to appear opposite Jimmy again, but prior commitments prevented her from doing so. Shirley Jones was signed, but this spoof of union politics turned out to be a sorry mish-mash of comedy, drama and songs. It was rough going at the box office.

This was to be followed up with *Bon Voyage* for the Disney organization with Greer Garson playing his wife, but both of them must have read *that script.*

An excellent story of the Irish revolution was next on the Cagney schedule and he went to Ireland to film it. Michael Anderson directed *Shake Hands With the Devil* for Pennebaker Productions. The script was based on the 1934 novel by Rearden Conner. Most of the filming was done at the Ardmore Studios in Bray, Ireland.

Its theme was one of violence becoming an end in itself, and Cagney was extremely effective as Sean Lenihan, a surgical professor in the Royal College of Surgeons associated with the underground movement. A top-notch international cast included Don Murray, Dana Wynter, Glynis Johns, Michael Redgrave, Sybil Thorndike and Cyril Cusack. Erwin Hillier's breathtaking photography of the Irish countryside was a tremendous asset.

At the Royal Theatre in Dublin on September 23, 1958, Cagney turned legit again briefly by making a rare stage appearance, doing his famous George M. Cohan routine for a benefit performance of Ireland's Variety Club.

Upon his return from Ireland, Jimmy joined Robert Montgomery in the production of *The Gallant Hours,* which depicted Admiral William F. ("Bull") Halsey's role in the winning of the Battle of Guadalcanal. Montgomery directed in a somber tone and the effect was most interesting. The film contained no battle scenes, just the tension that exists on the top level of command. Cagney gave a performance of dignity and profound understanding. His usual vivacity was replaced by compassion and a warm understanding for Halsey the man and Halsey the admiral. This film was also unique in its narrative style. The background of each character was given the viewer as he came into the story. Montgomery's one mistake was having the Roger Wagner Chorale provide the musical interludes—it was out of place in a war drama.

Although he had threatened to "retire" in the mid-fifties, a rash of good parts kept him from taking that step. After *The Gallant Hours* was completed, he de-

At the White House with William Halsey, III (presenting Vice-President Richard M. Nixon with his father's service cap), and Robert Montgomery

cided to retire again, but he couldn't turn down Billy Wilder's offer to star as C. P. MacNamara in *One, Two, Three*. It was filmed on location in West Berlin and at the Bavaria Studios in Munich, from June to September 1961.

His soft drink executive was a chip off his old block. Like his early films at Warners, *One, Two, Three* was directed in the feverish pace Cagney knew so well, and he shouted nearly every step of the way. The cast included Horst Buchholz, Pamela Tiffin, Arlene Francis, Lilo Pulver and Hanns Lothar.

One, Two, Three was the first all-out Cagney comedy since *Boy Meets Girl* (1938). Said Cagney: "As long as it's fun and the stories are good." Rumors circulated that he and Eleanor Parker would make something called *The Park Avenue Story*, but plans never jelled.

In 1961, the New York Film Critics awarded their Best Actor prize to Maximilian Schell for his work in *Judgment at Nuremberg*, seconded by Cagney in *One,*

Two, Three. Had Jimmy won, he would have been the first actor to have won three of the Critics' awards. This was, unhappily, his final appearance *before* the camera. Behind the camera he continued as a narrator. In 1962, he narrated a grisly instruction film on the history of Communism which bristled with firing squads and purges.

He supplied the voice for a central character in the television special, *The Ballad of Smokey the Bear* in November 1966. The program, dealing with the fire prevention bear, was taped in the Animagic process, in which three-dimensional puppet-like characters are moved in a stop-motion photography system. Joseph Schrank wrote the story and Johnny Marks composed the music. The one-hour show was produced by the U. S. Forest Service.

In his *New York Times* review, Jack Gould stated: "The animated mechanical puppetry was often erratic and cluttered, and not always successful at capitalizing on several attractive ideas, such as the whisper of the tall trees pleading for their lives. Smokey, whose voice was provided by Barry Pearl, and the big brother bear, for which James Cagney was the voice, were not endowed with too much personality, either in the lines they had to say or in the design of their faces."

Cagney also narrated A. C. Lyles' *Arizona Bushwhackers*, a second-rate Western in 1968, which starred Howard Keel, Yvonne DeCarlo and Marilyn Maxwell.

Offers still came in, but he refused them all. He had been offered the role of Alfred Doolittle in George Cukor's classy production of *My Fair Lady*, for which Warner Bros. paid a fabulous amount to get the rights to film. Two years later, in 1965, he was offered a part in Samuel Bronston's production *The French Revolution*, but he never accepted and it never materialized.

Asked if he planned to return to acting, he quickly replied: "In this business you need enthusiasm. I don't have the enthusiasm for acting anymore. Acting is not the beginning and the end of everything." He also told columnist Dorothy Manners: "Just forget any little rumors you may hear that the famous old grapefruit thrower will be back in front of a camera."

In 1969, Cagney visited Hollywood, stayed in his Beverly Hills home, and was offered $150,000 for a ten-second TV commercial which he could have done in a few hours. He refused. "I'm busy studying painting with Sergei Bongart, the famous Santa Monica artist," was his reply.

From the time Cagney was a small boy in the sweltering city streets of New York, he yearned for the country. "I had an aunt who lived out at Sheepshead Bay.

We used to go out there; I saw them making those early movies in Brooklyn with John Bunny and Flora Finch." Of those sojourns to the "wild" country of Brooklyn, he later stated: "I'm so thoroughly happy in the country and so thoroughly unhappy in the city," and added, "Like most city kids I was country-crazy. I still am."

He is an expert on soil conservation, and much of his movie wealth has been invested in scientific farm research. He used to claim that the best way to keep from going Hollywood was to stay away from it between pictures. Said Cagney at the height of his career: "Give me a couple days on a farm branding cattle, fixing fences or milking cows and I can recharge my batteries completely."

In the thirties, the Cagneys paid $85,000 for a house that was built in 1728 in Edgartown on Martha's Vineyard, the resort island off the coast of Massachusetts.

Jimmy is a gentleman farmer in the truest sense of the phrase. He is also reportedly a millionaire, with four farms that pay for themselves, a home in Beverly Hills and a New York City apartment.

Two of his farms are in California. In the East, he owns a 700-acre dairy farm near Millbrook (Dutchess County), New York, where he crossbreeds Scots Highland cattle with Shorthorns and Herefords. He has a milk herd of Friesian-Holstein cows and sells more than 1,000 quarts of milk daily.

He and Billie, his wife of fifty years, divide most of their time between their farm near Millbrook and the place on Martha's Vineyard. Their adopted son, James, Jr., married a girl he met while in the Marine Corps named Jilly Lisbeth Inness, of South Portland, Maine, in 1962. Cagney's daughter Cathleen ("Casey") is now Mrs. Jack Thomas. The Cagneys are proud grandparents.

Cagney was once asked to address the students of the University of Maine concerning soil conservation, and he has narrated many radio programs on this subject during the past few years. He came out fighting to preserve the Hudson Valley from Consolidated Edison's proposed power plant at Storm King Mountain in the mid-sixties. He identified himself in his telegrams to Robert F. Kennedy (N.Y.), Thomas H. Kuchel (Cal.) and Rep. Richard L. Ottinger (N.Y.) as a long-time conservationist joining other Hudson Valley residents in fighting particularly to preserve the spawning grounds of striped bass.

Which only goes to prove that James Cagney may have retired from films, but he never retired from life.

With Mae Clarke thirty years after the "grapefruit incident"

A recent picture of the Cagneys

ROGUES GALLERY

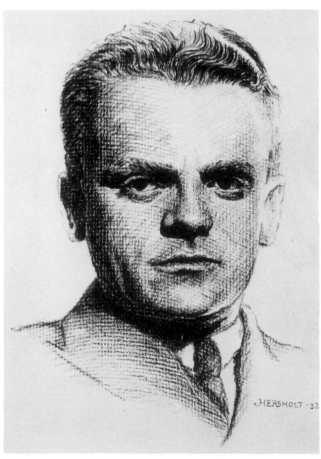

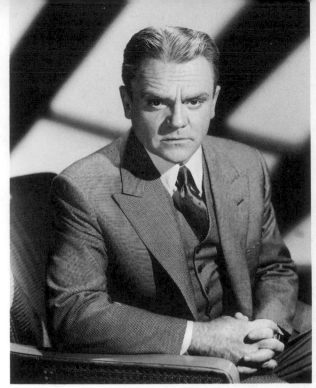

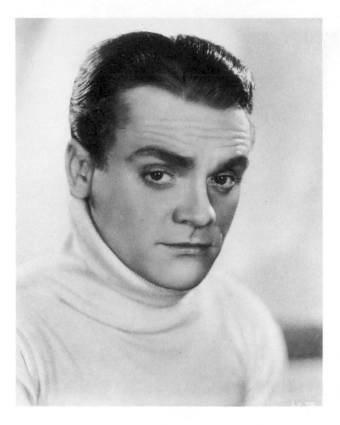

FILMOGRAPHY

THE SHORTER FILMS

During the big studio days of movie-making, most screen players appeared at one time or another in short subjects. Some of these concerned Hollywood and offered "inside" glimpses of stars at work and play, while others were little playlets devised for various industry charities.

At the time of World War II, actors not only appeared in training films and documentaries of every description but also narrated films.

James Cagney was no exception. Since this phase of the motion picture business was scantily recorded (for posterity or whatever), the following listing does not pretend to be complete. It is hoped, however, that Cagney's major shorter films are included:

1) *Practice Shots* (No. 11 of Bobby Jones' "How I Play Golf" series.) 1931. Directed by George Marshall. With James Cagney, Anthony Bushell, Donald Cook, Louise Fazenda. This short subject was one of many semi-instructional films golf pro Bobby Jones made during the height of his popularity. Cagney appeared on the green with Bobby and proceeded to ask him questions about his game, thus supplying comedy and continuity along with the other cast members.

2) *Hollywood on Parade #8.* 1933. A candid look at James Cagney, Frankie Darro and Joe E. Brown on the Warner Bros. lot.

3) *Screen Snapshots #11.* 1934. Columbia. Coverage of a Hollywood frolic for charity. Stars included Boris Karloff, Bela Lugosi, Genevieve Tobin, Pat O'Brien, James Cagney, Maureen O'Sullivan and Eddie Cantor.

4) *The Hollywood Gad-About.* 1934. Skibo Productions, Inc. Produced by Louis Lewyn. Presented by E. W. Hammons. An Educational Films Corp. of America Treasure Chest Short. The plot concerned a missing necklace and the glittering cast included Gary Cooper, Eddie Cantor, Mary Astor, Shirley Temple, Alice White, James Cagney, Chester Morris and Walter Winchell.

5) *A Trip Through a Hollywood Studio.* 1935. Warner Bros. 10 minutes. Cameras roamed in and around various Warners sets during filming of current movie fare. The notables included Dolores Del Rio, Ann Dvorak, Hugh Herbert, Wini Shaw, Rudy Vallee, Pat O'Brien, Busby Berkeley and James Cagney.

6) *For Auld Lang Syne.* 1938. Warner Bros. Directed by George Bilson, assisted by Marshall Hageman. Leo F. Forbstein conducted the Vitaphone Orchestra. A tribute to Will Rogers (sponsored by the Motion Picture Industy for the Will Rogers Memorial Commission). With Paul Muni, James Cagney, Dick Powell (and his Cowboy Octette), Benny Goodman and his Band, Rudy Vallee, Bonita Granville, Pat O'Brien,

As the air-raid warden in Mervyn LeRoy's superb *You, John Jones*

Johnny Davis, Allen Jenkins, Marie Wilson, Mabel Todd, Hugh Herbert, Frank McHugh, and the Schnikkelfritz Band.

7) *Show Business at War* (Issue #10; Volume IX of "The March of Time.") 20th Century-Fox. 1943. 23 min. Compilation of film stars entertaining or working toward entertaining U.S. servicemen; radio broadcasts, troop shows, highlights from both the Hollywood Canteen and the Stage Door Canteen. With Bette Davis, Humphrey Bogart, Ginger Rogers, James Cagney, Myrna Loy, Rita Hayworth, Kay Francis, Frank Sinatra, Alexis Smith, Gertrude Lawrence, the Mills Brothers, Jack Benny, Bob Hope, Fred MacMurray and Ginny Simms.

8) *You, John Jones.* 1943. Metro-Goldwyn-Mayer. Directed by Mervyn LeRoy. Cagney played an air-raid warden who shows America what might happen to his wife (Ann Sothern) and daughter (Margaret O'Brien) if the U.S. were invaded.

9) *Battle Stations.* 1944. 20th Century-Fox. A documentary short concerning SPARS produced for the U. S. Coast Guard. Cagney narrated along with Ginger Rogers. Vernon Duke furnished the music.

With pro golfer Bobby Jones in short subject "Practice Shots"

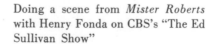

Doing a scene from *Mister Roberts* with Henry Fonda on CBS's "The Ed Sullivan Show"

SINNER'S HOLIDAY

A Warner Bros. & Vitaphone Picture

—1930—

CAST

Angel Harrigan: GRANT WITHERS; *Jennie Delano:* EVALYN KNAPP; *Harry Delano:* JAMES CAGNEY; *Myrtle:* JOAN BLONDELL; *Ma Delano:* LUCILLE LaVERNE; *Buck:* NOEL MADISON; *George:* OTTO HOFFMAN; *Mitch McKane:* WARREN HYMER; *Sikes:* PURNELL B. PRATT; *Joe Delano:* RAY GALLAGHER; *Happy:* HANK MANN

CREDITS

Director: JOHN G. ADOLFI; *Scenarists:* HARVEY THEW, GEORGE ROSENER; *Based on the Play* PENNY ARCADE *by:* MARIE BAUMER; *Photographer:* IRA MORGAN; *Editor:* JAMES GIBBONS; *Sound Recorder:* CLARE A. RIGGS; *Musical Director:* LEO F. FORBSTEIN; *Makeup Artist:* PERC WESTMORE

SYNOPSIS

Ma Delano, the owner of a penny arcade, lives above it with her sons, Joe and Harry, and her daughter Jennie. Mitch McKane, Harry's employer, makes a pass at Jennie, who is rescued by Angel Harrigan, Mitch's barker. Angel then quits Mitch and, at Jennie's urging, is hired by Ma Delano.

Harry is mixed-up with Mitch in his rum-running exploits and, during a heated argument, Harry accidentally kills Mitch. He confesses his guilt to Ma and together they plan to frame Angel. However, Jennie, overhearing the plot, clears Angel by informing on her brother.

CRITICS' CIRCLE

"In a season in which many features, for no good reason, are being allowed to run over an hour and a half, *Sinner's Holiday* has been compressed to fifty-

With Lucille LaVerne

five minutes. Concentration gives it pith; it tells its little story compactly and credibly. Although the action involves liquor-running and murder, it is less a picture of action than of character, made so by the skill of Lucille La Verne and James Cagney."

TIME

"The romance of a carnival barker and the daughter of a penny arcade proprietress is well told in the screen version of Marie Baumer's play *Penny Arcade*, now known as *Sinner's Holiday*. . . . Grant Withers as Angel Harrigan and Lucille LaVerne as Ma Delano are well cast, but the most impressive acting is done by James Cagney in the role of Harry Delano. His fretful tenseness during the closing scenes is conveyed with sincerity."

Mordaunt Hall, THE NEW YORK TIMES

"Cagney has by no means an easy role in his portrayal of a highly nervous youth who by nature cannot go straight. It is the type of part which can be spoiled by the slightest shade of over-acting, but Cagney carries his characterization in each sequence just far enough."

EXHIBITOR'S HERALD-WORLD

NOTES

When Al Jolson stipulated to Warner Bros., to whom he sold the screen rights to Marie Baumer's play *Penny Arcade*, that they hire Cagney and Joan Blondell, it was undecided just what roles they might do on the screen. Both players were tested for the leading roles, but the parts did not benefit from their interpretations.

Thus, Cagney and Blondell re-created their "character" roles and did them well. Since the "talkies" were firmly established by 1930, these two stage-trained actors were well on their way. The production itself was a quickie, filmed in just three weeks.

With Warren Hymer   With Lucille LaVerne

With Joan Blondell

With Purnell B. Pratt, Grant Withers, Evalyn Knapp and Lucille LaVerne

DOORWAY TO HELL

A Warner Bros. & Vitaphone Picture

—1930—

CAST

Louis Ricarno: LEWIS (LEW) AYRES; *Sam Marconi:* CHARLES JUDELS; *Doris:* DOROTHY MATHEWS; *Jackie Lamar:* LEON JANNEY; *Captain O'Grady:* ROBERT ELLIOTT; *Steve Mileway:* JAMES CAGNEY; *Captain of Military Academy:* KENNETH THOMSON; *Joe:* JERRY MANDY; *Rocco* NOEL MADISON; *Bit:* BERNARD "BUNNY" GRANVILLE; *Machine Gunner:* FRED ARGUS; *Girl:* RUTH HALL; *Gangsters:* DWIGHT FRYE, TOM WILSON, AL HILL

CREDITS

Director: ARCHIE MAYO; *Scenarist:* GEORGE ROSENER; *Based On the Story* A HANDFUL OF CLOUDS *by:* ROWLAND BROWN; *Photographer:* BARNEY "CHICK" MC GILL; *Editor:* ROBERT CRANDALL; *Sound Recorder:* DAVID FORREST; *Musical Director:* LEO F. FORBSTEIN; *Makeup Artist:* PERC WESTMORE

SYNOPSIS

Louis Ricarno appoints himself czar of the underworld's bootlegging rackets in his city's districts and warns the other racketeers to keep out. When all is running smoothly, he turns operations over to his lieutenant, Steve Mileway, marries the girl he loves and goes straight. However, the rival beer barons get to him anyway. His wife betrays him and his brother, who is attending military school, is kidnapped and later run over by a truck while trying to escape his captors. Louis returns to the rackets, to avenge the death of his little brother, but his decline is a swift one.

CRITICS' CIRCLE

"An excellent gangster film. While it may have a few weaknesses, it is always fast, colorful and exciting,

With Lew Ayres and Thomas Jackson

43

With Richard Purcell, Dorothy Mathews and Lew Ayres

With Lew Ayres and Dorothy Mathews

With Lew Ayres

has a definite story to tell and does not lapse into a maudlin, sentimental ending. Lewis Ayres as the main figure, Ricarno, is a promising young actor. He made you follow him intently to his bitter and tragic end. . . . But how much of this conviction was due to his acting and how much to Mr. Mayo's brilliant and skillful direction is open to discussion. Among others in the cast were James Cagney and Robert Elliott."

Marguerite Tazelaar, NEW YORK HERALD TRIBUNE

"Archie Mayo directed and handled this yarn without kid gloves. There's nothing especially soft-toned about the script, anyway, and Mayo hasn't impelled the theme by holding it down. It's practically an all-male picture, with Dorothy Mathews, as the girl, having little to do. The remaining men, and Miss Mathews too, handle themselves ably."

VARIETY

"The supporting cast is uniformly good, with honors going to James Cagney as Mileway. . . . Cagney is excellent in this role, his work being nearly on a par with the splended performance he gave in the screen version of *Penny Arcade*.

EXHIBITOR'S HERALD-WORLD

NOTES

Once his work in *Sinner's Holiday* had been completed, Cagney was rushed into a film that was already shooting, Rowland Brown's *A Handful of Clouds* (a gangster term), starring Lew Ayres, then riding the crest of the wave after his sensitive portrayal of the young soldier in *All Quiet on the Western Front*.

Advertised as "the picture gangdom dared Hollywood to make," its title was finally changed to *Doorway to Hell*. When viewing it today, it is obvious, almost from the beginning, that Ayres and Cagney should have switched roles. Ayres, a good actor, seemed more like a pathetic L'Aiglon rather than the indomitable little Napoleon that the script called for.

The leading lady, Dorothy Mathews, was selected from the extra ranks during the filming of one of the early crowd scenes. The production was commendable and Archie Mayo's direction was excellent, as was the camera work. Rowland Brown's original story won an Academy Award nomination.

With Lew Ayres and Dorothy Mathews

OTHER MEN'S WOMEN

A Warner Bros. & Vitaphone Picture

—1931—

CAST

Bill: GRANT WITHERS; *Lily:* MARY ASTOR; *Jack:* REGIS TOOMEY; *Ed:* JAMES CAGNEY; *Marie:* JOAN BLONDELL; *Haley:* FRED KOHLER; *Pegleg:* J. FARRELL MAC DONALD; *Waitress:* LILLIAN WORTH; *Bixby:* WALTER LONG; *Railroad Workers:* BOB PERRY, LEE MORGAN, KEWPIE MORGAN, PAT HARTIGAN

CREDITS

Director: WILLIAM A. WELLMAN; *Scenarist & Dialogue:* WILLIAM K. WELLS; *Based on a story by:* MAUDE FULTON; *Photographer:* BARNEY "CHICK" MC GILL; *Editor:* EDWARD MC DERMOTT; *Musical Director:* LEO F. FORBSTEIN; *Makeup Artist:* PERC WESTMORE

SYNOPSIS

Jack, a railroad engineer, and his wife Lily take in Jack's close pal Bill, a railroad fireman, as a boarder. Soon the friendship between Lily and Bill turns to love, and Bill leaves, but not before Jack suspects their attachment. On a long run together, the boys have a heated argument, which results in Jack's being hurled from the train and blinded. Retribution follows when Bill visits Jack's bedside and sees Lily's true love for her husband.

Great floods come to the area and Bill determines to take the train onto a bridge to give it weight to weather the storm. Hearing this, blind Jack jumps aboard and hurls his pal off the train and rides it to the bridge—and to his death.

CRITICS' CIRCLE

"*Other Men's Women* adds another item to the list of tawdry and misleading titles with which certain of the bright young men of Hollywood have sought to woo the mystical box office this season. . . . Mr. Toomey acts the husband, Mr. Withers is the best friend and Miss Astor is the wife. Joan Blondell, James Cagney and J. Farrell MacDonald are among the assistant players."

Andre D. Sennwald, THE NEW YORK TIMES

With Grant Withers, Bob Perry and Walter Long

"Underneath this old-fashioned title (*The Steel Highway*) . . . is hidden one of the surprises of the cinematic year. Not the least part of the surprise is the work of Grant Withers who, as the burly, boisterous fireman who is shocked into sobriety when he discovers that he has fallen in love with his pal's wife, does the best—the first real acting of his career. . . . It's a great picture disguised as an unimportant one."

PHOTOPLAY

NOTES

William A. Wellman's railroad melodrama was originally called *The Steel Highway*, a much better title, and had even been previewed for the press as such. As with *Sinner's Holiday*, Grant Withers had the leading role. By the time the first camera started rolling, Regis Toomey had replaced James Hall and Mary Astor had replaced Marian Nixon.

Cagney and Joan Blondell appeared briefly. Jimmy was an extra-gang workman for the railroad, while Blondell was the lunchroom's flip waitress. *Other Men's Women* had plenty of thrills and action, but when it came to the love-triangle, it was boring.

With Grant Withers, Bob Perry and Walter Long

THE MILLIONAIRE

A Warner Bros. & Vitaphone Picture

—1931—

CAST

James Alden: GEORGE ARLISS; *Barbara Alden:* EVALYN KNAPP; *Bill Merrick:* DAVID MANNERS; *Schofield:* JAMES CAGNEY; *Carter Andrews:* BRAMWELL FLETCHER; *Mrs. Alden:* FLORENCE ARLISS; *Peterson:* NOAH BEERY; *Dr. Harvey:* IVAN SIMPSON; *McCoy:* SAM HARDY; *Dan Lewis:* J. FARRELL MAC DONALD; *Briggs:* TULLY MARSHALL; *Doctor:* J. C. NUGENT

CREDITS

Director: JOHN G. ADOLFI; *Scenarists:* JULIAN JOSEPHSON, MAUDE T. POWELL; *Based on* IDLE HANDS *by:* EARL DERR BIGGERS; *Dialogue by:* BOOTH TARKINGTON; *Photographer:* JAMES VAN TREES; *Editor:* OWEN MARKS; *Musical Director:* LEO F. FORBSTEIN; *Makeup Artist:* PERC WESTMORE

SYNOPSIS

Self-made millionaire James Alden retires from the presidency of Alden Motor Works at his doctor's orders. However, a brash young insurance salesman warns Alden against inactivity and the millionaire sets out for California. In an effort to fight boredom, he takes half-interest in the Mission Filling Station with young Bill Merrick. Merrick, who happens to be in love with Alden's daughter Barbara, is studying to be an architect at night while running the gas station by day. It is not long before Alden realizes how to be happy even though he is rich.

CRITICS' CIRCLE

"Mr. Arliss . . . is an artist who is an actor, an actor

With George Arliss

With George Arliss

who is an artist. Thanks to the artistry of the erst-
while Disraeli, it (*The Millionaire*) assumes an importance it does not, at bottom, merit. . . . And that's
why you sit back and enjoy the fundamentally foolish
yarn!"

Robert Garland, NEW YORK WORLD-TELEGRAM

"Mr. Arliss's every action is wonderfully natural. He
examines a motor as if he were a mechanic from youth
and when he puts his pipe in his mouth—an ill omen
for those who do not see eye to eye with Alden—he
lights it as if he were really relishing every puff. This
stylist in histrionics makes it rather difficult for some
of those who play opposite him, for few of them can
hold their own while he is on the screen."

Mordaunt Hall, THE NEW YORK TIMES

NOTES

After three parts of varying sizes, Jimmy took George
Arliss' advice and accepted a one-scene role as Schofield,
the brash young life insurance salesman, in this film.
That was all he needed; anyone who saw *The Millionaire* came away remembering his energetic and forceful pitch to the old man.

Based on *"Idle Hands"* by Earl Derr Biggers, it was
well directed by John G. Adolfi, who had directed
Cagney in *Sinner's Holiday*. Warners remade it in
1947, as *That Way With Women*, starring Sydney
Greenstreet, Martha Vickers and Dane Clark.

THE PUBLIC ENEMY

A Warner Bros. & Vitaphone Picture

—1931—

CAST

Tom Powers: JAMES CAGNEY; *Gwen Allen:* JEAN HAR-
LOW; *Matt Doyle:* EDWARD WOODS; *Mamie:* JOAN
BLONDELL; *Ma Powers:* BERYL MERCER; *Mike Powers:*
DONALD COOK; *Kitty:* MAE CLARKE; *Jane:* MIA MARVIN;
Nails Nathan: LESLIE FENTON; *Paddy Ryan:* ROBERT
EMMETT O'CONNOR; *Putty Nose:* MURRAY KINNELL;
Bugs Moran: BEN HENDRICKS, JR.; *Molly Doyle:* RITA
FLYNN; *Dutch:* CLARK BURROUGHS; *Hack:* SNITZ ED-
WARDS; *Mrs. Doyle:* ADELE WATSON; *Tommy as a Boy:*
FRANK COGHLAN, JR.; *Matt as a Boy:* FRANKIE DARRO;
Officer Pat Burke: ROBERT E. HOMANS; *Nails' Girl:*
DOROTHY GEE; *Officer Powers:* PURNELL PRATT; *Steve
the Bartender:* LEE PHELPS; *Little Girls:* HELEN PAR-
RISH, DOROTHY GRAY, NANCI PRICE; *Bugs as a Boy:*
BEN HENDRICKS, III; *Machine Gunner:* GEORGE DALY;
Joe the Headwaiter: EDDIE KANE; *Mug:* CHARLES SUL-
LIVAN; *Assistant Tailor:* DOUGLAS GERRARD; *Black
Headwaiter:* SAM MC DANIEL; *Pawnbroker:* WILLIAM
H. STRAUSS

CREDITS

Director: WILLIAM A. WELLMAN; *Scenarists:* KUBEC
GLASMON, JOHN BRIGHT; *Adaptation & Dialogue:*
HARVEY THEW; *Based on the original story* BEER AND
BLOOD *by:* JOHN BRIGHT; *Photographer:* DEV JENNINGS;
Art Director: MAX PARKER; *Editor:* ED MC CORMICK;
Musical Director: DAVID MENDOZA; *Costumer:* EARL
LUICK; *Makeup Artist:* PERC WESTMORE

SYNOPSIS

Tom Powers, the son of a cop, and his boyhood pal,
Matt Doyle, grow up in pre-World War I slums with
little regard for law and order. His life of crime begins
simply with petty thievery and eventually moves to
more profitable jobs, until Tom becomes a notorious
rum-runner. His brother Mike, just back from the War,
warns him to go straight, but to no avail.

Tom takes Kitty as his moll, but later dumps her for

With Lee Phelps

With Edward Woods

With Mia Marvin

Gwen, whom he feels has more class. When a rival gang kills his pal Matt, he goes on a rampage, getting badly shot up in the process. To make sure they are not bothered by him again, the gang kidnaps him from the hospital and delivers him dying to his mother's doorstep.

CRITICS' CIRCLE

"Recently I re-viewed, at the National Film Theatre in London, William Wellman's 1931 film *The Public Enemy*. I had remembered it as good, but not as good as it now appears to be.

"It is, of course, James Cagney's picture. His performance is as great as anything I've seen in movies; his balletlike control of his body, every movement at once precise and free; his extraordinary command of expression.

"His Tom Powers is a human wolf, with the heartlessness and grace and innocence of an animal, as incapable of hypocrisy as of feeling; the smiling, unreflective delight with which he commits mayhem and murder makes Humphrey Bogart look like a conscience-stricken Hamlet.

"Wellman uses Cagney with subtlety, keeping him in the background much of the time while secondary characters occupy the foreground. (This development of secondary characters is usually a sign of a good movie.) So it is all the more powerful when Cagney moves up into the foreground at the big moments; our taste for this extraordinary actor has not been blunted by seeing too much of him."

Dwight MacDonald, ESQUIRE (1961)

"It is just another gangster film, weaker than most in its story, stronger than most in its acting, and like most maintaining a certain level of interest through the last burst of machine-gun fire. . . .

"Edward Woods and James Cagney, as Matt and Tom, respectively, give remarkably lifelike portraits of young hoodlums. . . . The audience yesterday laughed frequently and with gusto as the swaggering Matt and Tom went through their paces, and this rather took the edge off the brutal picture the producers appeared to be trying to serve up."

Andre D. Sennwald, THE NEW YORK TIMES

"In detail *The Public Enemy* is nothing like that most successful of gangster pictures (*Little Caesar*), but its central idea is identical—dissection of the criminal mind by reconstruction of one criminal's career. . . . *The Public Enemy* is well-told and its intensity is relieved by scenes of the central characters slugging bartenders and slapping their women across the face. U.S. audiences, long trained by the press to glorify thugs, last week laughed loudly at such comedy and sat spellbound through the serious parts. Unlike *City Streets*, this is not a Hugoesque fable of gangsters fighting among themselves, but a documentary drama of the bandit standing against society. It carries to its ultimate absurdity the fashion for romanticizing gangsters, for even in defeat the public enemy is endowed with grandeur. Best shot: two young gangsters scared to death on their first 'job.' "

TIME

"In telling their story Mr. Kubec Glasmon and Mr. John Bright have painted the racketeer as the rat he is pretty apt to be. And, in his direction, Mr. William Wellman has stuck by their guns. From the first reel to the last Tom Powers goes his way without romance or allure. The innate charm which was *Little Caesar's* is nowhere to be found. It's only with an effort that the pretty killer is decent to his dear old mother. [But] homicidal rodents are born, not made.

"It seems to me that Mr. Cagney is a rising young talking-picture actor to keep an eye on. He photographs well, his voice records effectively, he has an undeniable flair for getting inside a character and remaining there. Up to now, his characters have been what even he might call standardized and I trust he will do everything he can to keep from being forced into a gangster mould. Anyway, he's well worth watching."

Robert Garland, NEW YORK WORLD-TELEGRAM

"*The Public Enemy* is one of the very few films in which the script is the principal positive factor. Daring the little-used episodic form, this biography of a criminal traces his career from its origins in middle-class destitution through the petty crimes of boyhood to full-scale metropolitan racketeering. Acting as chorus, the wardheelers, bartenders, and big-time gang of South Side Chicago bosses approvingly look on at his progress and profit by it, even as they anticipate the inevitable moment when his corpse is delivered to his mother's door like a slab of meat. The bleak reality and cold nihilism of this film still have the power to impress the thoughtful student of society."

Richard Griffith

NOTES

It was Cagney's complete comprehension of the kind of boy that produced the man that made the murderer

With Murray Kinnell and Edward Woods

With Edward Woods

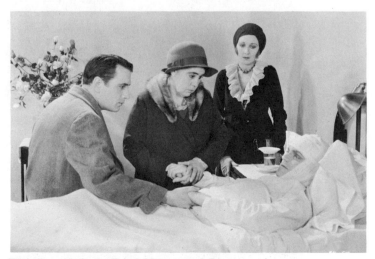

With Donald Cook, Beryl Mercer and Rita Flynn

On the set with Jean Harlow and Edward Woods

With Joan Blondell and Edward Woods

who would inevitably end up with his bullet-ridden body tottering into his mother's foyer which made this the shattering, brutal manifestation of gangster glory that it was. Tom Powers was not just a man, as the prologue to the film pointed out, he was a *problem!*

William A. Wellman was just the right director for this realistic treatment of Glasmon and Bright's original story "Beer and Blood." He made full use of newsreel material of New York City to set the tone of the picture, the action of which started in 1909. It is to Wellman's credit that most of the actual killings were not seen—they were out of camera range and only the sound track carried the message to the audience. The notable exception was when Eddie Wood was shot down in the street, a scene that set off the fantastic Cagney finale.

It's strange that the one scene that everyone remem-

With Mae Clarke

bers from this picture rich in "scenes" is the grapefruit bit with Mae Clarke. Said Cagney: "We took it from a real life incident in which a gangster named Hymie Weiss hit his girl in the face with an omelette."

The original story by John Bright and Kubec Glasmon was nominated for an Academy Award. Although Jean Harlow and Louise Brooks were signed on the same day (March 7, 1931), the latter was dropped from the cast soon after shooting began. In England it was called *Enemies of the Public*.

Just before *The Public Enemy* was to be shown in New York City, Cagney wrote his mother a letter warning her against the gruesome finish and impressing upon her that she must keep in mind that the mother and boy in the picture were only make-believe people; that she mustn't mustn't confuse them with Mrs. Cagney and her boy James.

With Jean Harlow

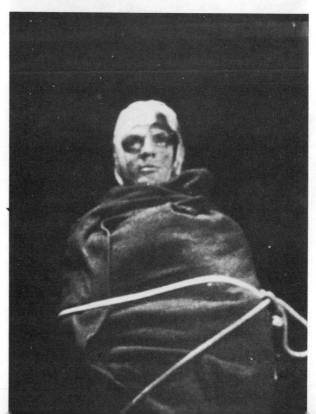

The chilling climax

SMART MONEY

A Warner Bros. & Vitaphone Picture

—1931—

With Edward G. Robinson and Noel Francis

CAST

Nick Venizelos: EDWARD G. ROBINSON; *Irene Graham:* EVALYN KNAPP; *Jack:* JAMES CAGNEY; *Marie:* NOEL FRANCIS; *District Attorney:* MORGAN WALLACE; *Mr. Amenoppopolus:* PAUL PORCASI; *Greek Barber:* MAURICE BLACK; *D. A.'s Girl:* MARGARET LIVINGSTON; *Schultz:* CLARK BURROUGHS; *Salesman:* BILLY HOUSE; *Two-Time Phil:* EDWIN ARGUS; *Sleepy Sam:* RALF HAROLDE; *Sport Williams:* BORIS KARLOFF; *Small Town Girl:* MAE MADISON; *Dealer Barnes:* WALTER PERCIVAL; *Snake Eyes:* JOHN LARKIN; *Lola:* POLLY WALTERS; *Hickory Short:* BEN TAGGART; *Cigar Stand Clerk:* GLADYS LLOYD; *Matron:* EULALIE JENSEN; *Desk Clerk:* CHARLES LANE; *Reporter:* EDWARD HEARN; *Tom, a Customer:* EDDIE KANE; *George, the Porter:* CLINTON ROSEMOND; *Machine Gunner:* CHARLES O'MALLEY; *Joe, Barber Customer:* GUS LEONARD; *Cigar Stand Clerk:* WALLACE MAC DONALD; *Dwarf on Train:* JOHN GEORGE; *Gambler:* HARRY SEMELS; *Girl at Gaming Table:* CHARLOTTE MERRIAM; *with:* LARRY MC GRATH, SPENCER BELL, ALLAN LANE

CREDITS

Director: ALFRED E. GREEN; *Scenarists:* KUBEC GLASMON, JOHN BRIGHT; *Additional dialogue by:* LUCIEN HUBBARD, JOSEPH JACKSON; *Based on an original story by:* LUCIEN HUBBARD, JOSEPH JACKSON; *Photographer:* ROBERT KURRLE; *Editor:* JACK KILLIFER; *Musical Director:* LEO F. FORBSTEIN; *Makeup Artist:* PERC WESTMORE

SYNOPSIS

Knowing Nick's particular weakness for blondes, the district attorney plants countless suitable young ladies in his path, in an effort to gain information. Nick is consistently too wily for them, but, one day, an act of kindness does him in. He saves a girl from committing suicide, unaware that she is wanted for blackmail and that the D. A. has threatened to prosecute her unless she gets the goods on Nick.

With Billy House, Boris Karloff, Edward G. Robinson, Harry Semels and Maurice Black

CRITICS' CIRCLE

"In the effort to vary, however slightly, the frayed formula for underworld pictures, Warner Brothers stumbled into the environment of illegal gambling, a field so fertile it is hard to see how it had hitherto been neglected. Nick is played by Edward G. Robinson, an actor with the face of a depraved cherub and a voice which makes everything he says seem violently profane.

"In *Smart Money* he does again several of the things he did in *Little Caesar* but not so many that the role is repetitious. His pal, who dies after Nick has hit him for suggesting that his last bad blonde is a stoolpigeon, is James Cagney (*Public Enemy*)."

TIME

"James Cagney, who figured as the officious gangster in *The Public Enemy*, is to be seen in this current contribution ever ready with his short-arm jab. His role is of minor importance, for the boastful barber is the limelight in most of the scenes."

Mordaunt Hall, THE NEW YORK TIMES

NOTES

The logical action for Warner Bros. to take, once *Little Caesar* had been released and *The Public Enemy* had been completed, was to put Edward G. Robinson and James Cagney into the same flick. It was a dynamic combination. While the leading role was Robinson's, Jimmy held his own throughout.

Warners' production values were in full evidence. Director Alfred E. Green and photographer Robert Kurrle came up with some unusual ideas and angles. Lucien Hubbard's and Joseph Jackson's original story "The Idol" was nominated for an Academy Award.

With Edward G. Robinson and Charlotte Merriam

55

Evalyn Knapp and Edward G. Robinson

BLONDE CRAZY

A Warner Bros. & Vitaphone Picture

—1931—

CAST

Bert Harris: JAMES CAGNEY; *Ann Roberts:* JOAN BLONDELL; *Dapper Dan Barker:* LOUIS CALHERN; *Helen Wilson:* NOEL FRANCIS; *A. Rupert Johnson, Jr.:* GUY KIBBEE; *Joe Reynolds:* RAYMOND MILLAND; *Peggy:* POLLY WALTERS; *Four-Eyes, Desk Clerk:* CHARLES (LEVINSON) LANE; *Colonel Bellock:* WILLIAM BURRESS; *Dutch:* PETER ERKELENZ; *Mrs. Snyder:* MAUDE EBURNE; *Lee:* WALTER PERCIVAL; *Hank:* NAT PENDLETON; *Jerry:* RUSSELL HOPTON; *Cabbie:* DICK CRAMER; *Detective:* WADE BOTELER; *Bellhops:* RAY COOKE, EDWARD MORGAN; *Conman:* PHIL SLEMAN

CREDITS

Director: ROY DEL RUTH; *Scenarists:* KUBEC GLASMON, JOHN BRIGHT; *Based on an original story by:* KUBEC GLASMON, JOHN BRIGHT; *Photographer:* SID HICKOX; *Editor:* RALPH DAWSON; *Musical Director:* LEO F. FORBSTEIN; *Makeup Artist:* PERC WESTMORE; *Songs—* *"When Your Lover Has Gone"* by: E. A. SWAN; *"I Can't Write the Words"* by: GERALD MARKS, BUDDY FIELDS; *"Ain't That the Way It Goes?"* by: ROY TURK, FRED AHLERT; *"I'm Just a Fool in Love With You"* by: SIDNEY MITCHELL, ARCHIE GOTTLER, GEORGE W. MEYER

SYNOPSIS

Bert, an enterprising bellhop, lives handsomely on his wits. Together with Ann, a world-wise chambermaid, he sets out to take the world for all it is worth. In this pursuit, they cheat cheaters and trim the big shots. Eventually, they are swindled by Dapper Dan Barker and his sassy accomplice, Helen, so Bert and Ann travel to New York to avenge themselves.

Eventually, Ann decides to go straight and marries Reynolds, a young bond salesman, while Bert is caught and goes to jail. Later, Ann visits him there and tells him she is divorcing Reynolds and will be waiting for his release.

CRITICS' CIRCLE

"A chipper, hardboiled, amusing essay on petty thievery. In his first starring performance, James Cagney has a role in which he is more mischievous than wicked. He makes rascality seem both easy and attractive as he did in *The Public Enemy* and *Smart Money*."

TIME

"Unedifying though the incidents are and feeble as is the attempt at a moral, the greater part of James

Cagney's new picture, *Blonde Crazy*, is lively and cleverly acted. . . . Mr. Cagney is as alert and pugnacious as Bert Harris as he was the quick-thinking, young gangster of *The Public Enemy*."

Mordaunt Hall, THE NEW YORK TIMES

"James Cagney's entertaining performance lifts the picture out of the gutter and makes it amusing in spite of its subject matter."

PHILADELPHIA RECORD

NOTES

Larceny Lane, this film's original title, certainly made use of the personalities of both Cagney and Joan Blondell (who had replaced Marian Marsh). Jimmy's ambitious Bert Harris is a study in how to succeed in anybody's book, while Blondell's Ann Roberts was typical of the wisecracking, gum-chewing spitfire. They complemented one another beautifully.

It was directed in a zippy style by Roy Del Ruth and, once again, Kubec Glasmon and John Bright did the scenario and original story. The supporting cast was extremely effective; Ray Milland, Noel Francis, Louis Calhern and Polly Walters, who replaced Dorothy Burgess as Peggy, were standouts.

With Louis Calhern and Noel Francis

With Joan Blondell

With Joan Blondell

With Ray Milland

TAXI!

A Warner Bros. & Vitaphone Picture

—1932—

CAST

Matt Nolan: JAMES CAGNEY; *Sue Reilly:* LORETTA YOUNG; *Skeets:* GEORGE E. STONE; *Pop Reilly:* GUY KIBBEE; *Buck Gerard:* DAVID LANDAU; *Danny Nolan:* RAY COOKE; *Ruby:* LEILA BENNETT; *Marie Costa:* DOROTHY BURGESS; *Joe Silva:* MATT MC HUGH; *Father Nulty:* GEORGE MAC FARLANE; *Polly:* POLLY WALTERS; *Truckdriver:* NAT PENDLETON; *Mr. West:* BERTON CHURCHILL; *William Kenny:* GEORGE RAFT; *Monument Salesman:* HECTOR V. SARNO; *Cleaning Lady:* AGGIE HERRING; *Onlooker:* LEE PHELPS; *Cabbie:* HARRY TENBROOK; *Cop With Jewish Man:* ROBERT EMMETT O'CONNOR; *Dance Judges:* EDDIE FETHERSTONE, RUSS POWELL; *Cop:* BEN TAGGART; THE COTTON CLUB ORCHESTRA

CREDITS

Director: ROY DEL RUTH; *Scenarists:* KUBEC GLASMON, JOHN BRIGHT; *Based on the play* THE BLIND SPOT *by:* KENYON NICHOLSON; *Photographer:* JAMES VAN TREES; *Art Director:* ESDRAS HARTLEY; *Editor:* JAMES GIBBONS; *Musical Director:* LEO F. FORBSTEIN; *Makeup Artist:* PERC WESTMORE; *Assistant Director:* WILLIAM CANNON

SYNOPSIS

Matt Nolan, the leader of an insurgent group of cab drivers, openly defies the powerfully organized taxi trust. His sweet wife, Sue, struggles to curb her husband's dangerous pugnacity, but without success. One of the racketeers accidently shoots Matt's brother in a nightclub. There's no stopping Matt as he avenges his brother's death by going after the killer.

CRITICS' CIRCLE

"Unquestionably there is no young man on the screen today who has the faculty of portraying sincerely, of living, the part of the typical New York young man of a certain part of the city. Whether or not Cagney was born and brought up in New York does not particularly matter. Suffice it to say that he has the typical young, hairtrigger-tempered fighting lad of the big town's streets down to the last innuendo. There is something different in his rapid speech and more rapid actions, something which takes an audience by storm, perhaps because it is so refreshing."

HOLLYWOOD HERALD

"If you have seen *The Public Enemy, Smart Money* or *Blonde Crazy,* you have some idea what to expect of *Taxi!.* Authors Kubec Glasmon and John Bright are camera-minded writers and their stories, which usually deal in an offhand way with violent happenings, have speed, vigor and assurance. Fortunately for all concerned, James Cagney attracted Hollywood's attention at about the same time as authors Bright and Glasmon. When he appears in one of their inventions the result is often brilliantly successful. . . . *Taxi!* is a sordid but amusing observation on minor metropolitan endeavors."

TIME

"Written for the screen by that team of movie realists, Kubec Glasmon and John Bright, the film is . . . a fast-moving and hard-punching drama, but perhaps its chief distinction is Mr. Cagney's lively portrayal of the scrappy young hackman."

William Bilmore, BROOKLYN DAILY EAGLE

"We believe Cagney's popularity could equal or overrun Gable's this 1932. He has a grand sense of humor and he's one swell actor. Movie audiences are thrilled. Will hold your attention until the final Cagney wisecrack."

New York DAILY NEWS

"James Cagney, the terrier of the screen, is to be seen in another belligerent role. This film, which bears the title of *Taxi!,* affords the alert young actor heaps of opportunities for his slang and his short-arm jabs. Mr. Cagney misses no chance to make his characterization tell. Loretta Young is sympathetic and able as Sue."

Mordaunt Hall, THE NEW YORK TIMES

With Dorothy Burgess

With Loretta Young

With Loretta Young

With Loretta Young, Leila Bennett, George E. Stone, Polly Walters
and Ray Cooke

NOTES

Taxi! continued in the tradition of earlier Cagney films
by capitalizing on his energetic and forceful acting.
The hard-fisted action was also due to Roy Del Ruth's
direction. This Glasmon-Bright scenario had two working titles during its filming: *The Blind Spo*t, from the
Kenyon Nicholson play of the same name, and *Taxi,
Please!*

Cagney danced for the first time in this film—with
Loretta Young in the dance contest scene. The excellent
cast included: George E. Stone, Dorothy Burgess,
David Landau and Ray Cooke, among others.

Taxi! was one of Cagney's biggest hits, and Warners
gave it national re-issue (with *Smart Money*) in May
1936. Bland Johaneson, in the New York *Daily Mirror*,
noted on this occasion that "a swarm of Cagney en-
thusiasts in leather jackets visited the Strand yesterday to applaud its revival."

The movie-within-a-movie sequence, when Loretta
and Jimmy go to the movies, contained Donald Cook
and Evalyn Knapp in *Side Show*.

As things usually turned out at Warners, Loretta
Young replaced Nancy Carroll who replaced Joan Blondell who replaced Dorothy Mackaill.

THE CROWD ROARS

A Warner Bros. & Vitaphone Picture

—1932—

CAST

Joe Greer: JAMES CAGNEY; *Anne:* JOAN BLONDELL; *Lee:* ANN DVORAK; *Eddie Greer:* ERIC LINDEN; *Dad Greer:* GUY KIBBEE; *Spud Connors:* FRANK MC HUGH; *Bill Arnold:* WILLIAM ARNOLD; *Jim:* LEO NOMIS; *Mrs. Spud Connors:* CHARLOTTE MERRIAM; *Dick Willshaw:* REGIS TOOMEY; *Auto Drivers:* HARRY HARTZ, RALPH HEPBURN, FRED GUISSO, FRED FRAME, PHIL PARDEE, SPIDER MATLOCK, JACK BRISKO, LOU SCHNEIDER, BRYAN SALSPAUGH, STUBBY STUBBLEFIELD, SHORTY CANTLON, MEL KENEALLY, WILBUR SHAW; *Mechanic:* JAMES BURTIS; *Ascot Announcer:* SAM HAYES; *Tom, Counterman:* ROBERT MC WADE; *Official:* RALPH DUNN; *Announcer:* JOHN CONTE; *Red, Eddie's Pitman:* JOHN HARRON

CREDITS

Director: HOWARD HAWKS; *Scenarists:* KUBEC GLASMON, JOHN BRIGHT, NIVEN BUSCH; *Based on a story by:* HOWARD HAWKS, SETON I. MILLER; *Photographers:* SID HICKOX, JOHN STUMAR; *Art Director:* JACK OKEY; *Production Supervisor:* RAYMOND GRIFFITH; *Editor:* THOMAS PRATT; *Musical Director:* LEO F. FORBSTEIN; *Makeup Artist:* PERC WESTMORE; *Assistant Director:* DICK ROSSEN

SYNOPSIS

Triumphant racing star Joe Greer wants to keep his kid brother Eddie from a racing career. When Eddie becomes infatuated with Anne, a blonde who frequents the tracks, Joe gives him an earful about her past. However, this only encourages the young man. Joe is eaten up by these two concerns and eventually breaks with his girl Lee. Eddie eventually marries Anne. Later, at the track, he causes the death of an old pal who has tried to patch things up between the brothers. He then goes into a remorseful decline. Meanwhile, his brother becomes a successful driver, but is injured during a championship race. Joe replaces him and wins.

With Ann Dvorak and Joan Blondell

With Ann Dvorak

With Eric Linden and Frank McHugh

CRITICS' CIRCLE

"In the old days the late Wallace Reid played the hero of every racing drama and whirled about the track to the roar of the crowd. Now it is Mr. Cagney, who, I suspect, is a better actor than his closest competitor as an 'it' boy, Clark Gable. At any rate, *The Crowd Roars* is an enormously successful picture. . . Mr. Cagney is again superb. Forceful, bantamlike, he is required to play a sympatico second fiddle after knocking his little brother down and threatening his girl. True, the motivation of his role is so thin and simplike that one almost loses sympathy with him despite his unquestioned power as an actor and as a personality."

John S. Cohen, Jr., NEW YORK SUN

"Having assumed such truly American types as the bootlegger and murderer for profit, James Cagney turns his attention to the comparatively harmless sport of automobile racing. . . . Cagney, as usual, is intensely believable as a racing driver, but it is a shallow part and it permits him little opportunity for the sharpness of characterization which distinguish his earlier roles."

Thornton Delehanty, NEW YORK EVENING POST

"For one thing, *The Crowd Roars* represents the only feeble and undistinguished dialogue that the Messrs. Glasmon and Bright have yet arranged for the screen. The film . . . is never dramatic or convincing and it depends upon its noise for its excitement. Mr. Cagney is, of course, believable, but this is his weakest performance and the other players are lost, save Miss Joan Blondell, who, in a small part, manages to register forthrightly."

NEW YORK HERALD TRIBUNE

"The various episodes in this romance of the American motor racing track are at least as painful as they are exciting. No doubt this is partly due to the extremely unpleasant character of most of the protagonists. The hero, well acted by Mr. James Cagney, who is known as 'the hard-boiled he-man of the screen,' is certainly not obviously heroic. . . . The ugly emotions of the crowd which delights in such disasters are represented with some accuracy, but it is not explained what we are to think of ourselves if we enjoy this film. Nevertheless these continuous excitements do have a certain fascination, which is increased by the sound construction of the film."

THE TIMES (London)

"Having recorded the buzzing of airplanes, the rattle of gangster pistols, the slow thunder of artillery, the drumming of horses' hoofs, the squealing of police sirens and other disturbing decibels, it was time for the cinema to investigate the uproars of the common motor car. In this picture, the automobiles are small, slim, built for racing. Less sleek and decorative than the vehicles in which the late Wallace Reid transported himself as the hero of similar sagas about motor racing, they are more exciting and dangerous. There are three races in the course of the picture, two serious accidents, innumerable skids, two gasoline tank fires. All this, photographed brilliantly and from every angle, is enough to make *The Crowd Roars* a dreadful and stimulating spectacle."

TIME

NOTES

Action, blood and guts were again the formula for this Howard Hawks production. Jimmy was a self-centered auto racer with a nasty disposition when it came to "women of the track" being around his kid brother. He played this attitude to the hilt. Blondell was back as the gal who marries the kid brother, well played by Eric Linden. Ann Dvorak, another fine actress on the Warner payroll, was properly histrionic as Jimmy's girl.

The Crowd Roars, originally called *The Roar of the Crowd,* then *The Roaring Crowd,* was filmed at the Indianapolis, Ventura and Ascot race tracks to give it just the right brand of realism. Besides the other famous drivers partaking in this picture, Billy Arnold, the real winner of the Indianapolis 500 race in 1930, played the part of Bill, who talks to Cagney in the pits before the race.

Howard Hawks directed with skill and set his sights on the sport and the people of the sport. He had so much racing footage left that Lloyd Bacon utilized it for an unofficial remake called *Indianapolis Speedway* in 1939.

With Frank McHugh
and Eric Linden

63

WINNER TAKE ALL

A Warner Bros. & Vitaphone Picture

—1932—

CAST

Jim Kane: JAMES CAGNEY; *Peggy Harmon:* MARIAN NIXON; *Joan Gibson:* VIRGINIA BRUCE; *Pop Slavin:* GUY KIBBEE; *Rosebud, The Trainer:* CLARENCE MUSE; *Dickie Harmon:* DICKIE MOORE; *Monty:* ALLAN LANE; *Roger Elliott:* JOHN ROCHE; *Legs Davis:* RALF HAROLDE; *Forbes:* ALAN MOWBRAY; *Ben Isaacs:* CLARENCE WILSON; *Butler:* CHARLES COLEMAN; *Ann:* ESTHER HOWARD; *Lois:* RENEE WHITNEY; *Al West:* HARVEY PERRY; *Pice:* JULIAN RIVERO; *Ring Announcer:* SELMER JACKSON; *Manager:* CHRIS PIN MARTIN; *Interne:* GEORGE HAYES; *Tijuana Referee:* BOB PERRY; *Second:* BILLY WEST; *Reporter:* PHIL TEAD; *Waiter:* ROLFE SEDAN; *Boxing Spectator:* JOHN KELLY; *Ring Announcer, Championship:* LEE PHELPS; *Society Man:* JAY EATON; *Blonde:* CHARLOTTE MERRIAM

CREDITS

Director: ROY DEL RUTH; *Scenarists:* WILSON MIZNER, ROBERT LORD; *Based On The Magazine Story* "133 AT 3" *by:* GERALD BEAUMONT; *Photographer:* ROBERT KURRLE; *Art Director:* ROBERT HAAS; *Editor:* THOMAS PRATT; *Musical Score:* W. FRANKE HARLING; *Musical Director:* LEO F. FORBSTEIN; *Costumer:* ORRY-KELLY; *Makeup Artist:* PERC WESTMORE

SYNOPSIS

Jim Kane, a prize-fight idol, goes broke on wine and women, whereupon his fans collect money to send him to a health resort in New Mexico. While there, he meets Peggy, who is about to be evicted, and to pay her rent

With Clarence Muse

he undertakes a "winner take all" bout, in which his nose is broken. Flushed with success, he arrives in New York, where he eventually meets Joan, a society lady who is slumming.

He falls for Joan in a big way and even has his nose mended. Now careful not to injure his nose, his boxing becomes tedious and he is soon unpopular, not only with the crowds, but also with the society lady. When his nose is broken again in a subsequent fight, he finds that she does not love him and he returns to Peggy.

CRITICS' CIRCLE

"Like Actor Cagney's previous impersonations, this one has a quality of effortless authenticity. It is not exactly acting—no one could be taught to say 'bhointt up' as Cagney says it without being raised in sight of Brooklyn Bridge."

TIME

"In essentials the story is very familiar, but the details are a little unusual, and it is the details which count and make this film by no means so trite as it sounds. Not only do the adventures of his nose make a curious theme, but Mr. Cagney gives such a fascinating picture of the boxer's conceit and stupidity that the original plot, which might have come from a novelette, is lost in the intricacies of his character."

THE TIMES (London)

"How much of an actor is Cagney is a matter that sage critics dispute, though I for one can't help but recall that he did a splendid bit as a blind boy in that stage play of Mary Boland's some years back. However, it is true that his screen roles have been all of a piece. Apparently, his bosses say he shall go out there and be tough—and is he tough! This is one of those roles. Yet it seems to me it is a more finely drawn characterization than most of his cinema portraits."

"He carries with him a veritable smell of the shower room, of sweating body and sodden leather. He walks like a punch-drunk fighter. He does things with his eyes and his lips. He gets an inimitable inflection and accent into his voice."

Gerald Breitgam, NEW YORK WORLD-TELEGRAM

"After having been highly successful in his portrayals as a gangster, a gambler, a taxicab driver, a confidence man and an automobile racer, James Cagney, the stormy petrel of the Warner Brother's Studio, turns his attention, in *Winner Take All*, to impersonating a prizefighter. . . . In the various ring encounters, Mr.

With Guy Kibbee and Clarence Muse

With Dickie Moore and Marian Nixon

With Virginia Bruce

With Charlotte Merriam
and Marian Nixon

With Charles Coleman

Cagney is far more convincing that most players who elect to impersonate pugilists."

Mordaunt Hall, THE NEW YORK TIMES

"This Cagney boy registers heavily in the midst of his latest squabble with the Warner boys. He is unerring in his portrayal of the 'mugg' type. . . . Story may sound like a familiar pattern, but it proves what good handling will do. All good stories, for that matter, come from familiar patterns, same as cloaks and suits. But what a difference the tailoring makes!"

HOLLYWOOD HERALD

NOTES

In *Winner Take All*, Cagney was excellent as pugnacious fighter Jim Kane, who lets glory go to his head. The Wilson Mizner-Robert Lord scenario approached the prize fighting game and, together with Roy Del Ruth's knowing direction and Robert Kurrle's fine photography, Warners had another Cagney hit.

The supporting cast included Marian Nixon, Guy Kibbee, and Virginia Bruce. Cagney trained for the fight sequences with ex-welterweight fighter Harvey Perry, who also played a role in the picture. Here, again, they used a movie-within-a movie sequence: a scene from *Queen of the Night Clubs* (1929) with Texas Guinan and George Raft was shown. *Winner Take All* was Cagney's first fight picture, but not his last. He was to enter the ring in *The Irish in Us* and *City for Conquest*.

With Virginia Bruce

HARD TO HANDLE

A Warner Bros. & Vitaphone Picture

—1933—

CAST

Lefty Merrill: JAMES CAGNEY; *Ruth Waters:* MARY BRIAN; *Lil Waters:* RUTH DONNELLY; *Radio Announcer:* ALLEN JENKINS; *Marlene Reeves:* CLAIRE DODD; *John Hayden:* GAVIN GORDON; *Mrs. Hawks, Landlady:* EMMA DUNN; *Charles Reeves:* ROBERT MC WADE; *Ed McGrath:* JOHN SHEEHAN; *Joe Goetz:* MATT MC HUGH; *Mrs. Weston Parks:* LOUISE MACKINTOSH; *Antique Dealer:* WILLIAM H. STRAUSS; *Merrill's Secretary:* BESS FLOWERS; *Hash-Slinger:* LEW KELLY; *Colonel Wells:* BERTON CHURCHILL; *Colonel's Associate:* HARRY HOLMAN; *Fat Lady With Vanishing Cream:* GRACE HAYLE; *Dance Judge:* GEORGE PAT COLLINS; *District Attorney:* DOUGLASS DUMBRILLE; *Andy:* STERLING HOLLOWAY; *Jailer:* CHARLES WILSON; *with:* JACK CRAWFORD, STANLEY SMITH, WALTER WALKER *and* MARY DORAN

CREDITS

Director: MERVYN LE ROY; *Scenarists:* WILSON MIZNER, ROBERT LORD; *Based on a story by:* HOUSTON BRANCH; *Photographer:* BARNEY "CHICK" MC GILL; *Art Director:* ROBERT HAAS; *Editor:* WILLIAM HOLMES; *Musical Conductor:* LEO F. FORBSTEIN; *Costumer:* ORRY-KELLY; *Makeup Artist:* PERC WESTMORE

SYNOPSIS

Lefty Merrill is a fast-talking, irrepressible promoter who leaps from one high-pressure enterprise to another. At various points, he gets involved in the exploitation of marathon dances, eighteen-day diets, treasure hunts, fat-reducing lotions, putting a girl's college on the map and making America grapefruit-conscious.

With Mary Brian

With Allen Jenkins and Ruth Donnelly

With Mary Brian and Ruth Donnelly

His one big mistake comes about when his partner in the dance marathon absconds with the winner's money and the girl's mother tries to force him into marriage with her daughter—an eventuality that finally takes place.

CRITICS' CIRCLE

"Unlike Lee Tracy's somewhat similar picture, *The Half Naked Truth*, *Hard to Handle* depends less upon journalistic exaggerations about an exciting profession than upon the personality of its principal. Cagney, talking and galloping a little faster than usual, is still wholly successful in the character part which he discovered and which, with eloquent repetition, he has made peculiarly his own."

TIME

"It (*Hard to Handle*) is a violent, down-to-the-pavement, slangy affair which has many a mirthful moment. Although Mr. Cagney is the mainstay of the peppery tale, he is ably supported by Mary Brian, Ruth Donnelly, Allen Jenkins and others. The episodes fly by like the wind, or as fast as Lefty Merrill runs in several of the episodes."

Mordaunt Hall, THE NEW YORK TIMES

"Incidents are piled on in a frantic effort to keep the story apace with Mr. Cagney's dashings about, and they are piled on without much regard to plot or logical sequence. The result is that the picture is a scattered and disappointing jig-saw, with occasional bursts of comedy and a few intermittent surprises. . . . Even the able and high-speed direction of Mervyn LeRoy cannot cover up the uninspired action. The fact that he holds it admirably, and even magnificently at times, is not more than you would expect from an actor of Cagney's perfected style."

Thornton Delehanty, NEW YORK EVENING POST

"It's great to see Mr. Cagney change tempo so readily, and *Hard to Handle* opens up a new cinematic vista for him. He is a pleasing player always, and we have yet to see him in a role that has taxed his histrionic strength. In the present picture he's superb as ever, a thoroughly enjoyable entertainer."

Regina Crewe, NEW YORK AMERICAN

"Mr. Cagney obviously is an unusual performer. His versatility is quite remarkable. It is rare that one encounters in an actor the abilities to play a powerful role such as he had in *The Public Enemy* and then to turn around and play light farce and romance as he has since done. Here he gives one of his lighter but better performances. There is a freshness about it, a spontaneity in it."

John S. Cohen, Jr., NEW YORK SUN

"The reception of *Hard to Handle* will be marked by reviewers and public for its presentation of a new picture stealer who may very well become a leading screen comedienne in her own right. Remember the gal who played the secretary to Lee Tracy in *Blessed Event?* She stood out like a sore thumb in that part, and has been uniformly good in everything that has been handed her. But this time she got a fat part, and how she ran away with it! She means every bit as much to the picture as Cagney, and that is saying plenty. In the role of the promoting mother, anxious to get on Easy Street for her daughter's sake, and quite as much for her own, Miss (Ruth) Donnelly is nothing less than riotous. . . . Cagney is back with a bang, and brings a most promising comedienne along with him."

HOLLYWOOD HERALD

NOTES

Mervyn Le Roy's frantic direction and Jimmy's tremendously energetic performance as an unorthodox promoter make this script an uproarious occasion. Cagney dashed from one end of the screen to the other and from one end of the film to the other. He never stopped. As his schemes got wilder, the audience hardly had time to take a breath between laughs.

The Mizner-Lord scenario, from a story by Houston Branch, was Cagney's first film after winning a salary victory with the studio and, at first, had been called *Bad Boy*. It was then changed to *The Inside* and, finally, to *Hard to Handle*.

The supporting cast was extremely effective: Mary Brian was never better (being a blonde helped!), mainly because she was teamed with the delightfully funny Ruth Donnelly. Claire Dodd was around to give Cagney a break in pace, while Allen Jenkins was close at hand.

With Claire Dodd

With Ruth Donnelly

With Mary Brian and Ruth Donnelly

PICTURE SNATCHER

A Warner Bros. & Vitaphone Picture

—1933—

CAST

Danny Kean: JAMES CAGNEY; *McLean:* RALPH BELLAMY; *Patricia Nolan:* PATRICIA ELLIS; *Allison:* ALICE WHITE; *Jerry:* RALF HAROLDE; *Casey Nolan:* ROBERT EMMETT O'CONNOR; *Grover:* ROBERT BARRAT; *Hennessy, The Fireman:* GEORGE PAT COLLINS; *Leo:* TOM WILSON; *Olive:* BARBARA ROGERS; *Connie:* RENEE WHITNEY; *Colleen:* ALICE JANS; *Speakeasy Girl:* JILL DENNETT; *Reporter:* BILLY WEST; *Machine Gunner:* GEORGE DALY; *Head Keeper:* ARTHUR VINTON; *Prison Guard:* STANLEY BLYSTONE; *Hood:* DON BRODIE; *Reporter:* GEORGE CHANDLER; *Journalism Student:* STERLING HOLLOWAY; *Mike, Colleen's Boyfriend:* DONALD KERR; *Pete, A Drunken Reporter:* HOBART CAVANAUGH; *Reporter Strange:* PHIL TEAD; *Sick Reporter:* CHARLES KING; *Reporter Outside Prison:* MILTON KIBBEE; *Editors:* DICK ELLIOTT, VAUGHN TAYLOR; *Bartender:* BOB

With Alice White

With Alice White

With Ralph Bellamy

PERRY; *Barber:* GINO CORRADO; *Speakeasy Proprietor:* MAURICE BLACK; *Record Editor:* SELMER JACKSON; *Police Officer:* JACK GREY; *Captain:* JOHN INCE; *Little Girl:* CORA SUE COLLINS

CREDITS

Director: LLOYD BACON; *Scenarists:* ALLEN RIVKIN, P. J. WOLFSON; *Based on a story by:* DANNY AHERN; *Dialogue Director:* WILLIAM KEIGHLEY; *Additional Dialogue:* BEN MARKSON; *Photographer:* SOL POLITO; *Art Director:* ROBERT HAAS; *Editor:* WILLIAM HOLMES; *Musical Conductor:* LEO F. FORBSTEIN; *Costumer:* ORRY-KELLY; *Makeup Artist:* PERC WESTMORE; *Assistant Director:* GORDON HOLLINGSHEAD

SYNOPSIS

After being released from a three-year stretch at Sing Sing, former racketeer Danny Kean becomes a "picture snatcher," that is, a man employed by certain disreputable newspapers to secure photographs of those who are trying to escape notoriety. He soon falls in love with Patricia Nolan whose father, a police lieutenant, escorted Kean to jail. At Kean's instigation, a story about Nolan's excellent work gets the officer a promotion to captain and his attitude towards Kean changes.

Shortly thereafter, Danny steals a pass to an electrocution at Sing Sing and Nolan, who was in charge of the reporters for the occasion, is demoted to lieutenant after Danny takes a picture there. He hides in a sob-sister's apartment when everyone turns against him, but eventually restores himself to grace by taking a picture of a notorious killer.

CRITICS' CIRCLE

"*Picture Snatcher* is a vulgar but generally funny collection of blackouts. . . . This is the third successive Warner Brothers picture to be distinguished by lavatory scenes (the other two were *Baby Face* and *Central Airport*). A happy thought was the teaming of tough, noisy Alice White with tough, noisy Cagney. Without plot restrictions, it is doubtful who would have won the bout."

TIME

"The amazing ingenuity and freshness of James Cagney are revealed anew in *Picture Snatcher*. . . . Again it is

With Alice White

obvious that he is an exceptionally resourceful performer. His acting is filled with touches that heighten and throw him in sharp setoff to—well, most of Hollywood."

John S. Cohen, Jr., NEW YORK SUN

"Artistically, the best thing in the film is the consistency which Mr. Cagney discovers between the superficial cleverness and the extreme thoughtlessness of the snatcher. Mr. Cagney makes this character credible and interesting."

THE TIMES (London)

"James Cagney's latest production is fast, snappy, tough and packed with action. It is curious how this pugnacious little man dominates the screen so fiercely in all of his stories, regardless of their worth. Certainly *Picture Snatcher* is his film all the time, and it is his personality that puts much of it over."

Marguerite Tazelaar, NEW YORK HERALD TRIBUNE

"It is a loud, thumping melange of urban excitements, compounded with an evident desire to give the Cagney fans a selection of 'best moments' from his previous works, and, if its tincture is decidedly in the theatrical vein, it is at least saved from the tripe category by the persuasive sincerity and exuberance of its star."

Thornton Delehanty, NEW YORK EVENING POST

"Cagney is competent, of course, rather too much so, perhaps, too assured of the tricks which he has found successful in the past. I wish he would acquire a few others to express the mannerism of our hardboiled youth."

THE NEW YORKER

NOTES

Cagney was still being supplied with scripts calling for plenty of action and snappy dialogue—with a dash of romance to keep the ladies happy. But it was the men that Warners were appealing to with his movies.

Lloyd Bacon contributed the fast pace necessary to bring the action to a boil, while William Keighley, who had directed Jimmy on the stage in *Penny Arcade*, was dialogue director. Sol Polito's photography contributed to the total effect, as did William Holmes' swift editing.

Ralph Bellamy and Patricia Ellis were on hand in the chief supporting roles, along with pert Alice White (who had replaced Thelma Todd), who nearly stole the show. Her razzmatazz daffy blonde provided many laughs.

THE MAYOR OF HELL

A Warner Bros. & Vitaphone Picture

—1933—

CAST

Patsy Gargan: JAMES CAGNEY; *Dorothy Griffith:* MADGE EVANS; *Mike:* ALLEN JENKINS; *Mr. Thompson:* DUDLEY DIGGES; *Jimmy Smith:* FRANKIE DARRO; *Smoke:* FARINA; *Mrs. Smith:* DOROTHY PETERSON; *Hopkins:* JOHN MARSTON; *Guard:* CHARLES WILSON; *Tommy's Father:* HOBART CAVANAUGH; *Johnny Stone:* RAYMOND BORZAGE; *Mr. Smith:* ROBERT BARRAT; *Brandon:* GEORGE PAT COLLINS; *Butch Kilgore:* MICKEY BENNETT; *Judge Gilbert:* ARTHUR BYRON; *The Girl:* SHEILA TERRY; *Joe:* HAROLD HUBER; *Louis Johnston:* EDWIN MAXWELL; *Walters:* WILLIAM V. MONG; *Izzy Horowitz:* SIDNEY MILLER; *Tony's Father:* GEORGE HUMBERT; *Charlie Burns:* GEORGE OFFERMAN, JR.; *Tommy Gorman:* CHARLES CANE; *Johnson's Assistant:* WALLACE MAC DONALD; *Car Owner:* ADRIAN MORRIS; *Hemingway:* SNOWFLAKE; *Guard:* WILFRED LUCAS; *Collectors:* BOB PERRY, CHARLES SULLIVAN; *Sheriff:* BEN TAGGART

CREDITS

Director: ARCHIE MAYO; *Scenarist:* EDWARD CHODOROV; *Based on a story by:* ISLIN AUSTER; *Photographer:*

With Dudley Digges

BARNEY "CHICK" MC GILL; *Art Director:* ESDRAS HARTLEY; *Editor:* JACK KILLIFER; *Musical Director:* LEO F. FORBSTEIN; *Costumer:* ORRY-KELLY; *Makeup Artist:* PERC WESTMORE; *Assistant Director:* FRANK SHAW

SYNOPSIS

Patsy Gargan, a racketeer with friends in high places, allows himself to be sent to a state reform school as a "deputy inspector." He is touched by the predicament of the youngsters, as well as by Dorothy Griffith, the resident trained nurse. After deposing the institution's hard-boiled superintendent, he gets himself appointed to the post. Because he talks the boys' language, he gains their confidence and installs a system of self-government.

However, difficulties with his gang in New York bring him back to the city, where he is embroiled in a fight and kills a man. He goes into hiding and the boys at the reform school think he has deserted them, so a riot ensues. Soon Patsy returns and straightens everything out.

CRITICS' CIRCLE

"*The Mayor of Hell* is the Hollywood equivalent of a Russian picture called *The Road to Life* which was exhibited in the U.S. a year ago. The differences are interesting. *The Road to Life* was frankly propaganda for Soviet reform schools; as such, its earnest enthusiasm made it valid, exciting. *The Mayor of Hell*, far more adroit, far more cleverly invented, is propaganda for nothing. Like most of what comes out of Hollywood it is entertaining trash."

TIME

"Purportedly a social document, a sort of case study in reformatory methods, it is actually a wild hodgepodge of melodrama and sentiment. Even the splendid performances of James Cagney and Dudley Digges and a score of excellent boy actors are powerless to shape the work to distinctive or artistic form."

NEW YORK HERALD TRIBUNE

"So persuasive is Mr. Cagney's performance as a coldblooded ward-heeler, intent on cleaning up the vicious aspects of a reform school, that it excuses many of the film's shortcomings."

"Mr. James Cagney has the necessary slickness and self-confidence to make him not only a gangster but a reformer, and should *Nicholas Nickleby* ever be filmed, Mr. Dudley Digges is the obvious choice for the part of Mr. Squeers."

THE TIMES (London)

"The story is badly balanced because of an obtrusive gangster element and it bulges here and there to make room for Madge Evans, who is too sensitive and feminine for the role of nurse in a reform school. But the power, the vigor, the surge and flow of real issues and important psychological problems make *The Mayor of Hell* an interesting and stimulating drama in spite of itself.

"Mr. Cagney fills the part of the reformed wardheeler with the gusto and swagger one expects of him."

A. D. S., THE NEW YORK TIMES

"There is an odd mixture of excellent and bad treatment in *The Mayor of Hell*. The occasional passages of effective drama are marred by a loose and meandering continuity. Though Cagney is nominally the star, his role is not as important as that of the youthful gang leader, superbly played by Frankie Darro, on which the story would normally focus. The picture has been pulled out of proportion in order to force the Cagney roll to the foreground."

Thornton Delehanty, NEW YORK EVENING POST

NOTES

Cagney's characterization of Patsy Gargan, mobster turned ward-heeler, is the main reason for seeing this film. Islin Auster's original story, "Reform School," was fairly well scripted by Edward Chodorov, but Archie Mayo's direction lacked punch. *The Mayor of Hell* was realistic enough, but could not make up its mind whether to be a social-comment picture or a searing melodrama; the middle ground did not work.

Madge Evans, Jimmy's leading lady, was a replacement for Glenda Farrell, who was a replacement for the studio's original choice, Joan Blondell. Farrell or Blondell would have been more interesting and certainly better suited to the Cagney brand of action and sass.

Dudley Digges, who headed the supporting cast, was mean enough to be good and gave a memorable performance. Young Frankie Darro also contributed greatly to this film's success. Humphrey Bogart later starred in the re-make entitled *Crime School* (1938).

With Madge Evans, Dudley Digges and William V. Mong

With Allen Jenkins and Madge Evans

With Frankie Darro and Madge Evans

FOOTLIGHT PARADE

A Warner Bros. & Vitaphone Picture

—1933—

In a bevy of chorus girls

CAST

Chester Kent: JAMES CAGNEY; *Nan Prescott:* JOAN BLONDELL; *Bea Thorn:* RUBY KEELER; *Scotty Blair:* DICK POWELL; *Silas Gould:* GUY KIBBEE; *Harriet Bowers Gould:* RUTH DONNELLY; *Vivian Rich:* CLAIRE DODD; *Charlie Bowers:* HUGH HERBERT; *Francis:* FRANK MC HUGH; *Al Frazer:* ARTHUR HOHL; *Harry Thompson:* GORDON WESTCOTT; *Cynthia Kent:* RENEE WHITNEY; *Joe Farrington:* PHILIP FAVERSHAM; *Miss Smythe:* JULIET WARE; *Fralick, The Music Director:* HERMAN BING; *George Appolinaris:* PAUL PORCASI; *Doorman:* WILLIAM GRANGER; *Cop:* CHARLES C. WILSON; *Gracie:* BARBARA ROGERS; *Specialty Dancer:* BILLY TAFT; *Chorus Girls:* MARJEAN ROGERS, PAT WING, DONNA MAE ROBERTS; *Chorus Boy:* DAVE O'BRIEN; *Drugstore Attendant:* GEORGE CHANDLER; *Title-Thinker-Upper:* HOBART CAVANAUGH; *Auditor:* WILLIAM V. MONG; *Mac, The Dance Director:* LEE MORAN; *Mouse in "Sittin' on a Backyard Fence" number:* BILLY BARTY; *Desk Clerk in "Honeymoon Hotel" number:* HARRY SEYMOUR; *Porter:* SAM MC DANIEL; *Little Boy:* BILLY BARTY; *House Detective:* FRED KELSEY; *Uncle:* JIMMY CONLIN; *Sailor-Pal in "Shanghai Lil" number:* ROGER GRAY; *Sailor Behind Table:* JOHN GARFIELD; *Sailor on table:* DUKE YORK; *Joe, The Assistant Dance Director:* HARRY SEYMOUR; *Chorus Girls:* DONNA LA BARR, MARLO DWYER

CREDITS

Directors: LLOYD BACON, BUSBY BERKELEY; *Scenarists:* MANUEL SEFF, JAMES SEYMOUR; *Dialogue Director:* WILLIAM KEIGHLEY; *Photographer:* GEORGE BARNES; *Art Directors:* ANTON GROT, JACK OKEY; *Editor:* GEORGE AMY; *Musical Director:* LEO F. FORBSTEIN; *Costumer:* MILO ANDERSON; *Makeup Artist:* PERC WESTMORE; *Creator and Director of Numbers:* BUSBY BERKELEY; *Songs*—"By a Waterfall," "Ah, the Moon Is Here," "Sittin' on a Backyard Fence" *by:* SAMMY FAIN, IRVING KAHAL; "Shanghai Lil," "Honeymoon Hotel," *by:* HARRY WARREN, AL DUBIN

SYNOPSIS

Chester Kent, who stages prologues for movie theaters that are sent out over the country, has to outdo himself to beat a rival prologue concern. However, his ideas are stolen right and left by people his rivals have hired.

Kent is, therefore, eventually compelled to keep his troupe away from snoopers for three days, during which he works on three big numbers, and thus finally beats the competition.

With Joan Blondell and Claire Dodd

With Ruth Donnelly and Dick Powell

With Ruby Keeler

With Ruby Keeler and Joan Blondell

With Guy Kibbee, William Granger, Joan Blondell, Arthur Hohl and Paul Porcasi

With Ruby Keeler

With Ruby Keeler, Joan Blondell, Frank McHugh and Dick Powell

NOTES

for it by appearing in the last number himself—where-in he sings and tapdances with Ruby Keeler at the head of a parade of sailors. The number is 'Shanghai Lil.' Anyway, the film offers further proof of his refreshing versatility. Anyone who can project the power of *The Public Enemy* and the humor of *Picture Snatcher* and *Taxi!* and, in addition can dance with the best of them, can do anything, probably, except play *King Lear*. Indeed, in spite of the ordinary material of his last few pictures, Mr. Cagney remains one of the most interesting of the talkie stars."

John S. Cohen, Jr., NEW YORK SUN

"Mr. Cagney loses none of his dramatic vitality by his transference to musical comedy and his skill at tap-dancing and even his singing voice are immeasurably helpful. The languidly beautiful Miss Claire Dodd is of vast assistance, too, in an unfortunately small role which calls chiefly for her to be mauled about and generally mocked by her rival, Miss Joan Blondell."

Richard Watts, Jr., NEW YORK HERALD TRIBUNE

Footlight Parade is one of the best examples of the fantastic Hollywood musical of the thirties. Its ability to provide extravagant, frantically spectacular chorus numbers, which could not possibly be presented on any stage in the theatre, is matched by a strange effort at realism, which gives the musical numbers a logical setting and reason for being.

Cagney officially became a movie song-and-dance man as Chester Kent when the director is forced to go on in the "Shanghai Lil" number when an actor shows up drunk. He was terrific and expanded his screen image another full notch.

Director Lloyd Bacon, who handled the storyline, and director Busby Berkeley, who handled the musical numbers, both deserve praise for a job well done. George Barnes, then Joan Blondell's husband, was responsible for the expert camera work.

Jimmy was joined by Blondell for the sixth time. Ruby Keeler and Dick Powell were swiftly becoming Warners' little love birds. The major cast included such stalwarts as Guy Kibbee, Ruth Donnelly, Claire Dodd, Frank McHugh and Cagney's old vaudeville crony, Hugh Herbert. Renee Whitney was the original Shanghai Lil but was replaced by Ruby Keeler.

LADY KILLER

A Warner Bros. & Vitaphone Picture

—1933—

CAST

Dan Quigley: JAMES CAGNEY; *Myra Gale:* MAE CLARKE; *Duke:* LESLIE FENTON; *Lois Underwood:* MARGARET LINDSAY; *Ramick:* HENRY O'NEILL; *Conroy:* WILLARD ROBERTSON; *Jones:* DOUGLAS COSGROVE; *Pete:* RAYMOND HATTON; *Smiley:* RUSSELL HOPTON; *Williams:* WILLIAM DAVIDSON; *Mrs. Wilbur Marley:* MARJORIE GATESON; *Brannigan:* ROBERT ELLIOTT; *Kendall:* JOHN MARSTON; *Spade Maddock:* DOUGLASS DUMBRILLE; *Thompson:* GEORGE CHANDLER; *The Escort:* GEORGE BLACKWOOD; *Oriental:* JACK DON WONG; *Los Angeles Police Chief:* FRANK SHERIDAN; *Jeffries, Theater Manager:* EDWIN MAXWELL; *Usher Sargeant Seymour:* PHIL TEAD; *Movie Fan:* DEWEY ROBINSON; *Man With Purse:* H. C. BRADLEY; *J. B. Roland:* HARRY HOLMAN; *Dr. Crane:* HARRY BERESFORD; *Butler:* OLAF HYTTEN; *Ambulance Attendant:* HARRY STRONG; *Casino Cashier:* AL HILL; *Man in Casino:* BUD FLANAGAN (DENNIS O'KEEFE); *Hand-Out:* JAMES BURKE; *Jailer:* ROBERT HOMANS; *Lawyer:* CLARENCE WILSON; *Porter:* SAM MC DANIEL; *Los Angeles Cop:* SPENCER CHARTERS; *Western Director:* HERMAN BING; *Letter-Handler:* HAROLD WALD-RIDGE; *Director:* LUIS ALBERNI; *Property Man:* RAY COOKE; *Hood:* SAM ASH

CREDITS

Director: ROY DEL RUTH; *Production Supervisor:* HENRY BLANKE; *Scenarist:* BEN MARKSON; *Based on* THE FINGER MAN *by:* ROSALIND KEATING SHAFFER; *Adaptation:* BEN MARKSON, LILLIE HAYWARD; *Photog-*

With Mae Clarke

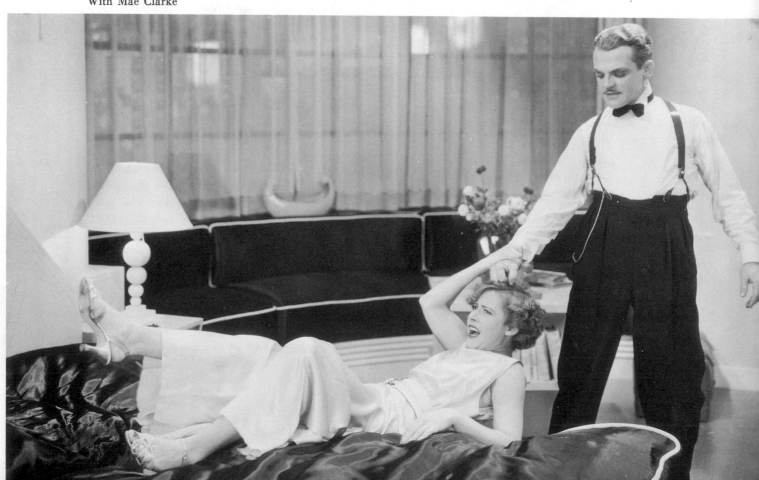

rapher: TONY GAUDIO; *Art Director:* ROBERT HAAS; *Editor:* GEORGE AMY; *Musical Conductor:* LEO F. FORBSTEIN; *Costumer:* ORRY-KELLY; *Makeup Artist:* PERC WESTMORE; *Assistant Director:* CHUCK HANSEN

SYNOPSIS

Soon after young Dan Quigley, an usher in a movie palace, is fired, he turns to crime. In no time at all, he is the leader of a gang involved in a profitable "come-on" racket. In Hollywood hiding from the New York police, Quigley gets a film bit as an Indian chief and, as it sometimes happens in Hollywood, he swiftly rises to stardom. As might be expected, his old gang shows up out of the blue and tries to involve him in a new racket, robbing movie stars' homes.

CRITICS' CIRCLE

"The reason for the picture's existence seems to have been due to a desire to give the versatile and gifted Mr. Cagney a chance to show himself in an all-around way, and *Lady Killer* is therefore a kind of résumé of everything he has done to date in the movies. His method is straight from the shoulder and decisive, and though the grapefruit trick is omitted, his activities leave no doubt in the end that his attitude toward women is of the rough-and-ready variety."

NEW YORK EVENING POST

"Cagney again plays the combination comedian-tough guy and has seldom appeared to better advantage. Roy Del Ruth's direction makes the most of a good story and cast."

LOS ANGELES TIMES

"James Cagney's memorable exploit with a grapefruit is tame by comparison with his activities as Dan Quigley in *Lady Killer*. There are few peaceful moments in this film, which shows Mr. Quigley as an insolvent usher, a burglar and a cinema player . . . while suspense is not its strong point, it at least affords enough opportunities for Mr. Cagney to display his characteristic outbursts."

Mordaunt Hall, THE NEW YORK TIMES

"*Lady Killer* illustrates its makers' theory that a James Cagney picture requires less plot than movement. Tired of bashing his ladies on the chin, Cagney in this picture drags Myra (Mae Clarke) out of bed by the hair, hurls her twelve feet down a corridor."

TIME

With Mae Clarke

With Raymond Hattan, Douglass Dumbrille, Russell Hopton and Leslie Fenton

With Margaret Lindsay

"New Cagney picture is an all-time high in roughneck character work even for this rough and tumble star. Assault and battery and a modicum of mayhem committed upon a woman character tops anything yet, this episode having the treat-'em-rough star drag his girl friend by the hair across the room, pitch her emphatically through the door, climaxing the treatment with an enthusiastic sample of booting.

"Crook angle is handled with a cheerful style of humor and there is a certain spirit about the Cagney character, played in his energetic way, that carries its own persuasive charm. Comedy is first rate."

VARIETY

"In *Lady Killer*, there is a complete and unashamed exploitation of a star. James Cagney, who plays the title role in the motion picture, gives so vigorous, exciting and captivating a performance that one pays scant heed to the episodic and frequently implausible qualities of the narrative. Tough, arrogant and likeable, he infuses shopworn material with glamour and makes the work a lively and gusty melodrama."

LITERARY DIGEST

"Skillfully mixing farce, satire and melodrama and affording Mr. Cagney a role in which he is thoroughly at home, this *Lady Killer* turns out to be a sprightly, more or less daring, thoroughly entertaining film—the best Mr. Cagney has made in some time."

NEW YORK WORLD-TELEGRAM

"It is my suspicion that a great deal of the narrative is inclined to be implausible and that its decidedly episodic manner has a way of weakening its force. Nevertheless, it is so vigorously managed, so attractively played, and, above all, so pleasantly filled with the Cagney vitality that it emerges as agreeable entertainment. Neither in taste or in high ethical standards is this *Lady Killer* a thing to be rapturously admired. I wish, too, that Mr. Cagney would let poor Miss Clarke alone for a while. But the film is fun. . . . I still want to see Mr. Cagney play an Irish revolutionist of the Black-and-Tan days though."

Richard Watts, Jr., NEW YORK HERALD TRIBUNE

NOTES

This was hardly a glamorous look at Hollywood life—inside or outside of the studio. But Hollywood was always the first to satirize itself and this was one of the attempts. Originally entitled *The Finger Man*, this

82

Ben Markson scenario contained bite and hit many nails squarely on the head.

Roy Del Ruth kept everything moving briskly along, but it was a first-rate cast that delivered the wallop: Mae Clarke, this time being dragged across a room by her hair, Leslie Fenton and Margaret Lindsay. In the final analysis, it must be agreed that all concerned with this production, whether before or behind the camera, had fun.

With Margaret Lindsay

With Margaret Lindsay

With Mae Clarke

JIMMY THE GENT

A Warner Bros. & Vitaphone Picture

—1934—

CAST

Jimmy Corrigan: JAMES CAGNEY; *Joan Martin:* BETTE DAVIS; *Mabel:* ALICE WHITE; *Louie:* ALLEN JENKINS; *Joe Rector (Monty Barton):* ARTHUR HOHL; *James J. Wallingham:* ALAN DINEHART; *Ronnie Gatston:* PHILIP REED; *The Imposter:* HOBART CAVANAUGH; *Gladys Farrell:* MAYO METHOT; *Hendrickson:* RALF HAROLDE; *Mike:* JOSEPH SAWYER; *Blair:* PHILIP FAVERSHAM; *Posy Barton:* NORA LANE; *Judge:* JOSEPH CREHAN; *Civil Judge:* ROBERT WARWICK; *Jitters:* MERNA KENNEDY; *Bessie:* RENEE WHITNEY; *Tea Assistant:* MONICA BANNISTER; *Man Drinking Tea:* DON DOUGLAS; *Chester Coote:* BUD FLANAGAN (DENNIS O'KEEFE); *Man in Flower Shop:* LEONARD MUDIE; *Justice of the Peace:* HARRY HOLMAN; *File Clerk:* CAMILLE ROVELLE; *Pete:* STANLEY MACK; *Grant:* TOM COSTELLO; *Ferris:* BEN HENDRICKS; *Halley:* BILLY WEST; *Tim:* EDDIE SHUBERT; *Stew:* LEE MORAN; *Eddie:* HARRY WALLACE; *Irish Cop:* ROBERT HOMANS; *Ambulance Driver:* MILTON KIBBEE; *Doctor:* HOWARD HICKMAN; *Nurse:* EULA GUY; *Viola:* JULIET WARE; *Blonde:* RICKEY NEWELL; *Brunette:* LORENA LAYSON; *Second Young Man:* DICK FRENCH; *Third Young Man:* JAY EATON; *Reverend Amiel Bottsford:* HAROLD ENTWISTLE; *Bailiff:* CHARLES HICKMAN; *Ticket Clerk, Steamship:* LEONARD MUDIE; *Steward:* OLAF HYTTEN; *Second Steward:* VESEY O'DAVOREN; *Chalmers:* LESTER DORR; *Secretary:* PAT WING

With Bette Davis

CREDITS

Director: MICHAEL CURTIZ; *Executive Producer:* JACK L. WARNER; *Scenarist:* BERTRAM MILHAUSER; *Based on an original story by:* LAIRD DOYLE, RAY NAZARRO; *Dialogue Director:* DANIEL REED; *Photographer:* IRA MORGAN; *Art Director:* ESDRAS HARTLEY; *Editor:* THOMAS RICHARDS; *Musical Conductor:* LEO F. FORBSTEIN; *Costumer:* ORRY-KELLY; *Makeup Artist:* PERC WESTMORE

SYNOPSIS

Jimmy Corrigan is a semi-respectable racketeer, whose business it is to hunt up missing heirs to large unclaimed estates. If a genuine heir is unobtainable, he conveniently supplies one. He aspires to gentility when he beholds the glittering offices of Wallingham, his competitor, who is more sanctimonious about his trade, no less shifty.

Corrigan's one time assistant, Joan, is now working for Wallingham, for she believes him to be honest. Jimmy soon begins a campaign to prove to Joan that Wallingham is also a scoundrel. Once he has accomplished that, he tells Joan that he will reform if she comes back to work with him.

CRITICS' CIRCLE

"*Jimmy the Gent*, hard and amusing, is no more incredible than a racket picture should be. Good Shot: Cagney and colleagues drilling 'you-alls' and 'yas-suhs' into an East-Sider who is to impersonate an heir to an Atlanta fortune."

TIME

"Fast and flip, rough and rowdy, peppered with a running fire of slang-spiced dialogue, the new James Cagney picture swaps laughs for every dime deposited at the box office.

"Cagney, head close-cropped, is the usual fast-talking tough guy, and gives a characterization which Broadway will love, and which, we fear, is too swift to be followed in the sticks. One of the girls, Alice White, is easily best."

Regina Crewe, NEW YORK AMERICAN

"Jimmy Cagney's latest pictorial feature, *Jimmy the Gent*, is a swift-paced comedy in which he gives another of his vigorous, incisive portrayals."

Mordaunt Hall, THE NEW YORK TIMES

With Allen Jenkins, Mayo Methot, Alice White and Arthur Hohl

With Bette Davis

With Alan Dinehart

"The reprehensible Mr. Cagney, who is sometimes alleged to be one of the cinema's subversive moral influences, is in top form in a rough and rowdy screen farce of dubious ethical value . . . it has the great virtue of some of the most vigorous and racily entertaining dialogue since the days when the Messrs. Glasmon and Bright wrote screen speeches for Mr. Cagney and promised to become the leading cinema playwrights of their time.

"Mr. Cagney, his hair cropped short and his manner as incisive as ever, plays the head of the heir-chasing industry with all of his engaging and forthright candor. . . . Best of the women is Miss Alice White, as a punch-drunk tool of the heir-chasing racketeer. Miss Bette Davis is satisfactory as the heroine."

Richard Watts, Jr., NEW YORK HERALD TRIBUNE

NOTES

Jimmy "the Gent" Cagney returned to the rackets with this film, but the presentation was far lighter than any previous racket picture. The emphasis was on comedy under the astute directorial eye of Michael Curtiz, who was to direct many of Cagney's finest pictures.

Originally called *The Heir Chaser* by Laird Doyle and Ray Nazarro, the scenario by Bertram Milhauser was first entitled *Always a Gent,* then *Blondes and Bonds* and finally became *Jimmy the Gent.* Whatever it was called, it was a rough and tough depiction of the con game. The excellent cast could not have been bettered. Bette Davis was zippy as his former assistant and, when Bette narrowed her expressive eyes and put her hand on her hip, you knew a chilling wisecrack was forthcoming. Alice White, who had appeared to advantage with Jimmy in *Picture Snatcher,* was delightful in another dumb blonde characterization. Alan Dinehart was properly pompous, while Mayo Methot displayed much razzle-dazzle toughness in two scenes.

With Allen Jenkins and Bette Davis

85

HE WAS HER MAN

A Warner Bros. & Vitaphone Picture

—1934—

CAST

Flicker Hayes: JAMES CAGNEY; *Rose Lawrence:* JOAN BLONDELL; *Nick Gardella:* VICTOR JORY; *Pop Sims:* FRANK CRAVEN; *J. C. Ward:* HAROLD HUBER; *Monk:* RUSSELL HOPTON; *Red Deering:* RALF HAROLDE; *Mrs. Gardella:* SARAH PADDEN; *Dutch:* J. M (JOHN) QUALEN; *Dan Curly:* BRADLEY PAGE; *Gassy:* SAMUEL S. HINDS; *Waiter:* GEORGE CHANDLER; *Whitey:* JAMES EAGLES; *Fisherman:* GINO CORRADO

CREDITS

Director: LLOYD BACON; *Scenarists:* TOM BUCKINGHAM, NIVEN BUSCH; *Based on a story by:* ROBERT LORD; *Photographer:* GEORGE BARNES; *Art Director:* ANTON GROT; *Editor:* GEORGE AMY; *Musical Director:* LEO F. FORBSTEIN; *Costumer:* ORRY-KELLY; *Makeup Artist:* PERC WESTMORE; *Song "My Only Romance" by:* SIDNEY MITCHELL, LEW POLLACK

With Joan Blondell

SYNOPSIS

Safe-cracker Flicker Hayes, just out of prison, agrees to do another job with Red and Dan, the men who had framed him. Once he gets the money, he blows the whistle on them. Dan is captured and later executed, while Red escapes and trails Flicker to San Francisco. Flicker meets a former prostitute named Rose, and accompanies her to a Portuguese fishing village, where she intends to marry a man named Nick.

Instead, she falls for Flicker and he leads her on and eventually runs out on her right into Dan's henchmen. He then returns to Rose, but the henchmen follow. They want to take both of them for a ride, but Flicker convinces them that Rose knows nothing about him, so they leave her when they take Flicker away. Rose levels with Nick and promises to be a good wife.

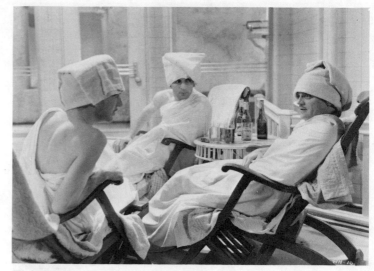

With Bradley Page and Ralf Harolde

CRITICS' CIRCLE

"It is James Cagney's gift to execute a characterization with such clarity and conviction that a poor plot becomes exciting and engaging through his participation. His presence was never more sorely needed than in 'He Was Her Man.' Through a preposterous saga of a safecracker, a streetwalker and a fisherman he moves with fine restraint and assurance, making the screen drama a rather effective hodgepodge of melodrama and sentiment.

"More than any other screen actor today, Mr. Cagney is the exponent of the school of acting of which George M. Cohan is the brilliant dean. Eschewing histrionic fireworks, he is adept at calculated understatement, in which the slightest gesture, the slightest inflection of the voice, is extremely significant. It is possible that you do not care for the disreputable and frequently vicious type of American citizenry he delineates, but you cannot quarrel with the manner in which he recreates them."

Howard Barnes, THE NEW YORK HERALD TRIBUNE

"Mr. Cagney once more reveals himself to be a genuinely expert actor. Miss Blondell does well as Rose."

Mordaunt Hall, THE NEW YORK TIMES

"Another variation of the gangster theme . . . with the always capable and entertaining James Cagney. The cast is good—the production excellent. But at best *He Was Her Man* is only so-so underworld melodrama."

William Boehnel, NEW YORK WORLD-TELEGRAM

With Joan Blondell

87

Robert Lord's original story, *Without Honor*, was used as the working-title throughout filming, as well as *Without Glory*. The scenario by Tom Buckingham and Niven Busch was no great shakes, nor was the direction of Lloyd Bacon. When released, the picture was entitled *He Was Her Man*, but critics and public were not particularly impressed.

Guy Kibbee was originally signed for the part of Pop Sims—it was to be his first straight part since *City Streets*—but by shooting time he was busy on another film. Frank Craven replaced him.

Blondell's role as a prostitute has probably been the major objection to this film's being shown on television. Although, the fact that it is not a very good film might be another reason. Nevertheless, it was Cagney's seventh, and last, picture with Joan Blondell.

With Sarah Padden, Joan Bondell, Victor Jory and Gino Corrado

With Joan Blondell

With James Eagles and George Chandler

88

HERE COMES THE NAVY

A Warner Bros. & Vitaphone Picture

—1934—

CAST

Chesty O'Connor: JAMES CAGNEY; Biff Martin: PAT O'BRIEN; Dorothy Martin: GLORIA STUART; Droopy: FRANK MC HUGH; Gladys: DOROTHY TREE; Commander Denny: ROBERT BARRAT; Lieutenant Commander: WILLARD ROBERTSON; Floor Manager: GUINN WILLIAMS; Droopy's Ma: MAUDE EBURNE; First Girl: MARTHA MERRILL; Second Girl: LORENA LAYSON; Aunt: IDA DARLING; Riveter: HENRY OTHO; Hat Check Girl: PAULINE TRUE; Porter: SAM MC DANIEL; Foreman: FRANK LA RUE; Recruiting Officer: JOSEPH CREHAN; C.P.O.: JAMES BURTIS; Supply Sergeant: EDWARD CHANDLER; Professor: LEO WHITE; Officer: NILES WELCH; Sailor: FRED "SNOWFLAKE" TOONE; Skipper: EDDIE SHUBERT; Admiral: GEORGE IRVING; Captain: HOWARD HICKMAN; Navy Chaplain: EDWARD EARLE; Lieutenant: EMMETT; Bit: GORDON (BILL) ELLIOTT; Workman: NICK COPELAND; Attendant: JOHN SWOR; Marine Orderly: EDDIE ACUFF; Hood at Dance: CHUCK HAMILTON; Sailor: EDDIE FETHERSTONE

With Pat O'Brien, Gloria Stuart and Frank McHugh

With Frank McHugh

CREDITS

Director: LLOYD BACON; *Scenarists:* BEN MARKSON, EARL BALDWIN; *Based on a story by:* BEN MARKSON; *Photographer:* ARTHUR EDESON; *Art Director:* ESDRAS HARTLEY; *Editor:* GEORGE AMY; *Musical Director:* LEO F. FORBSTEIN; *Costumer:* ORRY-KELLY; *Makeup Artist:* PERC WESTMORE; *Technical Adviser:* COMMANDER HERBERT A. JONES; *Song "Hey, Sailor!" by:* IRVING KAHAL, SAMMY FAIN

SYNOPSIS

Biff Martin fights Chesty O'Connor at a dance hall and steals his girl. Later, the hot-tempered, undisciplined Chesty joins the Navy and is assigned to duty on the U.S.S. *Arizona*, where Biff is Petty Officer. Chesty's rugged individualism upsets the traditions of the sea and soon leads to alienation from his fellow gobs.

Biff not only dislikes this young fellow's attitude toward the Navy, but objects to Chesty's romance with his sister Dorothy. When Chesty goes A.W.O.L., Biff has no alternative but to have him court-martialed. Chesty soon redeems himself with a heroic rescue, during which he gets burned to a crisp in a successful effort to save his comrades, and is restored to favor.

CRITICS' CIRCLE

"*Here Comes the Navy* puts James Cagney into a sailor suit aboard the U. S. S. *Arizona* where, as a rebellious, bantam egomaniac, he comports himself exactly as he has done before as a journalist, a taxi-driver, a gambler, an iron-puddler, a racetrack tout, a bellhop. . . . Rapid and reasonably authentic, *Here Comes the Navy* is a satisfactory addition to a series of cinema cartoons which, because their color and mood are indigenous and timely, may be more interesting than most current cinemas 20 years from now."

TIME

"The result is a tiresome rehash which not even the dynamo propulsions of James Cagney and Pat O'Brien are able to keep in motion. The interest of the picture lies rather in the pictorial excursions into the maneuvers of the fleet and the aircraft. . . . The pallidness of the story and dialogue work a hardship on Cagney, O'Brien and Gloria Stuart."

Thornton Delehanty, NEW YORK EVENING POST

"A fast-moving comedy enriched by an authentic naval setting, this Warner production has the added advantage, in these parlous times, of being beyond censorial reproach.

"This last is even more remarkable since the chief player is none other than James Cagney, whose rough-and-tumble antics in several earlier pictures have been held up to scorn by those who would reform the screen. Mr. Cagney has not changed his style in this picture; he still speaks and acts in the traditional Cagneyesque manner. But the restraining bond of the producer, writer, director (or all three), never is relinquished."

Frank S. Nugent, THE NEW YORK TIMES

"As one of the first signs of the new cinema uplift, there is Mr. James Cagney, who in his latest picture confines his punches to the men of his cast and learns that the United States Navy is a great character building organization. It is only fair to add, though, that the reform wave has not seriously softened Mr. Cagney, even though it apparently has had certain moderating effects on his vehicle. . . . Among those who are grateful for the enforced modification of Mr. Cagney's tactics is probably Miss Dorothy Tree who appears briefly in the film as a treacherous blonde. . . . You can imagine what would have happened to Miss Tree in the good old days, but yesterday when Mr. Cagney passed her with hardly a word it was brought to me once more that the new dispensation was here."

Richard Watts, Jr., NEW YORK HERALD TRIBUNE

NOTES

This was Cagney's first film after the inception of the Legion of Decency code, which set everyone wondering what would become of Mae West and Jimmy Cagney. *Here Comes the Navy*, originally called *Hey, Sailor*, was Warners' answer to the censors that Jimmy's personality and antics were to continue, even if certain modifications had to be made. The public didn't seem disturbed one bit—this became a bonanza at the box office.

Here Comes the Navy was filmed, with the cooperation of the U. S. Navy Department, aboard the U.S.S. *Arizona* (later sunk at Pearl Harbor on December 7, 1941) and at the Naval Training Station in San Diego. It was expertly directed by Lloyd Bacon, who had just misfired with *He Was Her Man*, and was well photographed by Arthur Edeson.

This was the first of eight pictures Cagney did with Pat O'Brien, and one of the best. The cast was good

enough to help *Here Comes the Navy* win an Academy Award nomination for Best Picture of 1934.

In case you were wondering why Cagney had two blonde ladies opposite him, it was because Margaret Lindsay, originally cast as Dorothy Martin, had to have an operation at the time shooting began and Warners borrowed Gloria Stuart to replace her. Since scenes with blonde Dorothy Tree, as Gladys, had already been filmed, Jimmy ended up with two blondes.

With Pat O'Brien

With Pat O'Brien, Guinn Williams and Dorothy Tree

THE ST. LOUIS KID

A Warner Bros. & Vitaphone Picture

—1934—

CAST

Eddie Kennedy: JAMES CAGNEY; *Ann Reid:* PATRICIA ELLIS; *Buck Willetts:* ALLEN JENKINS; *Farmer Benson:* ROBERT BARRAT; *Richardson:* HOBART CAVANAUGH; *Merseldopp:* SPENCER CHARTERS; *Brown:* ADDISON RICHARDS; *Gracie:* DOROTHY DARE; *Judge Jones:* ARTHUR AYLESWORTH; *Harris:* CHARLES WILSON; *Joe Hunter:* WILLIAM DAVIDSON; *Louie:* HARRY WOODS; *The* *Girlfriend:* GERTRUDE SHORT; *Pete:* EDDIE SHUBERT; *Gorman:* RUSSELL HICKS; *Sergeant:* GUY USHER; *Cops:* CLIFF SAUM, BRUCE MITCHELL; *Policeman:* WILFRED LUCAS; *Girl:* ROSALIE ROY; *Office Girl:* MARY RUSSELL; *Motor Cop:* BEN HENDRICKS; *Mike:* HARRY TYLER; *Paymaster:* MILTON KIBBEE; *Cook:* TOM WILSON; *Secretaries:* ALICE MARR, VICTORIA VINTON; *Farmer:* LEE PHELPS; *Girl in Car:* LOUISE SEIDEL; *Giddy Girl:* MARY TREEN; *First Girl:* NAN GREY; *Second Girl:* VIRGINIA

With Edna Bennett, Clay Clement and Patricia Ellis

GREY; *Third Girl:* MARTHA MERRILL; *Sheriff:* CHARLES B. MIDDLETON; *Prosecutor:* DOUGLAS COSGROVE; *First Deputy:* MONTE VANDERGRIFT; *Second Deputy:* JACK CHEATHAM; *Driver:* STANLEY MACK; *Attendant:* GROVER LIGGEN; *Broadcast Officer:* FRANK BULL; *Sergeant:* WADE BOTELER; *Policeman:* FRANK FANNING; *Second Policeman:* GENE STRONG; *Flora:* EDNA BENNETT; *Man:* CLAY CLEMENT; *Detective:* JAMES BURTIS and EDDIE FETHERSTONE, JOAN BARCLAY

CREDITS

Director: RAY ENRIGHT; *Producer:* SAMUEL BISCHOFF; *Scenarists:* WARREN DUFF, SETON I. MILLER; *Based on a story by:* FREDERICK HAZLITT BRENNAN; *Photographer:* SID HICKOX; *Dialogue Director:* STANLEY LOGAN; *Art Director:* JACK OKEY; *Editor:* CLARENCE KOLSTER; *Musical Director:* LEO F. FORBSTEIN; *Costumer:* ORRY-KELLY; *Makeup Artist:* PERC WESTMORE

SYNOPSIS

Pugnacious truck driver Eddie Kennedy, who is on a St. Louis-Chicago milk delivery run, becomes involved in a fight between a trucking firm and striking dairymen, who are determined that no milk shall be delivered through their district. While in a small town, Eddie is jailed for fighting, but sneaks out one night to visit his girl, Ann.

During the hours of his absence, a dairyman is killed by a thug hired by the trucking company. Eddie is accused of murder, and, to prove his innocence, he starts to track the real murderer down. Ann offers an alibi and is abruptly kidnapped by agents of the trucking firm. Through fast thinking and action, Eddie uncovers the villains' hideaway, rescues Ann, and exonerates himself.

CRITICS' CIRCLE

"*The St. Louis Kid* shows James Cagney receiving a cuff on the jaw from his leading lady instead of giving her one. . . . In other respects, the picture is standard Cagney entertainment, a rapid, realistic fantasy about a truck driver who wants a quiet weekend in the country."

TIME

"*St. Louis Kid* is the sort of film that Warner Brothers, and only Warner Brothers, do so well. With a swift pace that never lets down, and believable characters,

With Patricia Ellis, Eddie Fetherstone, Martha Merrill and Joan Barclay

With Allen Jenkins

93

never actors merely playing at tough mugs, the thing that gives this type film its unique flavor lies in the story background, its understanding of that background, and its timeliness."

LIBERTY

"*The St. Louis Kid* finds James Cagney in one of the most authentic and therefore most congenial roles he has had in a long while. [It] has the pace, the variety and the soundness of characterization to win wide appreciation. It is worthy of the Cagney talent for making himself likably hard-boiled, and it deserves a special cheer for affording Allen Jenkins, as Cagney's sidekick, the elbow room which his comic gift deserves."

Thornton Delehanty, NEW YORK EVENING POST

"Before marking *The St. Louis Kid* down as a disappointment, let its merits be duly acknowledged. It has the whistling velocity of the Cagney pictures and it hews to the excellent tradition of its kind by its vigor of method and directness of approach. . . . To be sure, it is still worth a filmgoer's time to watch Mr. Cagney hang one on somebody's button, but somehow the spectacle seems less than epic after you have watched the photoplay pussyfooting around a dramatic subject."

Andre Sennwald, THE NEW YORK TIMES

"The picture is at its best when it avoids melodrama and keeps away from its kid-gloved references to the farmer's rebellion. The Messrs. Cagney and Jenkins are, as everyone knows by now, two of the ablest of screen actors, and the plot manipulations of 'The St. Louis Kid' permit them to display their talents attractively. Mr. Cagney remains the most pleasant and yet believable of tough guys, performing the almost incredible feat of combining both realism and likableness in this dangerous type of role."

Richard Watts, Jr., NEW YORK HERALD TRIBUNE

NOTES

The St. Louis Kid brought Jimmy to grips with a major problem then very much in evidence throughout the country: the milk war! Various dairymen and truckers were constantly in the headlines, so Frederick Hazlitt Brennan's story was very timely.

Ray Enright directed with energy and never let the action lag. In fact, enough humor was injected into the proceedings to give Jimmy some wonderfully comic situations. His leading lady was Patricia Ellis, who had replaced Ann Dvorak, who had replaced Margaret Lindsay. It seems getting the right girl for Jimmy was

not as easy a task as it might seem. As usual, Allen Jenkins was his side kick. In England the title was *A Perfect Weekend*. Director Ray Enright replaced director Robert Florey.

With Patricia Ellis

DEVIL DOGS OF THE AIR

A Warner Bros. Picture
A Cosmopolitan Production

—1935—

CAST

Tommy O'Toole: JAMES CAGNEY; *Lieutenant William Brannigan:* PAT O'BRIEN; *Betty Roberts:* MARGARET LINDSAY; *Crash Kelly:* FRANK MC HUGH; *Ma Roberts:* HELEN LOWELL; *Mac:* JOHN ARLEDGE; *Commandant:* ROBERT BARRAT; *Captain:* RUSSELL HICKS; *Adjutant:* WILLIAM B. DAVIDSON; *Senior Instructor:* WARD BOND; *Fleet Commander:* SAMUEL S. HINDS; *Officer:* HARRY SEYMOUR; *Second Officer:* BILL BEGGS; *Mate:* BOB SPENCER; *Officers:* NEWTON HOUSE, RALPH NYE; *Medical Officer:* SELMER JACKSON; *Student:* BUD FLANAGAN

With Margaret Lindsay and Pat O'Brien

With Pat O'Brien

(DENNIS O'KEEFE); *Instructor:* GORDON (BILL) ELLI-OTT; *First Student:* DON TURNER; *Second Student:* DICK FRENCH; *Third Student:* CHARLES SHERLOCK; *Messenger:* CARLYLE BLACKWELL, JR.; *Girl:* MARTHA MERRILL; *Lieutenant Brown:* DAVID NEWELL; *Mrs. Brown:* OLIVE JONES; *Mrs. Johnson:* HELEN FLINT; *Communications Officer:* JOSEPH CREHAN

CREDITS

Director: LLOYD BACON; *Producer:* LOU EDELMAN; *Scenarists:* MALCOLM STUART BOYLAN, EARL BALDWIN; *Based on the story* AIR DEVILS *by:* JOHN MONK SAUN-DERS; *Photographer:* ARTHUR EDESON; *Art Director:* ARTHUR J. KOOKEN; *Editor:* WILLIAM CLEMENS; *Musical Director:* LEO F. FORBSTEIN; *Costumer:* ORRY-KELLY; *Makeup Artist:* PERC WESTMORE; *Technical Adviser:* MAJOR RALPH J. MITCHELL; *Assistant Director:* ERIC STACEY

SYNOPSIS

Tommy O'Toole, a well-heeled kid from Brooklyn, is encouraged to join the Marine Flying Corps by his boyhood pal, Lieutenant William Brannigan. Tommy, a crack stunt flyer, knows as much about flying as his instructors and quickly rises to first in his class, but makes enemies of the other students through his overbearing conceit and continual scoffing of the traditions and curriculum of Marine life.

A flirtation with Betty Roberts, a local waitress, brings about a bitter rivalry between O'Toole and Brannigan, but the wise guy soon gets his come-uppance and learns to respect his officers and the discipline of service life. In the process he finally wins Betty.

CRITICS' CIRCLE

"Any film in which Mr. James Cagney appears is certain to be a boisterous, boastful, full-blooded affair, with speed and Mr. Cagney's forceful personality dominating the action and moulding the pattern of the plot."

THE TIMES (London)

"In spite of its story, the film gains a certain interest due to the faultless authenticity of its background, its flying sequences—one of which has Cagney piloting a burning ship—and its understanding of customs and habits of military life and people."

LIBERTY

"*Devil Dogs of the Air* is thrilling as a bugle call, exciting as a big parade, entertainment through and through. The histrionic honors of the piece are pretty evenly divided between those twin stalwarts, the Messrs. Cagney and O'Brien, here so fortunately teamed. Each excellent, and if James merits a bit the best of it, it is only because his is the flashier role and more difficult of portrayal."

Regina Crewe, NEW YORK AMERICAN

"The co-starring team performs with an ease and naturalness due partly to constant repetitions of their roles. They can still play the hard-boiled officer and cocky recruit with sufficient vigor and comedy to make the picture a lively diversion. 'Devil Dogs of the Air,' content though it be with a well-worn plot, is an expert combination of thrills and fun."

Eileen Creelman, NEW YORK SUN

"It is to the vast credit of Mr. Cagney that he takes a role that might easily have been as unpleasant as one of those unlamented William Haines characters of the silent screen and actually makes it engaging. . . . In his quieter and more sympathetic role Mr. O'Brien is vigorous and ingratiating."

Richard Watts, Jr., NEW YORK HERALD TRIBUNE

"*Devil Dogs of the Air* is a loud and roughneck screen comedy which is distinguished by the most remarkable stunt flying and aerial photography the screen has seen in years. Even the most determined of the anti-militarists is likely to find his principals rolling under the seat when the photoplay is in the air.

"In the granite-jawed style that suits those two excellent actors, the Messrs. O'Brien and Cagney . . . the film is both amusing and exciting."

Andre Sennwald, THE NEW YORK TIMES

NOTES

Warner Bros. was great for saluting the armed services and the public also loved these films. They saluted West Point in *Flirtation Walk*, the Navy in *Here Comes the Navy* and, with *Devil Dogs of the Air*, they took care of the Marines. The film cost roughly $350,000 and took eight weeks to shoot. It was distinguished by fine aerial photography and the usual directorial verve of Lloyd Bacon.

Before giving this film its present title, Warners had come up with: *Air Devils, All Good Soldiers Have Wings, Flying Leathernecks* and *The Flying Marines*.

With Margaret Lindsay

The duo of Cagney and O'Brien, which was getting more fluent all the time, was enhanced by Margaret Lindsay. Frank McHugh, with his "ha, ha, ha" was a laugh-getter.

A previous picture about flying Marines in Nicaragua was Frank Capra's 1929 *Flight* for Columbia, with Ralph Graves and Jack Holt, so *Devil Dogs* was perhaps the second picture of any note made on this subject. It was re-issued nationally in 1941.

This was Jimmy's first Cosmopolitan Production, the company that Marion Davies transferred from MGM to Warner Bros. in 1934.

With Margaret Lindsay

With Margaret Lindsay

G-MEN

A Warner Bros. – First National Picture

—1935—

CAST

James "Brick" Davis: JAMES CAGNEY; *Jean Morgan:* ANN DVORAK; *Kay McCord:* MARGARET LINDSAY; *Jeff McCord:* ROBERT ARMSTRONG; *Brad Collins:* BARTON MAC LANE; *Hugh Farrell:* LLOYD NOLAN; *McKay:* WILLIAM HARRIGAN; *Danny Leggett:* EDWARD PAWLEY; *Gerard:* RUSSELL HOPTON; *Durfee:* NOEL MADISON; *Eddie Buchanan:* REGIS TOOMEY; *Bruce J. Gregory:* ADDISON RICHARDS; *Venke:* HAROLD HUBER; *The Man:* RAYMOND HATTON; *Analyst:* MONTE BLUE; *Gregory's Secretary:* MARY TREEN; *Accomplice:* ADRIAN MORRIS; *Joseph Kratz:* EDWIN MAXWELL; *Bill, The Ballistics Expert:* EMMETT VOGAN; *Agent:* JAMES FLAVIN; *Cops:* STANLEY BLYSTONE, PAT FLAHERTY; *Agent:* JAMES T. MACK; *Congressman:* JONATHAN HALE; *Bank Cashier:* ED KEANE; *Short Man:* CHARLES SHERLOCK; *Henchman at Lodge:* WHEELER OAKMAN; *Police Broadcaster:* EDDIE DUNN; *Interne:* GORDON (BILL) ELLIOTT; *Doctor at Store:* PERRY IVINS; *Hood Shot at Lodge:* FRANK MARLOWE; *Collins' Moll:* GERTRUDE SHORT; *Gerard's Moll:* MARIE ASTAIRE; *Durfee's Moll:* FLORENCE DUD-

With Robert Armstrong and Monte Blue

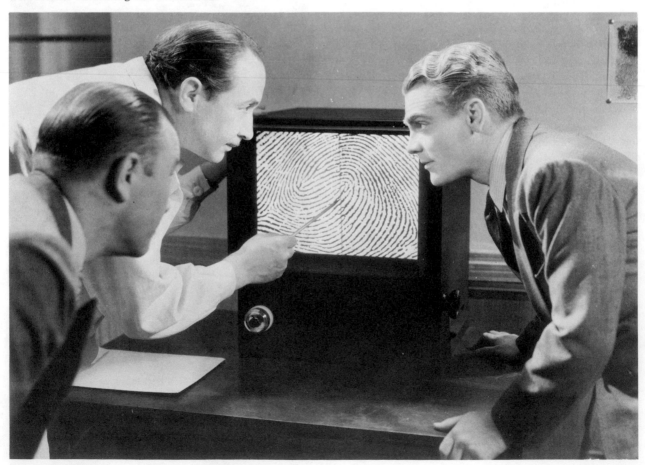

LEY; *Moll:* FRANCES MORRIS; *Hood:* AL HILL; *Gangster:* HUEY WHITE; *Headwaiter:* GLEN CAVENDER; *Tony:* JOHN IMPOLITO; *Sergeant:* BRUCE MITCHELL; *Deputy Sheriff:* MONTE VANDERGRIFT; *Chief:* FRANK SHANNON; *Announcer:* FRANK BULL; *Nurse:* MARTHA MERRILL; *Lounger:* GENE MORGAN; *J. E. Glattner, The Florist:* JOSEPH DE STEFANI; *Machine Gunners:* GEORGE DALY, WARD BOND; *Prison Guard:* TOM WILSON; *Police Driver:* HENRY HALL; *McCord's Aide:* LEE PHELPS; *Hood at Lodge:* MARC LAWRENCE; *Man:* BROOKS BENEDICT

CREDITS

Director: WILLIAM KEIGHLEY; *Scenarist:* SETON I. MILLER; *Based on* PUBLIC ENEMY NO. 1 *by:* GREGORY ROGERS; *Photographer:* SOL POLITO; *Art Director:* JOHN J. HUGHES; *Editor:* JACK KILLIFER; *Music Director:* LEO F. FORBSTEIN; *Costumer:* ORRY-KELLY; *Makeup Artist:* PERC WESTMORE; *Assistant Director:* MC GANN; *Dance Director:* BOBBY CONNOLLY; *Technical Adviser:* FRANK GOMPERT; *Song "You Bother Me an Awful Lot" by:* SAMMY FAIN, IRVING KAHAL

With Russell Hopton, Edward Pawley and Barton MacLane

SYNOPSIS

Brick Davis, a young lawyer who was befriended and educated by a big-shot racketeer, becomes a G-Man to avenge the murder of his best friend, who was shot while arresting a gangster. Since he is a slum boy himself, he is valuable to the department for his acquaintances with racketeers. At times, even his chief thinks he is a spy, because of these underworld associations, but Brick finally gets a chance to prove himself.

A old girl friend, Jean, who is now married to one of the gangsters, discloses their hiding place, a summer resort owned by the racketeer who brought him up. When he kills his former benefactor, he wants to quit the service but stays on to aid his girlfriend, Kay, who is being held hostage by the gang's leader. He shoots it out with them and saves Kay.

CRITICS' CIRCLE

"*G-Men* is James Cagney's best picture since *The Public Enemy.* An enormously exciting topical melodrama, adapted from the past few years' most violent

With Margaret Lindsay and Robert Armstrong

With Margaret Lindsay

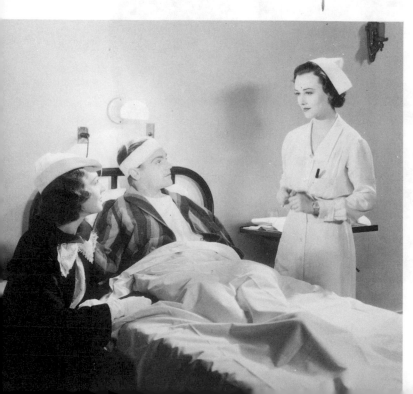

With Ann Dvorak
and Margaret Lindsay

headlines, it investigates the career of a Department of Justice agent with authenticity, enthusiasm, and enough bloodshed to cause cinema censors last week to consider banning the work from all Chicago theatres, on the ground that it might overstimulate small children."

TIME

"The first of many pictures of the same patriotic air now in feverish production at all the major studios, *G-Men* is one long, lusty paean in homage to our federal agents. It is also a violent, sanguinary, and highly exciting film—one packed with swiftly paced action. ... The beauteous Ann Dvorak and Margaret Lindsay attempt to inject a feminine note in the film, but *G-Men* remains as masculine as a bank robbery."

LIBERTY MAGAZINE

"The gangster is back, racing madly through one of the fastest melodramas ever made, scattering death and destruction over the screen, giving audiences enough excitement to last them for weeks, or until the next of the new cycle comes along. *G-Men* has started something."

Eileen Creelman, NEW YORK SUN

"James Cagney contributes another of his electrifying characterizations and is admirably aided by Robert Armstrong. ... The girls, naturally more or less subordinated in a drama of this genre, do well in their parts, with Miss Dvorak, perhaps, winning the nod."

Regina Crewe, NEW YORK AMERICAN

"With its rapid, explosive action continually punching you in the eyes *G-Men*—Warner Brothers' picturization of the government's campaign to exterminate gangsters by fighting fire with fire—emerges a swell show. ... Mr. Cagney has acted any number of superb characterizations in his screen career, but I think that here, as Brick Davis, he gives his most satisfactory performance. ... The construction of the film by Seton I. Miller, who wrote it, and William Keighley, who directed it, is swift and staccato."

William Boehnel, NEW YORK WORLD-TELEGRAM

"Mr. James Cagney, who has often found himself toughly and coolly resisting law and order, is here their champion—and a very vigorous, and courageous one he is. ... Mr. Cagney's desertion from one camp to another has not impaired his vitality, his air of having every situation in hand, however heavily loaded the dice may seem against him, his self-confidence,

Hollywood's Most Famous Bad Man Joins the "G-MEN" and Halts the March of Crime!

THE PICTURE OF THE MONTH

Leave it to Warner Bros. to make the first big picture of America's greatest battle in the war on crime!

The producers of "The Public Enemy" have trained their cameras on the men who trained their guns on the craftiest killers of this gang-ridden day and age.

They've brought the G-MEN, mighty man-hunters of the Department of Justice, out of the shadows of secrecy into the brilliant glare of the picture screen.

Yesterday's screaming headlines are a feeble whisper compared to the sensational revelations in this shot-by-shot dramatization of gangland's Waterloo — the last stand of the underworld!

It's all here! . . . every graphic detail of how the deadly trap was set — and sprung — on the Mad Dog of the Mobs, and of how the Big Shot no jail could hold kept his rendezvous with death!

"G-Men" is easily the *stand-out* for this month's highest honors. Our advice is to see it yourself before your friends begin to rave about it!

Yesterday
Public Enemy No. 1 in the never - to - be - forgotten Warner Bros. thriller, "The Public Enemy."

Today
he's on Uncle Sam's side, staging his own private war with the public enemies of 1935!

JIMMY CAGNEY revels in his return to the scenes of his greatest triumphs! . . . And Ann Dvorak, Margaret Lindsay, and Robert Armstrong score heavily in a big cast, superbly directed by William Keighley for First National Pictures.

On the set with dance director Bobby Connolly, Ann Dvorak and director William Keighley

and his gift for repartee. It has only limited them, and the very discipline of limitation has, oddly enough, given them an added significance."

THE TIMES (London)

NOTES

Warners put Jimmy on the side of the law in *G-Men*. He was his same old self, but his purpose had been redirected. Based on Gregory Roger's *Public Enemy No. 1*, Seton I. Miller's scenario still managed to throw in hold-ups, bank robberies, machine-gun massacres and miscellaneous "bumpings-off."

William Keighley superbly directed this actioner and, to this day, it remains one of Cagney's top films. Besides a huge cast, there were members of the staff of the then recently formed Federal Bureau of Investigation.

Cagney was now making $4500 weekly and it cost approximately $450,000 to film *G-Men* and six weeks to shoot it. This time Cagney had two leading ladies: Ann Dvorak, who sang and danced to "You Bother Me an Awful Lot," and Margaret Lindsay. The major men included Robert Armstrong, Barton MacLane, Lloyd Nolan and Russell Hopton. The working title was *The Farrell Case*.

G-Men was re-released in 1949 on the FBI's twenty-fifth anniversary, with an added prologue featuring David Brian as The Chief and Douglas Kennedy as an FBI agent.

THE IRISH IN US

A Warner Bros. — First National Picture

—1935—

CAST

Danny O'Hara: JAMES CAGNEY; *Pat O'Hara:* PAT O'BRIEN; *Lucille Jackson:* OLIVIA DE HAVILLAND; *Mike O'Hara:* FRANK MC HUGH; *Car-Barn McCarthy:* ALLEN JENKINS; *Ma O'Hara:* MARY GORDON; *Captain Jackson:* J. FARRELL MAC DONALD; *Doc Mullins:* THOMAS JACKSON; *Joe Delancy:* HARVEY PERRY; *Lady in Ring:* BESS FLOWERS; *Neighbor:* MABEL COLCORD; *Doctor:* EDWARD KEANE; *Cook:* HERB HAYWOOD; *Girl:* LUCILLE COLLINS; *Announcer:* HARRY SEYMOUR; *Chick:* SAILOR VINCENT; *Referee:* MUSHY CALLAHAN; *Messenger Boy:* JACK MC HUGH; *Men:* EDWARD GARGAN, HUNTLY GORDON, EMMETT VOGAN, WILL STANTON

102

With Mary Gordon

With Allen Jenkins and
Olivia de Havilland

CREDITS

Director: LLOYD BACON; *Producer:* SAMUEL BISCHOFF;
Scenarist: EARL BALDWIN; *Based on a story by:* FRANK
ORSATTI; *Photographer:* GEORGE BARNES; *Art Director:*
ESDRAS HARTLEY; *Editor:* JAMES GIBBONS; *Musical
Director:* LEO F. FORBSTEIN; *Costumer:* ORRY-KELLY;
Makeup Artist: PERC WESTMORE; *Assistant Director:*
JACK SULLIVAN; *Unit Manager:* BOB FELLOWS

SYNOPSIS

Ma O'Hara has raised three boys. Pat is a patrolman,
Mike is a dumb-bell city fireman, and Danny dislikes
work altogether, but occasionally acts as a fight manager. Pat falls for Lucille Jackson, the police captain's
daughter, who, it turns out, falls for his younger brother
Danny, thus causing a feud between the two brothers.
Meanwhile, Danny promotes a lame-brained fighter
dubbed Car-Barn, who gets all ginned up before a big
fight, which forces Danny to substitute for him. Need-
less to say, he gets the girl.

CRITICS' CIRCLE

"There is an atmosphere of standardization about this
film, and the director, Mr. Lloyd Bacon, has not been
imaginative in the use he has made of that well-tried
team Messrs. James Cagney, Pat O'Brien, and Frank
McHugh."

THE TIMES (*London*)

"The elastic Mr. Cagney has astonishingly little to do
for the first part of the comedy."

THE NEW YORK TIMES

"Cinemaddicts have learned that, in a picture in which
both James Cagney and Pat O'Brien appear, Pat O'Brien
is apt to fall clumsily in love with a girl whom James
Cagney, wrinkling his nose, putting his handkerchief to
his mouth and fingering his cheekbone, will take away
from him. *The Irish In Us* follows the pattern except
that, since it is full of sentiment and soft music, the
rivals perform with an unaccustomed restraint which
at times approaches boredom. O'Brien, a policeman,
Frank McHugh, a fireman, and Cagney, no occupation,
are brothers watched over by an extremely Irish mother
(Mary Gordon) whose brogue is so strong that, to the
possible improvement of the picture, half her lines are
virtually unintelligible."

TIME

103

"Fun, fight and frolic hold the screen divided three ways as befits a film the title of which is bestrewn with shamrocks as its dialogue is with brogue. The three musketeers of the sidewalks of New York, James, Pat and Frank, do nobly with fun faction allotted to them. The direction is breezy."

Regina Crewe, NEW YORK AMERICAN

"The film isn't an epic. It doesn't boast spectacular dance ensembles nor elaborate settings. It isn't even a particularly big story. But—it is high on human interest, plenty of hilarious gags and excellent on emoting. It's down-to-earth, and mellow and punch-packed."

Irene Thirer, NEW YORK POST

"Story and direction are decidedly at odds in [*The Irish in Us*], but fortunately for all concerned direction wins out, and what in other hands might have been a maudlin mixture of Irish tears and mother love turns out to be a fairly human and often snappy domestic comedy."

Winston Burdett, BROOKLYN DAILY EAGLE

With Olivia de Havilland

With Pat O'Brien and Frank McHugh

With Frank McHugh, Mary Gordon, Olivia de Havilland, Pat O'Brien and Bess Flowers

"Although the material is familiar, the acting and the direction are fresh and invigorating, and so the film becomes good-natured and satisfactory but by no means exceptional entertainment."

William Boehnel, NEW YORK WORLD-TELEGRAM

NOTES

The Irish in Us was sweetness and light time, under the direction of Lloyd Bacon. He didn't have to worry about Cagney and O'Brien doing their jobs well, so he concentrated on character actors like Mary Gordon, J. Farrell MacDonald and Frank McHugh, thus injecting loads of Celtic humor.

This was a minor, yet pleasant enough, opus, to be sure, and it benefitted greatly from the photography of George Barnes and the editing of James Gibbons.

A MIDSUMMER NIGHT'S DREAM

A Warner Bros. Picture

—1935—

CAST

Bottom: JAMES CAGNEY; *Lysander:* DICK POWELL; *Flute:* JOE E. BROWN; *Helena:* JEAN MUIR; *Snout:* HUGH HERBERT; *Theseus:* IAN HUNTER; *Quince:* FRANK MC HUGH; *Oberon:* VICTOR JORY; *Hermia:* OLIVIA DE HAVILLAND; *Demetrius:* ROSS ALEXANDER; *Egeus:* GRANT MITCHELL; *First Fairy (Prima Ballerina):* NINI THE-ILADE; *Hippolyta, Queen of Amazons:* VERREE TEAS-DALE; *Titania:* ANITA LOUISE; *Puck:* MICKEY ROONEY;

With Anita Louise

Snug: DEWEY ROBINSON; *Philostrate:* HOBART CAV-ANAUGH; *Starveling:* OTIS HARLAN; *Ninny's Tomb:* AR-THUR TREACHER; *Fairies: Pease-Blossom:* KATHERINE FREY; *Cobweb:* HELEN WESTCOTT; *Moth:* FRED SALE; *Mustard-Seed:* BILLY BARTY

CREDITS

Directors: MAX REINHARDT, WILLIAM DIETERLE; *Pro-ducer:* JACK L. WARNER; *Production Supervisor:* HENRY BLANKE; *Scenarists:* CHARLES KENYON, MARY MC CALL, JR.; *Based on the play by:* WILLIAM SHAKESPEARE; *Photographer:* HAL MOHR; *Art Director:* ANTON GROT; *Editor:* RALPH DAWSON; *Dialogue Director:* STANLEY LOGAN; *Sound Recorder:* MAJOR NATHAN LEVINSON; *Musical Score:* FELIX MENDELSSOHN; *Musical Director:*

LEO F. FORBSTEIN; *Musical Arrangement:* ERICH WOLF-GANG KORNGOLD; *Costumer:* MAX REE; *Dance Ensem-bles:* BRONISLAVA NIJINSKA, NINI THEILADE; *Makeup Artist:* PERC WESTMORE; *Special Photographic Effects:* FRED JACKMAN, BYRON HASKIN, H. E. KOENEKAMP; *Assistant Director:* SHERRY SHOURDS

SYNOPSIS

In Athens, Lysander and Demetrius love Hermia, while Helena futilely loves Lysander, until Puck, boy servant to fairy king Oberon, directs Lysander's love to Helena with a love potion. The same potion is used by Oberon to punish his queen, Titania, for her wandering affec-tions and she temporarily falls in love with Bottom, one of the tradesmen who are preparing a play, "Pyramus and Thisbe," to celebrate the wedding of

106

Theseus, Duke of Athens, to Hippolyta. By morning, the spells wear off and all is correctly restored.

CRITICS' CIRCLE

"Shakespeare produced with a spectacular scope he never dreamed of."

THE STAGE

"The chief fault of this production of *A Midsummer Night's Dream* is that it shows little or no regard for Shakespearean poetry. The rhythm and the verse are for the most part ignored. The lines are so broken up, so disconnected by intervening photographic shots intended to relieve the tedium of speech, that the metre is completely destroyed. . . . The most lamentable mistake in the cast was the Bottom of James Cagney. He seemed to me to misconceive the character, and only became tolerable in the scene where he discovers the ass's head on his shoulders."

Sydney W. Carroll, THE (London) TIMES

"Hollywood pursues the shapes and shadows of the unfettered imagination with courage, skill and heavy artillery in Max Reinhardt's film version of *A Midsummer Night's Dream*. . . . For the work is rich in aspiration and the sum of its faults is dwarfed against the sheer bulk of the enterprise. It has its fun and its haunting beauty.

"Joe E. Brown as Flute the Bellows-mender gives the best performance in the show. Mickey Rooney's remarkable performance as Puck is one of the major delights of the work. As Bottom, the lack-wit weaver whom Puck maliciously endows with an ass's head, James Cagney is too dynamic an actor to play the torpid and obstinate dullard. While he is excellent in the scenes in the wood, in the 'Pyramus and Thisbe' masque he belabors the slapstick of his part beyond endurance."

Andre Sennwald, THE NEW YORK TIMES

"With James Cagney's performance as Bottom we come to more controversial ground. The part of the self-confident weaver, who is decorated with an ass's head by Puck, has come to be associated with actors of greater bulk and considerably less dynamic power; so that Mr. Cagney strikes at most of our conceptions with revolutionary effect. I suspect that there is something disturbing, too, about the fact that it is excellently played, seemed to me a trifle disconcerting. It seems to me that Mr. Cagney is effective throughout the role, because he really is a first-rate actor. At the

With Joe E. Brown, Otis Harlan, Frank McHugh, Hugh Herbert, Dewey Robinson and Arthur Treacher

With makeup artist Perc Westmore

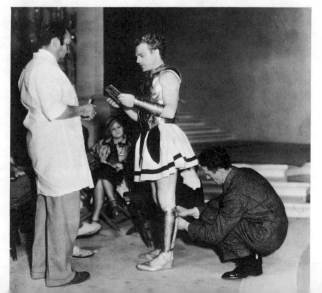

On the set with his wife Billie and makeup men

same time, he did disappoint me slightly. I thought he would be something more than just effective."

Richard Watts, Jr., NEW YORK HERALD TRIBUNE

NOTES

William Shakespeare's delightful comedy-fantasy was first produced (probably to celebrate a wedding at the court) in the Globe Playhouse somewhere between 1590 and 1596, and was first published in quarto form in 1600.

Max Reinhardt, the eminent European producer-director, left his homeland when Hitler came to power and Jack L. Warner welcomed him, in Burbank, with open arms. This was, to be sure, Warners' bid for "class." Because of Reinhardt's lack of cinematic experience, William Dieterle was assigned a co-directorship. Money was no object and the finest of everything was at Reinhardt's disposal.

Reinhardt brought Erich Wolfgang Korngold, the noted Viennese composer, to America to arrange the magnificent Mendelssohn music, and that single act was the greatest favor he could have done for the

With Hugh Herbert, Arthur Treacher, Dewey Robinson and Frank McHugh

brothers Warner. Korngold later wrote great rich musical scores for such Warner films as *Anthony Adverse, The Adventures of Robin Hood* and *Kings Row,* to name only a few.

Hal Mohr's deliriously beautiful photography won an Academy Award for Best Cinematography and Ralph Dawson's striking editing also won an Academy Award. Other outstanding achievements were Anton Grot's art direction, Max Ree's fantastic costumes, and the superb special effects. The film itself was nominated for an Academy Award as Best Picture, but lost to M-G-M's *Mutiny on the Bounty*.

Said Reinhardt: "The part of Bottom has always been played by a stout, middle-aged man. Why? James Cagney's type is perfect and his performance delights me."

With Joe E. Brown

110

FRISCO KID

A Warner Bros. — First National Picture

—1935—

CAST

Bat Morgan: JAMES CAGNEY; *Jean Barrat:* MARGARET LINDSAY; *Paul Morra:* RICARDO CORTEZ; *Bella Morra:* LILY DAMITA; *Charles Ford:* DONALD WOODS; *Spider Burke:* BARTON MAC LANE; *Solly:* GEORGE E. STONE; *William T. Coleman:* ADDISON RICHARDS; *James Daley:* JOSEPH KING; *Judge Crawford:* ROBERT MC WADE; *McClanahan:* JOSEPH CREHAN; *Graber:* ROBERT STRANGE; *Slugs Crippen:* JOSEPH SAWYER; *Shanghai Duck:* FRED KOHLER; *Tupper:* EDWARD MC WADE; *Jumping Whale:* CLAUDIA COLEMAN; *The Weasel:* JOHN WRAY; *First Lookout:* IVAR MC FADDEN; *Second Lookout:* LEE PHELPS; *Evangelist:* WILLIAM WAGNER; *Drunk:* DON BARCLAY; *Captain:* JACK CURTIS; *Miner:* WALTER LONG; *Man:* JAMES FARLEY; *Shop Man:* MILTON KIBBEE; *Salesman:* HARRY SEYMOUR; *Madame:* CLAIRE SINCLAIR; *Young Drunk:* ALAN DAVIS; *Dealer:* KARL HACKETT; *First Policeman:* WILFRED LUCAS; *Second Policeman:* JOHN T. (JACK) DILLON; *First*

111

With George E. Stone and Margaret Lindsay

With Fred Kohler

With Lily Damita and Ricardo Cortez

Man: EDWARD MORTIMER; *Second Man:* WILLIAM HOLMES; *Usher:* DON DOWNEN; *Mrs. Crawford:* MRS. WILFRED NORTH; *Speaker:* CHARLES MIDDLETON; *Man:* JOE SMITH MARBA; *Doctor:* LANDERS STEVENS; *Mulligan:* FRANK SHERIDAN; *Men:* J. C. MORTON, HARRY TENBROOK; *Dealer:* LEW HARVEY; *Rat Face:* EDDIE STURGIS; *Captain (Vigilante):* WILLIAM DESMOND; *Maid:* JESSIE PERRY; *Contractors:* EDWARD KEANE, EDWARD LE SAINT; *Vigilante Leaders:* ROBERT DUDLEY, DICK RUSH; *Doctor:* JOHN ELLIOTT; and HELENE CHADWICK, BILL DALE, DICK KERR, ALICE LAKE, VERA STEDMAN, JANE TALLENT

CREDITS

Director: LLOYD BACON; *Producer:* SAMUEL BISCHOFF; *Scenarists:* WARREN DUFF, SETON I. MILLER; *Based on an original story by:* WARREN DUFF, SETON I. MILLER; *Photographer:* SOL POLITO; *Art Director:* JOHN HUGHES; *Editor:* OWEN MARKS; *Musical Director:* LEO F. FORBSTEIN; *Costumer:* ORRY-KELLY; *Makeup Artist:* PERC WESTMORE; *Sound Recorder:* JAMES THOMPSON

SYNOPSIS

Bat Morgan, a poor sailor, is headed for the California gold fields when he becomes the victim of an attempted shanghai. In the ensuing free-for-all, he kills the notorious Shanghai Duck and, thus, becomes highly revered by the citizens of San Francisco's Barbary Coast. Morgan rises to power and riches by the sheer right of might, but experiences an almost helpless romance with Jean Barrat, a girl from the "right" side of the tracks.

CRITICS' CIRCLE

"Cagney is, as usual, forceful and aggressive, which is what the role calls for. Even in the serious love scenes, with no wisecracks or rough-house business to depend on, he carries himself well. But there are moments in which Cagney shows something he's never been guilty of before, and that's a tendency to go beyond the necessary histrionics and 'ham' it. Cagney's forte has always been a frank naturalness and a completely individualistic style of expression. Cluttering up a valuable formula with distracting business is poor judgment."

VARIETY

"Within the framework of American History Hollywood not infrequently moves with assurance and authority. At first Bat Morgan promised to be something more than the familiar type played so often by Mr. Cagney, but it is no more than a promise, and the film soon declines in interest, though the atmosphere remains triumphantly faithful to the period and the place. But atmosphere is not enough. With a little more imagination this story might have become impressive. Instead it is dragged along the pedestrian path cut out for Mr. Cagney."

LONDON DAILY TELEGRAPH

"Packed with action, the Cagney film offers a vigorous picture of early days along the San Francisco waterfront. Realistic fist fights, plenty of gunplay, and a tense climax bringing in the Vigilantes offer exciting entertainment that moves swiftly against the colorful backgrounds of a colorful era. The rowdy atmosphere of the hectic period is well sustained and the battling mob scenes toward the end of the film are effective. Cagney gives an interesting performance in his role."

Rose Pelswick, NEW YORK EVENING JOURNAL

"*Frisco Kid* is a carbon copy of *The Barbary Coast,* and a muddled one. It plays with vitality and frenzy, but it never gets close to the core of its subject. . . . The individual work is good, but in its entirety *The Frisco Kid* is disconcertingly unreal."

Thornton Delehanty, NEW YORK EVENING POST

"Although the film has little virtue as an historical canvas, it is a scrappy and bouncing melodrama full of the flaring, splashing color of its period, with a notably good performance in the title role by James Cagney."

William Boehnel, NEW YORK WORLD-TELEGRAM

"Gory, scrappy, feverish and melodramatic, this new Cagney picture restores the pugnacious hero to the realm of 'action.' Cagney in the quaint costumes of the 1850's may seem fanciful, but there is nothing fanciful about the way he puts on a brawl. Despite his wing collar, his curls, his brocaded waistcoat and his genteel lady-love, he gives the fighting show of his life in *The Frisco Kid.*"

Bland Johaneson, New York DAILY NEWS

NOTES

Cagney went from Elizabethan times to the Gay Nineties in one fell swoop. This Warren Duff-Seton I. Miller saga would not have been too bad, except for its timing. It followed on the heels of Samuel Goldwyn's more ambitious production of *Barbary Coast* and suffered in comparison.

His performance of Bat Morgan was vivid enough, and full of infinite variety, but the storyline provided little but the usual rough-and-ready action Cagney, himself, was getting tired of. He wanted more substance in his pictures.

The better-than-average cast included Margaret Lindsay, Ricardo Cortez, Lily Damita (who replaced Estelle Taylor), George E. Stone and Donald Woods.

The cast also included several actors and directors from the silent film era who were appearing as "extras" in *Frisco Kid*. Former director Dick Kerr was joined by former stars Helene Chadwick, Bill Dale, Alice Lake, Vera Stedman and Jane Tallent.

On the set with stars and directors from silent film era. Standing: Bill Dale, Vera Stedman, Jane Tallent and Dick Kerr. Seated: Helene Chadwick and Alice Lake

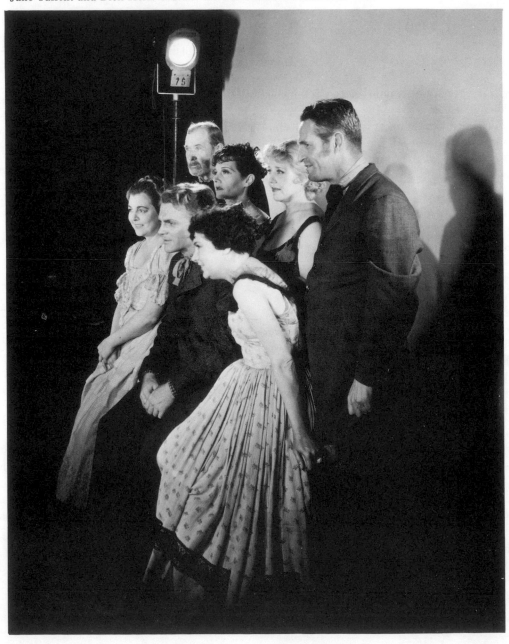

CEILING ZERO

A Warner Bros. — First National Picture
A Cosmopolitan Production

— 1935 —

CAST

Dizzy Davis: JAMES CAGNEY; *Jack Lee:* PAT O'BRIEN; *Tommy Thomas:* JUNE TRAVIS; *Texas Clark:* STUART ERWIN; *Tay Lawson:* HENRY WADSWORTH; *Lou Clark:* ISABEL JEWELL; *Al Stone:* BARTON MAC LANE; *Mary Lee:* MARTHA TIBBETTS; *Joe Allen:* CRAIG REYNOLDS; *Buzz Gordon:* JAMES H. BUSH; *Les Bogan:* ROBERT LIGHT; *Fred Adams:* ADDISON RICHARDS; *Eddie Payson:* CARLYLE MOORE, JR.; *Smiley Johnson:* RICHARD PURCELL; *Transportation Agent:* GORDON (BILL) ELLIOTT; *Baldy Wright:* PAT WEST; *Doc Wilson:* EDWARD GARGAN; *Mike Owens:* GARRY OWEN; *Mama Gini:* MATHILDE COMONT; *Birdie:* CAROL HUGHES; *Stunt Fliers:* FRANK TOMICK, PAUL MANTZ; *Pilots:* JIMMY AYE, HOWARD ALLEN, MIKE LALLY, HAROLD MILLER; *Mechanic:* JERRY JEROME; *Hostesses:* HELENE MC ADOO, GAY SHERIDAN, MARY LOU DIX, LOUISE SEIDEL, HELEN ERICKSON; *Office Workers:* DON WAYSON, DICK CHERNEY, JIMMIE BARNES, FRANK MC DONALD; *Teletype Operator:* J. K. KANE; *Tall Girl:* JAYNE MANNERS; *Girls:* MARYON CURTIZ, MARGARET PERRY

115

With Pat O'Brien and June Travis

With Pat O'Brien

CREDITS

Director: HOWARD HAWKS; *Producer:* HARRY JOE BROWN; *Scenarist:* FRANK WEAD; *Based on the play Ceiling Zero by:* FRANK WEAD; *Photographer:* ARTHUR EDESON; *Art Director:* JOHN HUGHES; *Editor:* WILLIAM HOLMES; *Musical Director:* LEO F. FORBSTEIN; *Costumer:* ORRY-KELLY; *Makeup Artist:* PERC WESTMORE; *Assistant Director:* LEE SELANDER; *Unit Manager:* BOB FELLOWS

SYNOPSIS

Irresponsible pilot Dizzy Davis returns to Federal Air Lines of Newark to get his old job back. His escapades are matched only by the loyalty shown him by the softhearted ground superintendent, Jake Lee. To keep an engagement with an aviatrix, he feins a heart attack, and his pal Texas Clark pilots his run and—as fate would have it—dies. Suddenly awakened to bitter reality, Davis braves a storm to test a newly invented de-icer device and crashes to his death a slightly tarnished hero.

CRITICS' CIRCLE

"You will probably find that the latter episodes of the film have too tearful a tone for so predominantly masculine a drama. I doubt very much whether Mr. Cagney himself put very much faith in the romantic finale. He acts with his customary gusto and vitality, and though his performance is by no means free of typical mannerisms he is an engaging and credible airman until he turns hero."

Winston Burdett, BROOKLYN DAILY EAGLE

"Howard Hawks, who is a master director when it comes to dealing with the drama of flying, has handled this latest aviation film with great skill. . . . Cagney plays the flamboyant character with amazing restraint."

Kate Cameron, New York DAILY NEWS

"Both O'Brien and Cagney are profoundly moving as the two friends linked by sentiment rather than mind. The characters are so human, ring so true that the tragedy of their association is doubly stirring."

Bland Johaneson, New York DAILY MIRROR

"James Cagney plays Dizzy, the irresponsible, courageous, outrageous Dizzy; and plays it better than he

116

has ever played anything before. His comedy crying scene is as expertly funny as his unspoken remorse is moving."

Eileen Creelman, NEW YORK SUN

"There is an element of tension in *Ceiling Zero* that sets it apart from the run-of-the-mill screen melodrama and, by the same token, relates it closely to the memorable gangster films which prevailed in the early days of Edward G. Robinson and James Cagney. Cagney is remarkably accurate in his portrayal of a loose-fibered daredevil whose major hobby is women. The picture owes a deal of its power to Howard Hawks' superb direction. Nor can one overlook the fine contributions of Isabel Jewell, Barton MacLane and June Travis in secondary roles."

Thornton Delehanty, NEW YORK EVENING POST

"The Americans are unsurpassed in the contrivance of films which bolster up improbable events and crude psychology with plausible detail. These films have little or no relation to art, but they are undeniably entertaining. This (*Ceiling Zero*) has Mr. James Cagney's graceful impudence to enlist our sympathy, and for victims the lively Miss June Travis, the wryly comic Mr. Stuart Erwin, and the dominating Mr. Pat O'Brien."

LONDON DAILY TELEGRAPH

"Packed with thrills, it has more than one given moment. It holds the interest all along and presents Cagney with a part he can get his teeth into. It also gives the tough but sympathetic Pat O'Brien a chance. Cagney and O'Brien know just how far to pull heartstrings. Chief credit for this telling entertainment goes to the actors."

THE TIMES (London)

"Cagney plays Dizzy with gusto, extracting sympathy from a role not over-blessed with that commodity. His well-known mixture of bounce, pugnacity, and appeal has been deftly exploited in a characterization his fellows will probably find much to their liking."

DAILY FILM RENTER

NOTES

Ceiling Zero (meaning fog on the ground), based on Frank Wead's Broadway play, provided Cagney with a fine drama of civil aviation. Under Howard Hawks' acute direction, this became the most powerfully dramatic aviation story since M-G-M's *Night Flight* two years before.

The play, as produced on the stage by Brock Pemberton and directed by Antoinette Perry, starred John Litel as Dizzy and Osgood Perkins as Jake. This was a very popular film with audiences and critics alike. The Cagney-O'Brien duo was again in full evidence and the supporting cast included such fine players as Stuart Erwin, Barton MacLane and Isabel Jewell (especially effective in a difficult role).

The author, Lt. Comdr. Wead, went through World War I as a naval aviator untouched. After the war, he fell off a chair and was paralyzed.

With Robert Light, Pat O'Brien, James Bush, June Travis and Isabel Jewell

With Pat O'Brien, Mathilde Comont, Martha Tibbetts, June Travis and Stuart Erwin

GREAT GUY

A Grand National Picture

—1936—

CAST

Johnny Cave: JAMES CAGNEY; *Janet Henry:* MAE CLARKE; *Pat Haley:* JAMES BURKE; *Pete Reilly:* EDWARD BROPHY; *Conning:* HENRY KOLKER; *Hazel Scott:* BERNADENE HAYES; *Captain Pat Hanlon:* EDWARD J. MC NAMARA; *Cavanaugh:* ROBERT GLECKLER; *Joe Burton:* JOE SAWYER; *Al:* ED GARGAN; *Tim:* MATTY FAIN; *Mrs. Ogilvie:* MARY GORDON; *Joel Green:* WALLIS CLARK; *The Mayor:* DOUGLAS WOOD; *Clerk:* JEFFREY SAYRE; *Meat Clerk:* EDDY CHANDLER; *Store Manager:* HENRY ROQUEMORE; *Client:* MURDOCK MAC QUARRIE; *Woman at Accident:* KATE PRICE; *Detective:* FRANK O'CONNOR; *Furniture Salesman:* ARTHUR HOYT; *Truck Driver:* JACK PENNICK; *Reporter:* LYNTON BRENT; *City Editor:* JOHN DILSON; *Guests:* BUD GEARY, DENNIS O'KEEFE; *Parker:* ROBERT LOWERY; *Grocery Clerk:* BOBBY BARBER; *Nurse:* GERTRUDE GREEN; *Burton's Girl Friend:* ETHELREDA LEOPOLD; *Cop at Accident:* BRUCE MITCHELL; *Party Guests:* JAMES FORD, FRANK MILLS, BEN HENDRICKS, JR.; *Deputy:* KERNAN CRIPPS; *2nd Meat Clerk:* BILL O'BRIEN; *Chauffeur:* LESTER DORR; *Receiving Clerk:* HARRY TENBROOK; *Mike the Cop:* LEE SHUMWAY; and GERTRUDE ASTOR, VERA STEADMAN, MILDRED HARRIS, BERT KALMAR, JR., WALTER D. CLARKE, JR.

With Mae Clarke

118

CREDITS

Director: JOHN G. BLYSTONE; *Producer:* DOUGLAS MAC-
LEAN; *Scenarists:* HENRY MC CARTHY, HENRY JOHNSON,
JAMES EDWARD GRANT, HARRY RUSKIN; *Based on "The
Johnny Cave Stories" by:* JAMES EDWARD GRANT; *Ad-
ditional Dialogue:* HORACE MC COY; *Photographer:*
JACK MC KENZIE; *Art Director:* BEN CARRE; *Editor:*
RUSSELL SCHOENGARTH; *Sound Recorder:* HAROLD
BUMBAUGH; *Musical Director:* MERLIN SKILES; *Cos-
tumer:* DOROTHY BEAL; *Assistant Director:* JOHN
SHERWOOD; *Presented by:* EDWARD L. ALPERSON

SYNOPSIS

Ex-prizefighter Johnny Cave, an honest public official,
is chief deputy of the Bureau of Weights and Measures.
He endeavors to fight a gang of short-weight chiselers,
who defraud shoppers by tactics such as weighing
down chickens with lead slugs and putting false bottoms in baskets of strawberries.

Johnny's girl friend, Janet Henry, is secretary to
one of the town's biggest grafters. In his campaign,
even though he's on the side of the law, Johnny does
not hesitate to use techniques which rival those of the
grafters.

CRITICS' CIRCLE

"*Great Guy* is James Cagney's first picture for the up
and coming young production company whose No. 1
box-office attraction he became after he broke with
Warner Bros. last year. As such, it goes a long way to
disprove the Hollywood theory that, given a free hand
in selecting stories and casts, an actor's vanity is sure
to lead him astray. *Great Guy* is vintage Cagney, ex-
hibiting him at all the shoulder-punching and *sotto
voce* wisecracking on which was founded his reputation as the cinema's No. 1 mick.

"In addition to delighting admirers of Actor Cagney, *Great Guy*, directed by John Blystone, produced
by onetime actor Douglas MacLean, sets the industry
an example of what a young company can do by spending its money on good actors and good writing instead
of big names, ponderous sets and over-pretentious
publicity."

TIME

"The film offers little that is new in the racket line,
but anyway it presents the same bustling, two-fisted

With James Burke and Bernadene Hayes

On the set with producer Douglas MacLean

119

Mr. Cagney who has fought so valiantly for law and order, or against them, in the past. If the story of *Great Guy* has about it a reminiscent and rather minor ring, at least it serves to remind us how much the screen has lost these past twelve months by Mr. Cagney's absence."

Winston Burdett, BROOKLYN DAILY EAGLE

"The photoplay itself is far from noteworthy, but Mr. Cagney invests it with such vigor and charm that it is distinctly worth attending. . . . He gives one of his most adroitly managed performances. If one is to quarrel with *Great Guy*, it is because it is not nearly worthy of Mr. Cagney's splendid gifts."

Howard Barnes, NEW YORK HERALD TRIBUNE

"In *Great Guy* James Cagney apparently is doing the things he likes best, but they are repetitious and apt to disappoint a public anticipating something finer from this star after his quite lengthy absence. It's all typical Cagney stuff, and that's the trouble with it. An actor of Cagney's ability should not be typed, either at the studio or in public estimation."

VARIETY

"With Mr. Cagney, then, allied with the forces of right for a change, *Great Guy* is an excellent vehicle for the talents the screen audience knows him for, it is crackling entertainment, and it bears unmistakable evidence of that Hollywood rarity, complete cooperation of the director and the story and casting departments, for there are interludes, deftly introduced, which permit Mr. Cagney to be the dynamic, knuckle-dusting Cagney of old."

J. T. M., THE NEW YORK TIMES

NOTES

When *Great Guy* was released, in December 1936, Cagney had been off the screen for one year. During this time he and Warner Bros. battled in court, with Jimmy finally becoming victorious.

This was his first picture (in a two-picture-a-year deal) with the independent outfit Grand National, and was based on the "Johnny Cave Stories" by James Edward Grant that had been appearing in the Saturday Evening Post. John G. Blystone neatly directed on a shoestring budget, which was all too apparent, since a Warners picture had definite production values that were missing here.

But, despite the budget, *Great Guy*, or *Pluck of the Irish* as it was called in England, was a nifty and ex-

citing melodrama. It was fun seeing Mae Clarke back in a Cagney picture. Mary Gordon replaced Grace Goodall, while Wallis Clark replaced Russell Hicks.

With Eddy Chandler, Henry Roquemore and James Burke

With Mae Clarke

SOMETHING TO SING ABOUT

A Grand National Picture

—1937—

CAST

Terry Rooney: JAMES CAGNEY; Rita Wyatt: EVELYN DAW; Hank Meyers: WILLIAM FRAWLEY; Stephanie Hajos: MONA BARRIE; Bennett O. Regan: GENE LOCKHART; Orchestra Soloist: JAMES NEWILL; Pinky: HARRY BARRIS; Candy: CANDY CANDIDO; Soloist: CULLY RICHARDS; Cafe Manager: WILLIAM B. DAVIDSON; Blaine: RICHARD TUCKER; Farney: MAREK WINDHEIM; Easton: DWIGHT FRYE; Daviani: JOHN ARTHUR; Ito: PHILIP AHN; Miss Robbins: KATHLEEN LOCKHART; Transportation Manager: KENNETH HARLAN; Studio

With John Arthur

With Evelyn Daw

Attorney: HERBERT RAWLINSON; *Edward Burns:* ERNEST WOOD; *Man Terry fights:* CHICK COLLINS; *Other Man:* DUKE GREEN; *Dancers:* HARLAND DIXON, JOHNNY BOYLE, JOHNNY (SKINS) MILLER, PAT MORAN, JOE BENNETT, BUCK MACK, EDDIE ALLEN; *Singer:* BILL CAREY; *Specialty:* THE VAGABONDS; *Girls:* ELINORE WELZ, ELEANOR PRENTISS; *Arthur Nelson's Fighting Cats:* PINKIE AND PAL; *Cabby:* FRANK MILLS; *Stuntman:* DUKE GREEN; *Studio Official:* LARRY STEERS; *Sailor in Drag:* JOHN (SKINS) MILLER; *S.F. Theatre Manager:* EDDIE KANE; *Studio Guard:* EDWARD HEARN; *Three Shades of Blue:* DOTTIE MESSMER, VIRGINIA LEE IRWIN, DOLLY WALDORF; *Ship's Captain:* ROBERT MC KENZIE; *Head Waiter:* ALPHONSE MARTEL; BO PEEP KARLIN and PAUL MC LARAND

CREDITS

Director: VICTOR SCHERTZINGER; *Producer:* ZION MYERS; *Scenarist:* AUSTIN PARKER; *Based on a story by:* VICTOR SCHERTZINGER; *Photographer:* JOHN STUMAR; *Art Directors:* ROBERT LEE, PAUL MURPHY; *Editor:* GENE MILFORD; *Musical Director:* C. BAKALEINKOFF; *Dance Director:* HARLAND DIXON; *Arrangements:* MYRL ALDERMAN; *Assistant Director:* JOHN SHERWOOD; *Production Manager:* HAROLD LEWIS; *Unit Manager:* GASTON GLASS; *Still Photographer:* TAD A. GILLUM; *Songs "Right or Wrong," "Any Old Love," "Something to Sing About," "Loving You," "Out of the Blue" by:* VICTOR SCHERTZINGER

SYNOPSIS

Terry Rooney, a Manhattan band leader, is called to Hollywood to star in a musical. Convinced by a scheming producer that his career is a flop, Terry marries his former soloist, Rita Wyatt, and they go off to the South Seas. Upon returning, he signs a seven-year contract which requires that he fake bachelorhood, with his wife agreeing to the subterfuge. However, trying to maintain this new image causes marital problems and Rita leaves for New York. Terry follows her and, together, they return to the band and freedom.

CRITICS' CIRCLE

"James Cagney leads with his left again, only in his newest picture the left is his foot instead of his fist. *Something To Sing About* is an entertaining piece, a light, gay and good-natured spoof of Hollywood. Cagney checks in a likeable performance and is ably assisted by William Frawley, who does a grand bit as the studio press agent; by Evelyn Daw, who sings well as the feminine lead; and by Mona Barrie, who does a smooth impersonation of a foreign star."

Rose Pelswick, NEW YORK JOURNAL-AMERICAN

"*Something To Sing About* is nothing to make a song about, but it returns two-fisted Cinemactor James Cagney to his theatrical nonage of 1924, when he was just one of the boys tapping routines in vaudeville. Though still unable to startle the dance world, he does unveil a new, more versatile Cagney. Now under Grand National management, free to create new roles, he is still most effective in the kind of thing he used to do. This venture into musical drama demands neither a repeat performance nor condemnation proceedings."

TIME

"James Cagney's second independently produced film for Grand National release is a first-class comedy with music giving him a chance to show himself in a more versatile part than provided in previous pictures. In this one, he sings, dances and plays a romantic juvenile. Cagney has brushed up on his tapping and handles himself easily and with assurance."

VARIETY

"The engaging Mr. Cagney, shrewd in the affairs of showmanship, conducts a thorough carnival in this rollicking musical comedy. His multiple accomplishments include hoofing and crooning as well as Cagney fisticuffs. He plays a role which requires all of these accomplishments in a rich story artfully fabricated out of show-business."

Bland Johaneson, New York DAILY MIRROR

"This is no *A Star is Born*, but a small musical about two singers whose marriage is almost broken up by success in the movies. The picture has James Cagney, of all people, as a glamour boy. . . . Miscast in a romantic role, he still plays briskly, keeping a certain liveliness in the film as long as he is on the screen. He dances well enough, too, in several unimaginative routines. His comedy scenes are more effective.

"*Something to Sing About* does not compare with Mr. Cagney's old films. This is a mild little piece, amusing mainly when it makes faces about Hollywood."

Eileen Creelman, NEW YORK SUN

"Jimmy Cagney's transition from a tough hombre to a romantic lead is accomplished with complete dexterity and without the loss of a single whit of the vigorous and dynamic qualities that always are a definite part of his screen characterizations in the eminently enjoyable song-and-dance film called 'Something To Sing About.' "

William Boehnel, NEW YORK WORLD-TELEGRAM

"That old grapefruit squasher, James Cagney, returned to the screen yesterday in an amusing farce entitled *Something To Sing About*. In this one he sings and dances to the delight of Cagney fans. Though admittedly not a Fred Astaire, there is a certain grace and agility about the man."

BROOKLYN DAILY EAGLE

On the set with director Victor Schertzinger and Evelyn Daw

Rehearsing

NOTES

Although *Something to Sing About* suffered from similar budget problems that were noticeable in *Great Guy*, it did provide audiences with some marvelous solo dancing by Cagney. The addition of music made the pace seem brisker than his first Grand National effort. The story was routine and the songs unmemorable. Director Victor Schertzinger, going against traditions, shot this musical comedy in continuity.

Evelyn Daw, a twenty-year-old from South Dakota, was Jimmy's co-star. Of the five songs, Miss Daw sang three, while Cagney and a trio named Three Shades of Blue did "Any Old Love." Despite the poor songs, C. Bakaleinikoff's musical score was nominated for an Academy Award. Of the serviceable cast only Mona Barrie lent class, in a blonde wig, as a foreign-born film star. Her two scenes with Cagney were well played.

Something to Sing About was re-issued in 1947 by Screencraft Pictures as "Battling Hoofer."

BOY MEETS GIRL

A Warner Bros. Picture

—1938—

CAST

Robert Law: JAMES CAGNEY; *J. C. Benson:* PAT O'BRIEN; *Susie:* MARIE WILSON; *C. Elliott Friday:* RALPH BELLAMY; *Rossetti:* FRANK MC HUGH; *Larry Toms:* DICK FORAN; *Rodney Bevan:* BRUCE LESTER; *Announcer:* RONALD REAGAN; *Happy:* PAUL CLARK; *Peggy:* PENNY SINGLETON; *Miss Crews:* DENNIE MOORE; *Songwriters:* HARRY SEYMOUR, BERT HANLON; *Major Thompson:* JAMES STEPHENSON; *B. K.:* PIERRE WATKIN; *Cutter:* JOHN RIDGELY; *Office Boy:* GEORGE HICKMAN; *Smitty:* CLIFF SAUM; *Commissary Cashier:* CAROLE LANDIS; *Dance Director:* CURT BOIS; *Olaf:* OTTO FRIES; *Extra:* JOHN HARRON; *Wardrobe Attendant:* HAL K. DAWSON; *Nurse:* DOROTHY VAUGHAN; *Director:* BERT HOWARD; *Young Man:* JAMES NOLAN; *Bruiser:* BILL TELAAK; *Cleaning Woman:* VERA LEWIS; *Nurses:* JAN HOLM, ROSELLA TOWNE, LOI CHEANEY; *L. A. Operator:* JANET SHAW; *Paris Operator:* NANETTE LAFAYETTE; *N. Y. Operator:* PEGGY MORAN; *Jascha:* EDDY CONRAD; and SIDNEY BRACY, WILLIAM HAADE, CLEM BEVANS

With Pat O'Brien and Marie Wilson

CREDITS

Director: LLOYD BACON; *Producer:* GEORGE ABBOTT; *Scenarists:* BELLA SPEWACK, SAM SPEWACK; *Photographer:* SOL POLITO; *Art Director:* ESDRAS HARTLEY; *Editor:* WILLIAM HOLMES; *Sound Recorder:* DOLPH THOMAS; *Musical Director:* LEO F. FORBSTEIN; *Costumer:* MILO ANDERSON; *Makeup Artist:* PERC WESTMORE; *Song "With a Pain in My Heart" by:* JACK SCHOLL, M. K. JEROME

SYNOPSIS

Robert Law and J. C. Benson, a pair of delirious and daffy scenario writers, endlessly embroider the "boy meets girl" theme in everything they do. However, their studio pranks are the despair of a stuffy supervisor and a conceited horse-opera star named Larry Toms.

For a gag, they write a part into Toms' new picture for the unborn son of Susie, a waitress in the studio commissary. When she is about to give birth, the pair volunteer to act as the infant's godfathers and to establish him in pictures. The child is named Happy and becomes a sensation, stealing scene after scene from the Western star.

CRITICS' CIRCLE

"In the case of *Boy Meets Girl* it is the performing rather than the adaptation or the direction, which has succeeded in changing a popular stage farce into an extremely amusing screen comedy. It seems to me, though, that it is the irrepressible clowning of James Cagney and Pat O'Brien which gives the show its fine comic flavor. The Messrs. Cagney and O'Brien have been wise, I think, in playing the travesty for straight laughs."

Howard Barnes, NEW YORK HERALD TRIBUNE

"The film version is prodigal. So is Mr. Cagney, who could be funnier if less fancy. A good actor all around, he embroiders his work with too much movement. Pat O'Brien is simpler but Cagney has the better material. . . . This is one of the funniest of films."

Arthur Pollock, BROOKLYN DAILY EAGLE

"*Boy Meets Girl* goes like a house afire when James Cagney and Pat O'Brien, as a pair of screwloose screenwriters, are expounding their Boy-Girl theory of cinema, imitating two British guardsmen, acting five parts at once in one of their screen plays, gener-

ally giving the impression of being possessed of a legion of March Hares. . . . After much thought last week on the question, Was the play better on screen or stage?, critics came to no concerted conclusion, felt sentimentally inclined to favor the Broadway version."

TIME

"A machine-gun pace explodes cracks and comic situations so fast that you have to sit forward for the laughs. (However) Cagney and O'Brien are not happily cast as writers; Cagney's staccato delivery is particularly at fault. . . . The same good lines and the same ludicrous situations are repeated. It ought to seem a lot better than it is when subjected to extreme high pressure."

Archer Winston, NEW YORK POST

"Comedy comes to Cagney as the years go on. As one of the pair of lunatic scenarists in *Boy Meets Girl* he is thoroughly comic. Along with Pat O'Brien, he upsets the whole studio, makes Hollywood seem far wilder than even the wildest dreams of those who never saw it, and, never letting down a moment, helps to make this one of the successful films of the season. I don't think that Cagney the comic, however, will ever achieve the success of Cagney the scoundrel, the hoodlum, the racketeer. There is possibly a kind of intensity in his countenance and in his manner a nervousness that don't quite belong in the sphere of light humor; but only at times is one aware of this, and his natural competence carries him well through any scene. Doubtless with the years he will grow gayer. He is still too young to be free of care."

John Mosher, THE NEW YORKER

"The picture is a succession of howls, of uproariously funny dialogue, of hugely amusing incidents and characters. Cagney and O'Brien check in expert performances."

Rose Pelswick, NEW YORK JOURNAL-AMERICAN

"It seemed impossible, but the Spewacks did it. They turned their madly funny stage plays of Hollywood into an equally and slightly wilder picture. . . . The tale is crammed with wisecracks, tripping lightly off the tongues of such experienced farceurs as Pat O'Brien, Marie Wilson, James Cagney, and even such unusually dignified personages as Ralph Bellamy and Dick Foran."

Eileen Creelman, NEW YORK SUN

"Although Mr. O'Brien gives a fine performance, his efforts do not come off as well as Mr. Cagney's for the

126

simple reason that he seems a little bewildered by the screwball antics in which he is supposed to indulge."

William Boehnel, NEW YORK WORLD-TELEGRAM

NOTES

Broadway's 1935 roaring satire on Hollywood's script writers was originally slated to be produced and directed by George Abbott after its purchase by Warner Bros. for Marion Davies. Miss Davies saw a few holes in the scenario Bella and Samuel Spewack had prepared from their own original and asked that certain changes be made. Warners had a fit and, in the end, Miss Davies retired from films and Warners agreed to pay Cagney $150,000 a picture (plus 10% of the gross) if he would return.

Return he did and this nutty farce took off like a shot, holes or not, as Lloyd Bacon, directing his eighth Cagney film, doubled the pace of any previous J. C. picture. George Abbott produced.

Cagney was supported by Pat O'Brien, Marie Wilson (in the role originally intended for Miss Davies), Ralph Bellamy, Dick Foran, and Penny Singleton as a manicurist. If you look closely at the Commissary Cashier, you will discover she's Carole Landis.

Olsen and Johnson were Warners' first choice to play the song writers, but the comedians were unavailable.

With Penny Singleton, Pat O'Brien, Dick Foran and Ralph Bellamy

With Bruce Lester, Marie Wilson and Pat O'Brien

With Pat O'Brien and Ralph Bellamy

With Pat O'Brien

On the set with Pat O'Brien and director Lloyd Bacon

With Marie Wilson

ANGELS WITH DIRTY FACES

A Warner Bros. Picture

—1938—

CAST

Rocky Sullivan: JAMES CAGNEY; *Jerry Connelly:* PAT O'BRIEN; *James Frazier:* HUMPHREY BOGART; *Laury Martin:* ANN SHERIDAN; *MacKeefer:* GEORGE BANCROFT; *Soapy:* BILLY HALOP; *Swing:* BOBBY JORDAN; *Bim:* LEO GORCEY; *Hunky:* BERNARD PUNSLEY; *Pasty:* GABRIEL DELL; *Crab:* HUNTZ HALL; *Rocky (As a Boy):* FRANKIE BURKE; *Jerry (As a Boy):* WILLIAM TRACY; *Laury (As a Girl):* MARILYN KNOWLDEN; *Steve:* JOE DOWNING; *Blackie:* ADRIAN MORRIS; *Guard Kennedy:* OSCAR O'SHEA; *Guard Edwards:* EDWARD PAWLEY; *Bugs, The Gunman:* WILLIAM PAWLEY; *Police Captain:* JOHN HAMILTON; *Priest:* EARL DWIRE; *Death Row Guard:* JACK PERRIN; *Mrs. Patrick:* MARY GORDON; *Soapy's Mother:* VERA LEWIS; *Warden:* WILLIAM WORTHING-

With Humphrey Bogart

With Ann Sheridan and Pat O'Brien

With the Dead End Kids

With Bernard Punsley, Gabriel Dell, Huntz Hall, Leo Gorcey, Bobby Jordan and Billy Halop

With Humphrey Bogart

With Pat O'Brien

TON; *R.R. Yard Watchman:* JAMES FARLEY; *Red:*
CHUCK STUBBS; *Maggione Boy:* EDDIE SYRACUSE; *Police-
man:* ROBERT HOMANS; *Basketball Captain:* HARRIS
BERGER; *Pharmacist:* HARRY HAYDEN; *Gangsters:* DICK
RICH, STEVEN DARRELL, JOE A. DEVLIN; *Italian Store-
keeper:* WILLIAM EDMUNDS; *Buckley:* CHARLES WILSON;
Boys in Poolroom: FRANK COGHLAN, JR., DAVID DU-
RAND; *Church Basketball Team:* BILL COHEE, LAVEL
LUND, NORMAN WALLACE, GARY CARTHEW, BIBBY MAYER;
Mrs. Maggione: BELLE MITCHELL; *Newsboy:* EDDIE
BRIAN; *Janitor:* BILLY MC LAIN; *Croupier:* WILBUR
MACK; *Girl at Gaming Table:* POPPY WILDE; *Adult
Boy:* GEORGE OFFERMAN, JR.; *Norton J. White:* CHARLES
TROWBRIDGE; *City Editor, Press:* RALPH SANFORD;
Police Officer: WILFRED LUCAS; *Guard:* LANE CHAND-
LER; *Cop:* ELLIOTT SULLIVAN; and LOTTIE WILLIAMS,
GEORGE MORI, DICK WESSELL, JOHN HARRON, VINCE
LOMBARDI, AL HILL, THOMAS JACKSON, JEFFREY SAYRE

CREDITS

Director: MICHAEL CURTIZ; *Producer:* SAM BISCHOFF;
Scenarists: JOHN WEXLEY, WARREN DUFF; *Based on an
original story by:* ROWLAND BROWN; *Photographer:* SOL
POLITO; *Art Director:* ROBERT HAAS; *Editor:* OWEN
MARKS; *Sound Recorder:* EVERETT A. BROWN; *Musical
Score:* MAX STEINER; *Orchestrator:* HUGO FRIEDHOFER;
Costumer: ORRY-KELLY; *Dialogue Director:* JO GRA-
HAM; *Makeup Artist:* PERC WESTMORE; *Assistant
Director:* SHERRY SHOURDS; *Technical Adviser:* FATHER
J. J. DEVLIN; *Song "Angels With Dirty Faces" by:*
FRED FISHER, MAURICE SPITALNY

SYNOPSIS

Rocky Sullivan, a noted criminal, comes back to his
old neighborhood and finds that he is the idol of the
gutter-bred youngsters there. The boys pattern themselves after him and avidly follow his career. The
parish priest, Jerry Connelly, who grew up with Rocky,
knows that the criminal's influence is nullifying all the
work he is trying to do.

Rocky soon has shoot-'em-up encounters with
Frazier, a crooked lawyer, and Keefer, a political
boss, and the law ultimately catches up with him. In
prison, Jerry pleads with Rocky to destroy the boys'
unhealthy adoration of him, and, at the last minute,
on the way to the electric chair, Rocky takes his chum's
advice.

CRITICS' CIRCLE

"Almost every aspect of the story has already been
heavily exploited by the cinema. The distinction of
Angels With Dirty Faces is that it tells an old tale well.
(It) could scarcely be called a significant motion picture, but it is always exciting and sometimes moving.
That it has the latter quality is due to the superlative
performing of James Cagney and Pat O'Brien. Even
when they are involved in what have become hackneyed situations, they succeed in making their characterizations vivid, convincing and provocative."

Howard Barnes, NEW YORK HERALD TRIBUNE

"With few exceptions the picture is skillfully and handsomely produced. While the story is undistinguished,
it is forcefully told. . . . For Cagney, the picture is
likely to bring added prestige, for the bantam rooster
of a racketeer is just the kind of part he plays best.
He has a swagger and an aw-go-to-hell pugnacity that
illumines a toughie characterization."

VARIETY

"Cagney's performance of Rocky is one of the most
impressive he has ever given."

Kate Cameron, New York DAILY NEWS

"It's a good title, and a better picture. Every time
gangster melodramas seem dead and gone, the Warners
make a better one than even they have attempted before. . . . The picture moves swiftly, with increasing
tension. There is not a lackluster moment in the film.
The finish is unexpectedly emotional. Mr. O'Brien,
wisely underplaying, and James Cagney, cocky as ever,
are at their best. *Angels With Dirty Faces* is a grand
melodrama and one to remember."

Eileen Creelman, NEW YORK SUN

"The picture is pretty much on the violent side, punc-
tuated with gunplay, vigorous action and crisp dialogue. But principally it's Cagney, the Cagney of the
gangster-film era, who has been given a role tailored
to his measure and who checks in a performance that's
swift and sure and electrical."

Rose Pelswick, NEW YORK JOURNAL-AMERICAN

"Cagney has a wonderful time performing the role
and you will have one watching him. He is supported
by the always interesting Pat O'Brien and Humphrey
Bogart. . . . A rousing, bloody, brutal melodrama,
Angels With Dirty Faces tops the crime cycle."

Bland Johaneson, New York DAILY MIRROR

"Jimmy Cagney plays Rocky with his usual amount of gusto. His character is occasionally muddy. We can't always be sure whether he is a bad boy trying to be good, or whether he is a hopeless case. That is probably script trouble and it's a minor failing.

"Michael Curtiz' direction is splendid—fast, imaginative and humorous—and the performances are uniformly polished."

Herbert Cohn, BROOKLYN DAILY EAGLE

"Jimmy Cagney is the slum's own; a ten-minute egg whose mind is as quick as his trigger finger. It's an all-Cagney portrait, crackling with nervous energy, and excellent."

Archer Winston, NEW YORK POST

"*Angels With Dirty Faces* is a fine job of cinema technique. Rowland Brown's story and Michael Curtiz' direction bring nothing new to racketeer melodrama, but the brisk rattle of Cagney's conversation and his associates' machine guns has a pleasantly nostalgic quality. The film lives up to one of the year's best titles."

TIME

NOTES

During his short time with Grand National, Rowland Brown sold them this story but, when Cagney left to return to Warner Bros., the rights reverted to Brown, who promptly re-sold his story to Warners.

While Cagney was filming *Boy Meets Girl*, scenarists John Wexley and Warren Duff were preparing *Angels*. Cagney returned to the gangster era with this one, and delighted everyone as hard-headed Rocky Sullivan. To watch Cagney in this role is sheer bliss, for he did everything physically, *i.e.*, to convey his gross discomfort in church, he shrugged his shoulders and tried to free himself from his starched collar as if it were growing tighter. Michael Curtiz was nominated for directing two Warner Bros. films: *Angels* and *Four Daughters*. He won with neither.

Angels With Dirty Faces followed the general plot lines of *Manhattan Melodrama*, *San Francisco* and *Dead End*, in that two childhood friends grow up to go their different ways. The cast was top notch; the production was outstanding and greatly complimented by a musical score by Max Steiner. The original working title was *Battle of City Hall*.

With Ann Sheridan and Pat O'Brien

THE OKLAHOMA KID

A Warner Bros. — First National Picture

—1939—

CAST

Jim Kincaid: JAMES CAGNEY; *Whip McCord:* HUMPHREY BOGART; *Jane Hardwick:* ROSEMARY LANE; *Hudge Hardwick:* DONALD CRISP; *Ned Kincaid:* HARVEY STEPHENS; *John Kincaid:* HUGH SOTHERN; *Alec Martin:* CHARLES MIDDLETON; *Doolin:* EDWARD PAWLEY; *Wes Handley:* WARD BOND; *Curley:* LEW HARVEY; *Indian Jack Pasco:* TREVOR BARDETTE; *Ringo:* JOHN MILJAN; *Judge Morgan:* ARTHUR AYLESWORTH; *Hotel Clerk:* IRVING BACON; *Keely:* JOE DEVLIN; *Sheriff Abe Collins:* WADE BOTELER; *Kincaid's Horse:* WHIZZER; *Professor:* RAY MAYER; *Deputy:* DAN WOLHEIM; *Juryman:* BOB KORTMAN; *Old Man in Bar:* TEX COOPER;

Secretary: JOHN HARRON; *President Cleveland:* STUART HOLMES; *Times Reporter:* JEFFREY SAYRE; *Land Agent:* FRANK MAYO; *Mail Clerk:* JACK MOWER; *Settler:* AL BRIDGE; *Drunk:* DON BARCLAY; *Bartenders:* HORACE MURPHY, ROBERT HOMANS, GEORGE LLOYD; *Manuelita:* ROSINA GALLI; *Pedro:* GEORGE REGAS; *Post Man:* CLEM BEVANS; *Indian Woman:* SOLEDAD JIMINEZ; *Foreman:* ED BRADY; *Homesteader:* TOM CHATTERTON; *Henchman:* ELLIOTT SULLIVAN; and JOE KIRKSON, WILLIAM WORTHINGTON, SPENCER CHARTERS

CREDITS

Director: LLOYD BACON; *Associate Producer:* SAMUEL BISCHOFF; *Scenarists:* WARREN DUFF, ROBERT BUCKNER, EDWARD E. PARAMORE; *Based on an original story by:* EDWARD E. PARAMORE, WALLY KLEIN; *Photographer:* JAMES WONG HOWE; *Art Director:* ESDRAS HARTLEY; *Editor:* OWEN MARKS; *Sound Recorder:* STANLEY JONES; *Musical Score:* MAX STEINER; *Orchestrators:* HUGO FRIEDHOFER, ADOLPH DEUTSCH, GEORGE PARRISH, MURRAY CUTTER; *Costumer:* ORRY-KELLY; *Makeup Artist:* PERC WESTMORE; *Assistant Director:* DICK MAYBERRY; *Technical Advisor:* AL JENNINGS

SYNOPSIS

During the settlement of the Cherokee Strip, in 1893, John Kincaid runs as a reform candidate for Mayor of Tulsa and his eldest son, Ned, campaigns for sheriff on the same ticket. However, an outlaw gang frames Kincaid for murder and he is railroaded by a bought jury and hanged. His youngest son, Jim, better known as the Oklahoma Kid, then thumbs his nose at the law.

Believing that the law is unjust to the underdog, the Oklahoma Kid makes his own law with his fast draw, stealing from the strong who have already stolen from the weak. He eventually avenges his family honor by killing Whip McCord, the leader of the gang that framed his father.

CRITICS' CIRCLE

"All the unbelievable hoke of a small-time western are included in this film. To cap this, Cagney, the star and in the title role, plays a western Robin Hood without variation of his Hell's Kitchen manner and it's incongruous in the chaps-and-spurs setting. A weak screenplay and dialogue, plus slow paced direction, don't help matters, and the film falls into the class of just another horse opera."

VARIETY

With Rosemary Lane

135

"This week's disappointment is surely the latest Cagney. *The Oklahoma Kid* is a straight 'Western' of the old school, not quite old-school enough though, to be comic, and a ten-gallon hat doesn't set so well on Mr. Cagney's urban head."

John Mosher, THE NEW YORKER

"The redoubtable James Cagney has put on a ten-gallon hat, spurs and shooting irons in *The Oklahoma Kid* and has amply earned the right to wear them. He has neither the accent nor the lingo for a hard-riding, rough-and-tumble Western, but he succeeds in giving such a dynamic portrayal that the (picture) has continual suspense and excitement. . . . His performance can only be described as a tour-de-force. . . . Of the supporting cast Humphrey Bogart takes the chief honors."

Howard Barnes, NEW YORK HERALD-TRIBUNE

"Mr. Cagney is on a horse at the Strand. It is almost the only thing that distinguishes his picture from any one of five other past Cagney films. . . . There's something entirely disarming about the way he has tackled horse opera, not pretending a minute to be anything but New York's Jimmy Cagney all dressed up for a dude ranch. He cheerfully pranks through every outrageous assignment his script writers and director have given him. . . . Mr. Cagney doesn't urge you to believe him for a second; he's just enjoying himself; and, if you want to trail along, so much the better for you. The rest of the cast plays it with almost as straight a face, but not quite the same jauntiness."

Frank S. Nugent, THE NEW YORK TIMES

"Westerns have always been a Hollywood staple. Lately, partly because of the success of Gene Autry and the Hopalong Cassidy series, partly because there is no other type of picture calculated to give so little offense to foreign countries, they have enjoyed a spectacular renaissance. . . . In *The Oklahoma Kid*, the current vogue of Western is dramatically exemplified by the fact that in it James Cagney, whose cinema career has taken him as far toward the great open spaces as gangsters' hideouts, appears equipped with sombrero, cowboy suit, lasso and two remarkably effective hoss pistols. Typical shot: Cagney—whose Bowery accent lends an admirably exotic touch to his impersonation of a badlands sharpshooter—blowing complacently through his pistol barrel when he shoots someone."

TIME

NOTES

There seemed to be only one place where the explosive and vital Cagney personality had not yet appeared— the Wild West. A large-scale, big-budgeted Western melodrama was created for him and Warners spared no expense. Lloyd Bacon directed with flair, James Wong Howe's photography was more than suitable to the occasion, and Max Steiner's rousing musical score neatly tied up the package.

Cagney, as Jim Kincaid, who goes out after his father's killers, was really quite good—if you could get used to seeing him in a ten-gallon hat. Humphrey Bogart was properly menacing and Rosemary Lane properly plain. Jimmy sang "Rockabye Baby" in both English and Spanish, as well as "I Don't Want to Play in Your Yard."

Besides its action-packed attributes, *The Oklahoma Kid* was a fun Western from start to finish and, in the best Warners tradition, the speed never stopped.

With Humphrey Bogart

With Irving Bacon, Rosemary Lane and Donald Crisp

With Charles Middleton, Donald Crisp and Rosemary Lane

With Trevor Bardette, Ward Bond, Ray Mayer and Humphrey Bogart

On the Warner lot with Humphrey Bogart

EACH DAWN I DIE

A Warner Bros.—First National Picture

—1939—

CAST

Frank Ross: JAMES CAGNEY; *Hood Stacey:* GEORGE RAFT; *Joyce Conover:* JANE BRYAN; *Warden John Armstrong:* GEORGE BANCROFT; *Fargo Red:* MAXIE ROSENBLOOM; *Mueller:* STANLEY RIDGES; *Pole Cat Carlisle:* ALAN BAXTER; *W. J. Grayce:* VICTOR JORY; *Pete Kassock:* JOHN WRAY; *Dale:* EDWARD PAWLEY; *Lang:* WILLARD ROBERTSON; *Mrs. Ross:* EMMA DUNN; *Garsky:* PAUL HURST; *Joe Lassiter:* LOUIS JEAN HEYDT; *Limpy Julien:* JOE DOWNING; *D. A. Jesse Hanley:* THURSTON HALL; *Bill Mason:* WILLIAM DAVIDSON; *Stacey's Attorney:* CLAY CLEMENT; *Judge:* CHARLES TROWBRIDGE; *Temple:* HARRY CORDING; *Lew Keller:* JOHN HARRON; *Jerry Poague:* JOHN RIDGELY; *Patterson:* SELMER JACKSON; *Mac:* ROBERT HOMANS; *Snake Edwards:* ABNER BIBERMAN; *Mose:* NAPOLEON SIMPSON; *Accident Witness:* STUART HOLMES; *Girl in Car:* MARIS WRIXON; *Men in Car:* GARLAND SMITH, ARTHUR GARDNER; *Policeman:* JAMES FLAVIN; *Gate Guard:* MAX HOFFMAN, JR.; *Turnkey:* WALTER MILLER; *Guard in Cell:* FRED GRAHAM; *Bailiff:* WILFRED LUCAS; *Jury Woman:* VERA LEWIS; *Prosecutor:* EMMETT VOGAN; *Judge Crowder:* EARL DWIRE; *Bud:* BOB PERRY; *Johnny, a Hood:* AL HILL; *Convict:* ELLIOTT SULLIVAN; *Court Officer:* CHUCK HAMILTON; and NAT CARR, WEDGEWOOD NOWELL, FRANK MAYO, DICK RICH, LEE PHELPS, JACK WISE, GRANVILLE BATES

CREDITS

Director: WILLIAM KEIGHLEY; *Associate Producer:* DAVID LEWIS; *Scenarists:* NORMAN REILLY RAINE, WARREN DUFF, CHARLES PERRY; *Based on the novel by:* JEROME ODLUM; *Photographer:* ARTHUR EDESON; *Art Director:* MAX PARKER; *Editor:* THOMAS RICHARDS; *Sound Recorder:* E. A. BROWN; *Musical Score:* MAX STEINER; *Musical Director:* LEO F. FORBSTEIN; *Costumer:* HOWARD SHOUP; *Makeup Artist:* PERC WESTMORE; *Assistant Director:* FRANK HEATH; *Technical Adviser:* WILLIAM BUCKLEY; *Narrator:* JOHN CONTE

SYNOPSIS

Cub reporter Frank Ross catches the district attorney burning the files of a construction company under investigation. When he prints the truth, they retaliate by dousing him with whiskey and framing him with a long-term sentence for manslaughter. Embittered by this episode and his inability to win a pardon, he develops into a hardened prisoner.

He meets and becomes friendly with Hood Stacey, a "lifer" who had been an underworld big shot. Eventually, he helps Hood go free by engineering a daring courtroom break, only to be double-crossed when the big-timer thinks Frank has squealed. The whole business ends in carnage, corpses scattered in every direction.

CRITICS' CIRCLE

"There are few screen actors who can touch James Cagney for that subtle combination of personality and artifice which constitutes motion-picture make-believe. Moreover, in a particular field of melodrama, it seems to me that he has no peers. . . . The story of *Each Dawn I Die* is rather rickety. . . . As it is, Mr. Cagney's assured and versatile portrayal carries the action through sequences which aren't properly motivated, steadies the melodrama when it threatens to get out of hand and sustains both dramatic sympathy and suspense.

"Next to his unerring sense of timing, I would say that the actor's restraint stood him in greatest stead in creating a credible melodramatic characterization. In *Each Dawn I Die* he has several scenes to play, such as the one in which he is brought out of solitary on the verge of being stir-crazy, when the temptation to indulge in acting pyrotechnics must have been very strong indeed. Nevertheless, he holds each scene in its proper focus so far as plot and character are concerned, adding a unity to the production which it badly needed. He could easily have been far more showy, but he was wise enough to know that flamboyant performing would have destroyed the slim dramatic continuity which (this film) boasts."

Howard Barnes, NEW YORK HERALD TRIBUNE

"Those who love Mr. Cagney for his quick, sharp, belligerence will find him a more subdued man this time, and perhaps be disappointed. . . . That is not to say that James Cagney does not give an excellent performance, a moving performance, in fact."

Arthur Pollock, BROOKLYN DAILY EAGLE

"*Each Dawn I Die* winks at the Hays Code, which frowns on teaching cinemaddicts how to commit crimes, by illustrating a practically foolproof way to commit one. . . . In addition to its crackling screen play, its sharp camera eye, *Each Dawn I Die* is made memorable by the easy mastery of its two principals. Cinemactors Cagney and Raft, the screen's two deadliest Ruffie MacTuffies, have been friends ever since they began their careers as vaudeville hoofers in Manhattan in the 20's. Cagney was responsible for one of Raft's earliest cinema parts, a dancing bit in Cagney's *Taxi!* Their appropriate reunion, also celebrating their return to the gangster movies where they belong, is a fierce slugfest in handcuffs."

TIME

"Director William Keighley covers up the numerous threadbare spots in the story with a patchwork of Raft-Cagney sequences that contain some of the best acting of the season. Warner Brothers, in teaming Cagney and Raft, have hit on a combination that will go far and win wide audiences. However, the danger that melodrama may prove a destructive vehicle for these fine stars is always present and their superb work in *Each Dawn I Die* serves notice that they are meant for better things."

Howard Rushmore, THE DAILY WORKER

"The men will rejoice to welcome as lusty a melodrama as *Each Dawn I Die*, which divests itself of glamour from its first shot and pursues the course of bloodthirsty and ruthless hatreds from its opening sequence. It is rich in horror and brutality, qualities which invariably charm the men. And the Messrs. Raft and Cagney never have been better."

Bland Johaneson, New York DAILY MIRROR

With Willard Robertson, George Bancroft and George Raft

With Stuart Holmes

With Emma Dunn and Jane Bryan

With George Raft

With Willard Robertson, George Raft, Henry Otho and George Bancroft

140

With George Raft

"There's certainly plenty of action in the picture, much of it on the tense and even gruesome side. Both Cagney and Raft check in convincing performances and are assisted by a large cast."

Rose Pelswick, NEW YORK JOURNAL-AMERICAN

NOTES

Each Dawn I Die, under the keen direction of William Keighley, is a rousing, better-than-average, prison drama. Jimmy's co-star, George Raft, had come full cycle. The boys met originally in vaudeville and then, in 1931, Cagney got Raft a small bit during the filming of *Taxi!*—the year before Raft came into his own at Paramount. John Garfield, then Fred MacMurray were set for the Raft role originally; Jane Bryan replaced Ann Sheridan.

Once again, the production was given every advantage by Arthur Edeson's photography, Thomas Richards' editing and Max Steiner's musical score. Scenes from *Wings of the Navy* were included in this production.

With George Bancroft

THE ROARING TWENTIES

A Warner Bros. — First National Picture

—1939—

CAST

Eddie Bartlett: JAMES CAGNEY; *Jean Sherman:* PRISCILLA LANE; *George Hally:* HUMPHREY BOGART; *Lloyd Hart:* JEFFREY LYNN; *Panama Smith:* GLADYS GEORGE; *Danny Green:* FRANK MC HUGH; *Nick Brown:* PAUL KELLY; *Mrs. Sherman:* ELISABETH RISDON; *Pete Henderson:* ED KEANE; *Sergeant Pete Jones:* JOSEPH SAWYER; *Lefty:* ABNER BIBERMAN; *Luigi, the Proprietor:* GEORGE HUMBERT; *Bramfield, the Broker:* CLAY CLEMENT; *Bobby Hart:* DON THADDEUS KERR; *Orderly:* RAY COOKE; *Mrs. Gray:* VERA LEWIS; *First Mechanic:* MURRAY ALPER; *Second Mechanic:* DICK WESSEL; *Fletcher, the Foreman:* JOSEPH CREHAN; *Bootlegger:* NORMAN WILLIS; *First Officer:* ROBERT ELLIOTT; *Second Officer:* EDDY CHANDLER; *Judge:* JOHN HAMILTON; *Man in Jail:* ELLIOTT SULLIVAN; *Jailer:* PAT O'MALLEY; *Proprietor of Still:* ARTHUR LOFT; *Ex-Cons:* AL HILL, RAYMOND BAILEY, LEW HARVEY; *Order-Takers:* JOE DEVLIN, JEFFREY SAYRE; *Mike:* PAUL PHILLIPS; *Masters:* GEORGE MEEKER: *Piano Player:* BERT HANLON; *Drunk:* JACK NORTON; *Captain:* ALAN BRIDGE; *Henchman:* FRED GRAHAM; *Doorman:* JAMES BLAINE; *Couple in Restaurant:* HENRY C. BRADLEY, LOTTIE WILLIAMS; *Commentator:* JOHN DEERING; *Soldier:* JOHN HARRON; *Bailiff:* LEE PHELPS; *Waiter:* NAT

With Frank McHugh

With Gladys George and Humphrey Bogart

With Humphrey Bogart and Jeffrey Lynn

With Gladys George

CARR; *Policeman:* WADE BOTELER; *Customer:* CREIGHTON HALE; *Saleswoman:* ANN CODEE; *Cab Drivers:* EDDIE ACUFF, MILTON KIBBEE, JOHN RIDGELY; and JAMES FLAVIN, OSCAR O'SHEA, FRANK WILCOX, THE JANE JONES TRIO, HARRY HOLLINGSWORTH, FRANK MAYO, EMORY PARNELL, BILLY WAYNE, PHILIP MORRIS, MAURICE COSTELLO, JOHN ST. CLAIR

CREDITS

Director: RAOUL WALSH; *Producer:* HAL B. WALLIS; *Associate Producer:* SAMUEL BISCHOFF; *Scenarists:* JERRY WALD, RICHARD MACAULAY, ROBERT ROSSEN; *Based on an original story by:* MARK HELLINGER; *Dialogue Director:* HUGH CUMMINGS; *Photographer:* ERNIE HALLER: *Art Director:* MAX PARKER; *Editor:* JACK KILLIFER; *Sound Recorder:* EVERETT A. BROWN; *Musical Score:* HEINZ ROEMHELD, RAY HEINDORF; *Musical Director:* LEO F. FORBSTEIN; *Orchestrator:* RAY HEINDORF; *Costumer:* MILO ANDERSON; *Makeup Artist:* PERC WESTMORE; *Special Effects:* BYRON HASKIN & EDWIN A. DUPAR; *Assistant Director:* DICK MAYBERRY; *Script Girl:* VIRGINIA MOORE; *Montages:* DON SIEGEL; *Songs:* "My Melancholy Baby" *by:* ERNIE BURNETT, GEORGE A. NORTON; "I'm Just Wild About Harry" *by:* EUBIE BLAKE, NOBEL SISSLE; "It Had to Be You" *by:* ISHAM JONES, GUS KAHN; "In A Shanty in Old Shanty Town" *by:* JACK LITTLE, JOSEPH YOUNG, JOHN SIRAS

SYNOPSIS

Eddie Bartlett, a former garage mechanic, comes back from the great war and finds jobs are tough to get. He takes a fling at taxi driving and then bootlegging. He helps Jean Sherman get a job in a nightclub and she does well, but does not return his affections. Instead, she falls for his buddy, a lawyer.

After the market crash wipes him out, Bartlett temporarily returns to driving a cab, before getting back into the rackets. One day Jean, who is now married and a mother of a four-year-old boy, is a passenger. It is a brief and unhappy reunion. Her husband is now on the D.A.'s staff, and is a target for the underworld.

CRITICS' CIRCLE

"*The Roaring Twenties*, which to Author Mark Hellinger, as he expresses it in a foreword, is 'a memory of the past.' (It) has been skillfully, bitterly, vitally written by Mr. Hellinger. . . . Cagney is ideally cast as the little tough guy with a heart of gold. And he comes through with another cracker-jack characterization, aided by Raoul Walsh's deft direction."

Irene Thirer, NEW YORK POST

"James Cagney has the top spot in the piece, back once again in the type of role that brought him fame in *The Public Enemy* and other such melodramas. For the film is an account of the speakeasy days, of wars between rival bootleggers, of underworld feuds and killings, of dizzy night spots and of sentimental tears."

Rose Pelswick, NEW YORK JOURNAL-AMERICAN

"*The Roaring Twenties* would be little better than a sentimental and synthetic gangster melodrama were it not for James Cagney's triumphant contribution to the show. The great actor has played this sort of role before, but he has never played it better. By virtue of his taut and knowing portrayal, Mark Hellinger's rather slipshod script becomes taut and vastly exciting on the screen."

Howard Barnes, NEW YORK HERALD TRIBUNE

"The mad, hectic prohibition era is dramatized in *The Roaring Twenties*. Written by Mark Hellinger, the outstanding recorder of those days, it has the glittering nervous journalistic quality, which distinguishes it from previous bootleg melodramas. . . . A further distinction is lent the film by the appearance of nervous, New Yorky, wild James Cagney in it."

Bland Johaneson, *New York* DAILY MIRROR

"As though it were not already the most thoroughly cinematized decade of our history, the Warners are presenting *The Roaring Twenties* with the self-conscious air of an antiquarian preparing to translate a cuneiform record of lost civilization.

"If it all sounds familiar, Mr. Hellinger will remind you that it all really happened, as he so gratefully remembers. If it also seems to be good entertainment of its kind (and it is, barring the false dignity the Warners have attached to it), credit it to James Cagney in another of his assured portrayals of a criminal career man; to Gladys George, who has breathed poignance into the stock role of the night club hostess who calls her customers 'chump'; to Raoul Walsh, who has kept his story of the hectic years spinning."

Frank S. Nugent, THE NEW YORK TIMES

NOTES

Mark Hellinger's prohibition saga was originally entitled *The World Moves On* (an earlier Fox title with

With Humphrey Bogart and Jeffrey Lynn

With Gladys George

With Priscilla Lane

On the set with director Raoul Walsh

With Gladys George

Madeleine Carroll and Franchot Tone) and it took three scenarists to condense it to 104 minutes of running time: Jerry Wald, Richard Macaulay and Robert Rossen. This Hal B. Wallis production had everything to recommend it and, through Raoul Walsh's superb directorial hand, the entire decade of the twenties is spread before us.

The storyline, which was nearly integrated into the newsreel-like documentary, held audience interest throughout. Cagney was excellent as a returning veteran who could not find work and who finally turned to the bootlegging racket. Only Cagney could have played the finale without causing laughter in the audience. His supreme style as an artist can be seen in that scene, as he stumbles down the street, fatally wounded, and dies on the church steps. It was terrific.

Gladys George was perfect as Panama; Bogart—in his third and last Cagney film—was most effective. Lovely Priscilla Lane, top-billed with Jimmy because Warners was pushing her, made a soapy role gleam with honesty.

Gladys George replaced Ann Sheridan who had replaced Lee Patrick who had replaced Glenda Farrell, Raoul Walsh replaced Anatole Litvak as Director.

THE FIGHTING 69TH

A Warner Bros. Picture

—1940—

CAST

Jerry Plunkett: JAMES CAGNEY; *Father Duffy:* PAT O'BRIEN; *Wild Bill Donovan:* GEORGE BRENT; *Joyce Kilmer:* JEFFREY LYNN; *Sergeant Big Mike Wynn:* ALAN HALE; *"Crepe Hanger" Burke:* FRANK MC HUGH; *Lieutenant Ames:* DENNIS MORGAN; *Lieutenant Long John Wynn:* DICK FORAN; *Timmy Wynn:* WILLIAM LUNDIGAN; *Paddy Dolan:* GUINN "BIG BOY" WILLIAMS; *The Colonel:* HENRY O'NEILL; *Captain Mangan:* JOHN LITEL; *Mike Murphy:* SAMMY COHEN; *Major Anderson:* HARVEY STEPHENS; *Private Turner:* DE WOLFE (WILLIAM) HOPPER; *Private McManus:* TOM DUGAN; *Jack O'Keefe:* GEORGE REEVES; *Moran:* JOHN RIDGELY; *Chaplain Holmes:* CHARLES TROWBRIDGE; *Lieutenant Norman:* FRANK WILCOX; *Casey:* HERBERT ANDERSON; *Healey:* J. ANTHONY HUGHES; *Captain Bootz:* FRANK MAYO; *Carroll:* JOHN HARRON; *Ryan:* GEORGE KILGEN; *Tierney:* RICHARD CLAYTON; *Regan:* EDWARD DEW; *Doctors:* WILFRED LUCAS, EMMETT VOGAN; *Sergeant:* FRANK SULLY; *Doctor:* JOSEPH CREHAN; *Supply Sergeant:* JAMES FLAVIN; *Jimmy:* FRANK COGHLAN, JR.; *Eddie:* GEORGE O'HANLON; *Major:* JACK PERRIN; *Alabama Men:* TREVOR BARDETTE, JOHN ARLEDGE, FRANK MELTON, EDMUND GLOVER; *Engineer Sergeant:* FRANK FAYLEN; *Engineer Officer:* EDGAR EDWARDS; *Medical Captain:* RALPH DUNN; *German Officers:* ARNO FREY, ROLAND VARNO; *Hefferman:* ROBERT LAYNE IRELAND; *O'Brien:* ELMO MURRAY; *Waiter:* JACQUES LORY; *Chuck:* JACK BOYLE, JR.; and CREIGHTON HALE, BENNY RUBIN, EDDIE ACUFF, JACK MOWER, NAT CARR, JACK WISE

With Pat O'Brien, George Reeves and Alan Hale

With Sammy Cohen, Tom Dugan and Frank McHugh

CREDITS

Director: WILLIAM KEIGHLEY; *Producer:* JACK L. WARNER; *Executive Producer:* HAL B. WALLIS; *Original Screenplay by:* NORMAN REILLY RAINE, FRED NIBLO, JR., DEAN FRANKLIN; *Photographer:* TONY GAUDIO; *Art Director:* TED SMITH; *Editor:* OWEN MARKS; *Sound Recorder:* CHARLES LANG; *Musical Score:* ADOLPH DEUTSCH; *Orchestrator:* HUGO FRIEDHOFER; *Musical Director:* LEO F. FORBSTEIN; *Makeup Artist:* PERC WESTMORE; *Special Effects:* BYRON HASKIN, REX WIMPY; *Assistant Director:* FRANK HEATH; *Technical Advisers:* CAPTAIN JOHN T. PROUT, MARK WHITE

SYNOPSIS

Jerry Plunkett, a tough little red-headed Irishman from Brooklyn, joins the fighting 69th. From the first, he sneers at the regiment's traditions, jeers at its chaplain, and defies its colonel. He displays sadistic delight in bayoneting dummies at Camp Mills but, later, when his unit is picked to be the first regiment to go overseas, he shrivels at the sight of dead bodies at the front. In an hysterical outburst, he reveals to the enemy the position of the unit and brings death down on his comrades by his cowardice. Before he dies, however, he proves himself a soldier worthy of the fighting 69th.

CRITICS' CIRCLE

"*The Fighting 69th*, a fictionized account of the intimate life and exploits of Manhattan's famed World War regiment continues, in slightly modified form, Warners' long time efforts to refine through suffering the character of their ace triggerman, James Cagney.

"*Aficionados* who know a first class carnage when they see and hear one ought to like this picture. There is seldom a dull moment. Others will be willing to take James Cagney's word for it. Asked during a lull in shooting the picture what was going to happen next, Cinemactor Cagney eyed his questioner, demanded incredulously: 'Are you really that interested?'"

TIME

"Despite the handicaps provided by a despicable role, Cagney scores with a highlight performance. William Keighley provides deft direction throughout, for both the dramatic motivation and the impressive and sweeping battle panoramas. Tony Gaudio's photography is also top grade throughout."

VARIETY

"James Cagney's performance, as Private Jerry Plunkett, overshadows all the others.

"Jimmy Cagney draws another of the tough-guy roles that he can play so well, making a frisky loudmouth of Private Jerry Plunkett."

Herbert Cohn, BROOKLYN DAILY EAGLE

"The acting is excellent, as indeed it would be with such fine players as Cagney, Pat O'Brien, George Brent, Alan Hale, Frank McHugh, Jeffrey Lynn and all the others in the cast. The lines are amusing, and the battle scenes are terrifying. But the virtues of the film are chiefly those provided by Mr. Cagney and Mr. O'Brien, who continue to be two of the finest actors in the movies."

William Boehnel, NEW YORK WORLD-TELEGRAM

"The picture is better if you can manage to forget the plot, with all its obvious theatrics, hokum and unoriginality, and think of it instead as the human, amusing and frequently gripping record of a regiments' marching off to war. . . . And this we maintain in the face of Mr. Cagney's vivid performance of the swaggering recruit who turned yellow in the trenches, and Pat O'Brien's dignified and eloquent portrayal of the famous fighting chaplain whose monument stands in Times Square. Performance cannot work too many wonders with a dog-eared script."

Frank S. Nugent, THE NEW YORK TIMES

"Mr. Cagney gives a terrifying real portrayal of a tough braggart whose worst instincts come to the fore under army discipline until a patient priest reminds him of faith. Mr. O'Brien handles the exceedingly difficult role of Father Duffy with conviction and good sense, endowing the figure with the courage and piety which endeared him to the war generation."

Howard Barnes, NEW YORK HERALD TRIBUNE

NOTES

At the same time Warners announced its plans to film a tribute to New York's crack Irish regiment, known as "the fighting 69th," Fox was negotiating with M-G-M to borrow Spencer Tracy for "Father Duffy of the Fighting 69th," a project they quickly abandoned.

The Fighting 69th was a factual presentation of the 69th's war record. Known as "the Fighting Irish" from the time of the Civil War, this regiment of Celtic national guardsmen was incorporated into the Rainbow Division in 1917. The exploits of these great civilian soldiers—now a part of history—were the basis of this film.

Cagney played a fictional character named Jerry Plunkett, an obnoxious young fellow, who had no discipline and shunned the tradition of the unit and the Army itself. This was the plot gimmick that would swiftly take the audience through typical training days to the battlefields (filmed at the Calabasas ranch). Again, Cagney had to suffer a fatal injury to vindicate his rotten behaviour. His performance was a straightforward piece of honest acting, and *The Fighting 69th* was one of the biggest money-makers of that year.

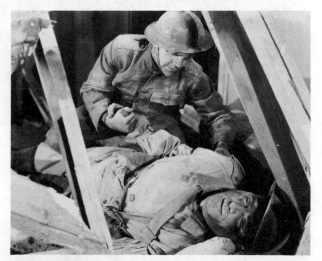

With Pat O'Brien

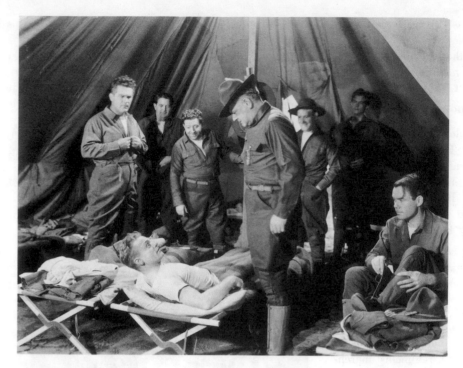

With Guinn "Big Boy" Williams, J. Anthony Hughes, Frank McHugh, Alan Hale, Tom Dugan, William Lundigan and John Ridgely

With Tom Dugan and Frank McHugh

150

TORRID ZONE

A Warner Bros. – First National Picture

—1940—

CAST

Nick Butler: JAMES CAGNEY; *Steve Case:* PAT O'BRIEN; *Lee Donley:* ANN SHERIDAN; *Wally Davis:* ANDY DEVINE; *Gloria Anderson:* HELEN VINSON; *Bob Anderson:* JEROME COWAN; *Rosario:* GEORGE TOBIAS; *Sancho:* GEORGE REEVES; *Carlos:* VICTOR KILIAN; *Rodriquez:* FRANK PUGLIA; *Gardner:* JOHN RIDGELY; *Sam:* GRADY SUTTON; *Garcia:* PAUL PORCASI; *Lopez:* FRANK YACONELLI; *Hernandez:* DICK BOTELER; *Shaffer:* FRANK MAYO; *McNama:* JACK MOWER; *Daniels:* PAUL HURST; *Sargeant of Police:* GEORGE REGAS; *Rita:* ELVIRA SANCHEZ; *Hotel Manager:* GEORGE HUMBERT; *First Policeman:* TREVOR BARDETTE; *Second Policeman:* ERNESTO PIEDRA; *Chico:* MANUEL LOPEZ; *Charley:* TONY PATON;

and MAX BLUM, BETTY SANKO, DON ORLANDO, VICTOR SABUNI, PAUL RENAY, JOE MOLINA

CREDITS

Director: WILLIAM KEIGHLEY; *Producer:* MARK HELLINGER; *Original screenplay by:* RICHARD MACAULAY, JERRY WALD; *Photographer:* JAMES WONG HOWE; *Art Director:* TED SMITH; *Set Decorator:* EDWARD THORNE; *Editor:* JACK KILLIFER; *Sound Recorder:* OLIVER S. GARRETSON; *Musical Score:* ADOLPH DEUTSCH; *Musical Director:* LEO F. FORBSTEIN; *Costumer:* HOWARD SHOUP; *Makeup Artist:* PERC WESTMORE; *Special Effects:* BYRON HASKIN, H. F. KOENEKAMP; *Technical Adviser:* JOHN MARI; *Song:* "Mi Caballero" by: M. K. JEROME, JACK SCHOLL

With Ann Sheridan and Helen Vinson

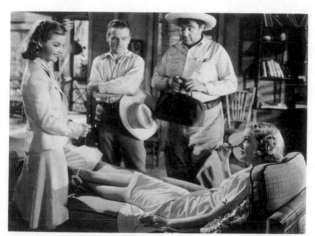

With Helen Vinson

With Ann Sheridan, Andy Devine and Helen Vinson

SYNOPSIS

In Central America, plantation boss Steve Case exiles stranded entertainer Lee Donley because she is a bad influence on his workers. On the boat, Lee meets Nick Butler, Case's ex-foreman, who is leaving for a better job in the States. She is intrigued by him. Case cons Butler into returning to the plantation, for a substantial bonus, if he can bring in the crop.

Problems at the plantation are multiplied when Gloria, one of the manager's wives, throws herself at Nick, trying to rekindle an old flame. Adding to the confusion, a local bandit, Rosario, stirs the workers into an open revolt against the plantation bosses.

CRITICS' CIRCLE

"*Torrid Zone* abounds in . . . robust action, in rowdy wisecracks by the men, catty wisecracks by the girls, skirmishes with a broad-minded bandit, falsetto funny business by Andy Devine, much sweltering and sweating by Messrs. Cagney and O'Brien. Oomph Girl Sheridan is never affected by the heat. She hops on and off moving banana trains, gets thrown in and out of jail, never even needs to change her one immaculate dress."

TIME

"If you want to forget the European situation completely for an hour and a half, go see *Torrid Zone*, Jimmy Cagney's new picture. Its accelerated pace, tough performance and rough humor are a combined guarantee against boredom."

Wanda Hale, New York DAILY NEWS

"Cagney, who can express a complete characterization with one little gesture, is just the person for the pugnacious plantation manager with a weakness for a shapely ankle, and few actors can interpret a fidgety, staccato role as well as O'Brien. Miss Sheridan is entirely at ease as the hardboiled torch singer, and when the occasion demands sentiment and simplicity that, too, is at her command."

William Boehnel, NEW YORK WORLD-TELEGRAM

"In *Torrid Zone* James Cagney again has a role suited to his combustible temperament and Ann Sheridan steps up a notch or two in our estimation as the femme fatale of the piece. . . . As the foreman Mr. Cagney again shows that he has more tightly muscled energy as an actor than half the Hollywood leads put together."

T. S., THE NEW YORK TIMES

With Pat O'Brien and Ann Sheridan

"Miss Ann Sheridan, in her second film as a star, is in good company, which is a fine thing for a young player who is learning why some actors are good and some bad. . . .

"Messrs. Cagney and O'Brien, with their rapid-fire talking and acting, keep the film from lagging."

Robert W. Dana, NEW YORK HERALD TRIBUNE

NOTES

William Keighley directed *Torrid Zone* in forty-one production days. The locale was fictional, but definitely Central America. A banana grove, jungle and tropical seaport setting were erected on exterior location in Warner Bros.'s thirty-acre annex. The complete set covered a five-acre tract, and 950 banana trees were planted in a make-believe grove to give it authenticity.

Normally, a story such as this would have been a "B" quickie but, under the aegis of Mark Hellinger, the direction of William Keighley and the camera technique of James Wong Howe, this Richard Macaulay-Jerry Wald original screenplay jumped into high gear. Not only did the action never cease, the wisecracks were given the same pace. *Torrid Zone* is a most enjoyable piece of hokum, but hardly more than that.

Cagney replaced George Raft, while Helen Vinson replaced Astrid Allwyn.

With Helen Vinson and Jerome Cowan

With Pat O'Brien and Grady Sutton

With Ann Sheridan

153

CITY FOR CONQUEST

A Warner Bros. – First National Picture

— 1941 —

CAST

Danny Kenny: JAMES CAGNEY; *Peggy Nash:* ANN SHERIDAN; *Old Timer:* FRANK CRAVEN; *Scotty McPherson:* DONALD CRISP; *Eddie Kenny:* ARTHUR KENNEDY; *Mutt:* FRANK MC HUGH; *Pinky:* GEORGE TOBIAS; *Dutch:* JEROME COWAN; *Murray Burns:* ANTHONY QUINN; *Gladys:* LEE PATRICK; *Mrs. Nash:* BLANCHE YURKA; *Goldie:* GEORGE LLOYD; *Lilly:* JOYCE COMPTON; *Max Leonard:* THURSTON HALL; *Cobb:* BEN WELDEN; *Salesman:* JOHN ARLEDGE; *Gaul:* ED KEANE; *Doctors:* SELMER JACKSON, JOSEPH CREHAN; *Callahan:* BOB STEELE; *Henchman:* BILLY WAYNE; *Floor Guard:* PAT FLAHERTY; *M. C.:* SIDNEY MILLER; *Dressing room Blonde:* ETHELREDA LEOPOLD; and LEE PHELPS, CHARLES WILSON, ED GARGAN, HOWARD HICKMAN, MURRAY ALPER, DICK WESSELL, BERNICE PILOT, CHARLES LANE, DANA DALE (MARGARET HAYES), ED PAWLEY, WILLIAM NEWELL, LUCIA CARROLL

CREDITS

Director and Producer: ANATOLE LITVAK; *Associate Producer:* WILLIAM CAGNEY; *Scenarist:* JOHN WEXLEY; Based on the novel *City for Conquest* by: ABEN KANDEL; *Photographers:* SOL POLITO, JAMES WONG HOWE; *Dialogue Director:* IRVING RAPPER; *Art Director:* ROBERT HAAS; *Editor:* WILLIAM HOLMES; *Sound Recorder:* E. A. BROWN; *Musical Score:* MAX STEINER; *Orchestrator:* HUGO FRIEDHOFER; *Musical Director:* LEO F. FORBSTEIN; *Dance Director:* ROBERT VREELAND; *Costumer:* HOWARD SHOUP; *Makeup Artist:* PERC WESTMORE; *Special Effects:* BYRON HASKIN, REX WIMPY; *Assistant Director:* CHUCK HANSEN

With Frank McHugh, Donald Crisp and George Tobias

SYNOPSIS

East Side truck driver Danny Kenny becomes a fighter to impress his girl Peggy. However, Peggy leaves on a dancing tour with Murray Burns and she begins to taste of success. Danny swiftly reaches the top in his new profession, but refuses to take Peggy back. His brother Eddie, who dreams only about symphonies, also "sells out" and writes popular music.

Once both Danny and Peggy have attained success, they both lose it; Danny spectacularly, Peggy slowly and bitterly. Danny is blinded in a fight and although he must sell papers on the street corner, he encourages his brother not to abandon his symphony. One evening, Peggy comes by Danny's newsstand and, together, they listen to Eddie's symphony over the radio.

CRITICS' CIRCLE

"The forceful personalities of James Cagney and Ann Sheridan are more than enough to make up for the deficiencies of *City For Conquest,* and whatever success the picture enjoys, which should be considerable, may be laid to the presence of these two stars in the cast, rather than to any ingenuity in plot, characterization or development. . . . Mr. Cagney stands forth in shining splendor with his performance of a truck driver turned prizefighter. Whatever subtleties the film had, he saw, and in playing the role, he somehow manages to invest it with a good deal more power than the character itself demands. Miss Sheridan turns on her celebrated "oomph" at every given opportunity, and on occasion, even does some fine acting on her own behalf, which is more than you'd expect."

Leo Mishkin, MORNING TELEGRAPH

"The film is unusual, too, because in the end the local boy does not make good in his worldly ambitions, although he gains something greater—peace, contentment and the satisfaction of knowing that he was able to help his brother, less material, to achieve his ambition. . . . It has Jimmy Cagney in it, and any film in which Cagney appears is bound to have merit, because there is no one like him to give vitality and credibility to a role. His performance . . . is among the best he ever has given."

William Boehnel, NEW YORK WORLD-TELEGRAM

"The picture is distinguished by many fine performances. Cagney's characterization of the prizefighter who is beaten blind in an unequal contest is one of

With Ann Sheridan

With Arthur Kennedy

With Anthony Quinn and Ann Sheridan

155

With George Tobias, Elia Kazan, Billy Wagner, Frank McHugh and Donald Crisp

With Frank McHugh

With Joyce Compton, Frank McHugh, Anthony Quinn, Ann Sheridan and George Tobias

his greatest contributions to the screen and Ann Sheridan is better than she has ever been before."

Kate Cameron, New York DAILY NEWS

"Cagney puts plenty of zest and vigor into his characterization, carefully shading romantic passages for utmost in audience attention. Miss Sheridan is excellent as the girl, displaying dancing abilities in several ballroom numbers with Quinn."

VARIETY

"*City For Conquest* is one of the best pictures ever made about New York and the people who intone pure New Yorkese. . . . But you always come back to the stunning performance of Cagney. It's like something he was born to do and no one else in the world could ever touch it. He fights, and he talks, and he acts, and he thinks like a guy from Delancey and Forsyth that you won't soon forget."

Archer Winston, NEW YORK POST

"Sometimes we wonder whether it wasn't really the Warners who got New York from the Indians, so diligent and devoted have they been in feeling the great city's pulse, picturing its myriad facets and recording with deep comparison the passing life of its seething population.

"Any picture that has Mr. Cagney and Miss Sheridan is bound to be tough and salty, right off the city's streets. And this one is. Miss Sheridan waxes quite emotional, and Mr. Cagney, as usual, gives the story the old one-two punch."

Bosley Crowther, THE NEW YORK TIMES

"A vivid portrayal and a terrific tempo are the distinguishing features of *City For Conquest*. James Cagney, who is certainly the first actor of the screen (not forgetting Spencer Tracy and James Stewart), gives one of his finest performances as a mugg from the lower East Side who goes places with his fists. . . . It is well worth seeing only because it has Mr. Cagney displaying the full range of his acting craftsmanship."

Howard Barnes, NEW YORK HERALD TRIBUNE

NOTES

City for Conquest represented what Warner Bros. did better than any other studio—a New York story. Based on Aben Kandel's novel, the John Wexley script about a prizefighter and his composer brother, under Anatole Litvak's inspired direction, was given an almost poetic production—complimented greatly by Max Steiner's musical score.

Jimmy Cagney's performance was at once poignant and forceful, and remains one of the finest acting chores of his career. He was ably supported by Ann Sheridan and young Arthur Kennedy, as his kid brother, besides the usual fine Warners stock company of players.

Sheridan once told an interviewer, "It was a very good part, and of course it was Cagney again. He sold like wildfire. To be in a picture with him was just the greatest."

Raoul Walsh was first set to direct, but was replaced by Litvak. Warners wanted Ginger Rogers to co-star with Jimmy, then Sylvia Sidney was actually signed, but finally replaced by Ann Sheridan. George Raft and Cesar Romero tested for Anthony Quinn's role.

On the set with director Anatole Litvak and Ann Sheridan

157

THE STRAWBERRY BLONDE

A Warner Bros. – First National Picture

— 1941 —

CAST

Biff Grimes: JAMES CAGNEY; Amy Lind: OLIVIA DE HAVILLAND; Virginia Brush: RITA HAYWORTH; Old Man Grimes: ALAN HALE; Nick Pappalas: GEORGE TOBIAS; Hugo Barnstead: JACK CARSON; Mrs. Mulcahey: UNA O'CONNOR; Harold: GEORGE REEVES; Harold's Girl Friend: LUCILE FAIRBANKS; Big Joe: EDWARD MC NA-MARA; Toby: HERBERT HEYWOOD; Josephine: HELEN LYND; Bank President: ROY GORDON; Street Cleaner Foreman: TIM RYAN; Official: ADDISON RICHARDS; Policeman: FRANK MAYO; Bartender: JACK DALEY; Girl: SUZANNE CARNAHAN (SUSAN PETERS); Boy: HERBERT ANDERSON; Baxter: FRANK ORTH; Inspector:

JAMES FLAVIN; *Sailor:* GEORGE CAMPEAU; *Singer:* ABE DINOVITCH; *Guiseppi:* GEORGE HUMBERT; *Secretary:* CREIGHTON HALE; *Treadway:* RUSSELL HICKS; *Warden:* WADE BOTELER; *Young Man:* PETER ASHLEY; *Bank President:* ROY GORDON; *Policemen:* MAX HOFFMAN, JR., PAT FLAHERTY; *Girl:* PEGGY DIGGINS; *Hanger-On:* BOB PERRY; *Woman:* DOROTHY VAUGHAN; *Dandy:* RICHARD CLAYTON; *Girl:* ANN EDMONDS; *Nurse:* LUCIA CARROLL; and HARRISON GREEN, EDDIE CHANDLER, CARL HARBAUGH, FRANK MELTON, DICK WESSELL, PAUL BARRETT, NORA GALE

CREDITS

Director: RAOUL WALSH; *Producers:* JACK L. WARNER, HAL B. WALLIS; *Associate Producer:* WILLIAM CAGNEY; *Scenarists:* JULIUS J. EPSTEIN, PHILIP G. EPSTEIN; Based on the play *One Sunday Afternoon* by: JAMES HAGAN; *Dialogue Director:* HUGH CUMMINGS; *Photographer:* JAMES WONG HOWE; *Art Director:* ROBERT HAAS; *Editor:* WILLIAM HOLMES; *Sound Recorder:* ROBERT E. LEE; *Musical Score:* HEINZ ROEMHELD; *Orchestrator:* RAY HEINDORF; *Costumer:* ORRY-KELLY; *Makeup Artist:* PERC WESTMORE; *Assistant Director:* RUSS SAUNDERS

SYNOPSIS

Young Biff Grimes, a correspondent school dentist, loses the neighborhood strawberry blonde, Virginia Brush, to a chiselling contractor, Hugo Barnstead. On the rebound, he marries her girl friend Amy Lind. Offered a job by the contractor, Biff is made the stooge for the firm's corruption and goes to jail for five years.

Out again, he rejoins his wife and sets up practice. When the contractor appears for emergency dentistry with his strawberry consort, Biff plans to do him in with dentist's gas. However, at the last minute, he decides that he is the luckier man—and extracts the contractor's tooth, without gas.

CRITICS' CIRCLE

"*Strawberry Blonde* is a blithe, sentimental, turn-of-the-century buggy ride. Cagney makes the hero a tough but obviously peachy fellow. But the strawberry humdinger, Rita Hayworth, takes the picture away from him, and dark-eyed Olivia de Havilland, with her electric winks, each followed by a galvanizing 'Exactly!' takes it away from both of them."

TIME

"The versatile James Cagney clowns his way through most of the *Strawberry Blonde* to remind one that he is as adept at comedy as melodrama. It's a big improvement on the original (*One Sunday Afternoon*), thanks to the acting and some bright dialogue, but it is still a rambling period piece. Without the brilliant make-believe of Cagney it would be trying as well as rambling. Since he dominates nearly every scene and has considerable assistance from the dialogue, *Strawberry Blonde* is moderately entertaining."

Howard Barnes, THE NEW YORK HERALD TRIBUNE

"Cagney and Miss de Havilland provide topnotch performances that do much to keep up interest in the proceedings. Rita Hayworth is an eyeful as the title character. Jack Carson is excellent as the politically ambitious antagonist of the dentist."

VARIETY

"James Cagney's Biff Grimes, for instance, is a great improvement over Gary Cooper's interpretation of the role and even betters Lloyd Nolan's fine performance in the stage play. Cooper was sadly miscast as the bragging, belligerent young dentist. . . . Cagney's performance of Biff is one of the best he's ever given on the screen. Olivia de Havilland's playing of Amy, too, is a fine thing to behold and is of great importance to the success of the film."

Kate Cameron, New York DAILY NEWS

"Both Cagney and Miss de Havilland have done fine acting jobs before but I think this is their tops."

Lee Mortimer, New York DAILY MIRROR

"*The Strawberry Blonde* is a delightful and amusing period piece in which the lighter talents of Cagney, de Havilland, Rita Hayworth, Alan Hale and George Tobias are displayed to excellent advantage."

Archer Winston, NEW YORK POST

"*Strawberry Blonde* is an unusual picture, a film with a definite individuality. It not only tells a very human story, it also creates an atmosphere, re-creates a period. . . . This is a comedy, with plenty of laughs; and it has James Cagney and Alan Hale, both at their best, playing fighting son and drunkard father. It is still a tender piece with more honest emotion than most. Olivia de Havilland's portrayal . . . accounts for part of the film's quality."

Eileen Creelman, NEW YORK SUN

"He (Cagney), always is vital and believable, equally at ease in both his comedy and serious scenes. But

With Pat Flaherty, Olivia de Havilland and Max Hoffman, Jr.

With Frank Melton and Rita Hayworth

With Rita Hayworth

then, all the acting is good, and so is the direction, which in Raoul Walsh's hands converts a serious story . . . into a friendly, informal, delightful and good-humored show."

William Boehnel, NEW YORK WORLD-TELEGRAM

NOTES

This was the second, of three, film versions of James Hagan's *One Sunday Afternoon.* The first starred Gary Cooper, Frances Fuller and Fay Wray in 1933 at Paramount. Warners re-made it as a musical in 1948 with Dennis Morgan, Janis Paige and Dorothy Malone.

The Strawberry Blonde is probably the best version. Raoul Walsh injected loads of energy and humor with his usual pacing, yet managed to maintain the quaintness of the 1910 setting. Cagney, too, seemed better suited to the role of Biff Grimes and gave a standout performance.

Rita Hayworth was borrowed from Columbia when Warner's own Ann Sheridan began feuding with the studio for better parts. Miss Hayworth, on the way to becoming the "love goddess" of the forties, supplied her own brand of "oomph."

This version switched the locale from a small town to New York City; otherwise the script followed the original closely. Heinz Roemheld won an Academy Award nomination for his musical scoring.

With Rita Hayworth and Alan Hale

On the set with Rita Hayworth and Olivia de Havilland

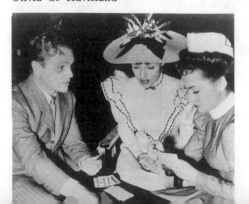

With Olivia de Havilland

THE BRIDE CAME C.O.D.

A Warner Bros. — First National Picture

—1941—

CAST

Steve Collins: JAMES CAGNEY; *Joan Winfield:* BETTE DAVIS; *Tommy Keenan:* STUART ERWIN; *Allen Brice:* JACK CARSON; *Peewee:* GEORGE TOBIAS; *Lucius K. Winfield:* EUGENE PALLETTE; *Pop Tolliver:* HARRY DAVENPORT; *Sheriff McGee:* WILLIAM FRAWLEY; *Hinkle:* EDWARD BROPHY; *Judge Sobler:* HARRY HOLMAN; *Reporters:* CHICK CHANDLER, KEITH DOUGLAS (later DOUGLAS KENNEDY), HERBERT ANDERSON; *Keenan's Pilot:* DE WOLFE (WILLIAM) HOPPER; *McGee's Pilot:* WILLIAM NEWELL; *Ambulance Driver:* CHARLES SULLIVAN; *Policemen:* EDDY CHANDLER, TONY HUGHES, LEE PHELPS; *Mabel:* JEAN AMES; *Headwaiter:* ALPHONSE MARTELL; *Dance Trio:* THE ROGERS DANCERS; *1st Operator:* PEGGY DIGGINS; *2nd Operator:* MARY BRODEL; *Valet:* OLAF HYTTEN; *Detective:* JAMES FLAVIN; *Announcer:* SAM HAYES; *Airline Dispatcher:* WILLIAM JUSTICE (later RICHARD TRAVIS); *Newsboys:* LESTER TOWNE, RICHARD CLAYTON, GARLAND SMITH, CLAUDE WISBERG; and LUCIA CARROLL, PETER ASHLEY, JOHN RIDGELY, SAUL GORSS, JACK MOWER, CREIGHTON HALE, GARRETT CRAIG

CREDITS

Director: WILLIAM KEIGHLEY; *Executive Producer:* HAL B. WALLIS; *Associate Producer:* WILLIAM CAGNEY; *Scenarists:* JULIUS J. EPSTEIN, PHILIP G. EPSTEIN; *Based on a story by:* KENNETH EARL, M. M. MUSSELMAN; *Photographer:* ERNEST HALLER; *Art Director:* TED SMITH; *Editor:* THOMAS RICHARDS; *Sound Recorder:* ROBERT E. LEE; *Musical Score:* MAX STEINER; *Musical Director:* LEO F. FORBSTEIN; *Orchestrator:* HUGO FRIEDHOFER; *Costumer:* ORRY-KELLY; *Makeup Artist:* PERC WESTMORE; *Special Effects:* BYRON HASKIN, REX WIMPY; *Assistant Director:* FRANK HEATH

SYNOPSIS

An elopement between Joan Winfield, daughter of a

With Bette Davis

With Bette Davis

With Bette Davis and Jack Carson

With Bette Davis

Texas oil tycoon, and band leader Allen Brice is promoted by a publicity-hungry broadcaster. Steve Collins, whose plane has been chartered for the elopers, phones Joan's father and agrees—for a fee, of course—to deliver his daughter to him the next morning, unmarried, C.O.D.

Steve kidnaps Joan, but the plane crashes in the desert. Steve tries to prevent Joan from signaling passing planes by chasing her into a deserted tunnel. Planes arrive nonetheless, and Steve lets Joan marry Allen, knowing the ceremony is not legal, and stalls the couple until her father arrives.

CRITICS' CIRCLE

"Despite Miss Davis's magnanimity, and Mr. Cagney's weighty allure, and the story's staggering under its sense of responsibility for such precious cargo, the movie has laughs because the brothers Epstein, who wrote the screenplay, write funny jokes and get screwy notions."

Cecelia Ager, P. M.

"*The Bride Came C.O.D.* is a hot-weather hors d'oeuvre. It offers the curious spectacle of the screen's most talented tough guy (James Cagney) roughhousing one of the screen's best dramatic actresses (Bette Davis) through ten reels of slapsticky summertime comedy. The result, seldom hilarious, is often funny."

TIME

"After a long succession of dramatic roles, Bette Davis is teamed with James Cagney in a broad farce that combines spontaneous gayety and infectious humor. Cagney grooves in a familiar role as the aggressive and two-fisted battler—manhandling the girl periodically for maximum results. Miss Davis clicks strongly as the oil heiress, displaying a flair for comedy that cannot be overlooked in future studio assignments."

VARIETY

"Of course the thing is far from standards set by either Bette Davis or James Cagney in their better pictures. It is to be hoped that, having proved themselves able to do comedy, as Cagney once disastrously proved himself able to be a song and dance man, they will return to the types of roles in which no one excels them. Then *The Bride Came C.O.D.* can be quickly forgotten and forgiven. Okay, Jimmie and Bette. You've had your fling. Now go back to work."

Archer Winston, NEW YORK POST

With Bette Davis and Harry Davenport

On the set with director William Keighley, Bette Davis and Harry Davenport

"*The Bride Came C.O.D.* is the stuff of which quickies are made. This is really a class B story screenplay. The presence of two of Warners' most publicized stars does not make it any more entertaining. Miss Davis is no great shakes at this sort of thing, although she plays with spirit. Mr. Cagney is far too mature to make his role appealing."

Eileen Creelman, NEW YORK SUN

"Both Miss Davis and Mr. Cagney are ideally cast, particularly the latter who has a role right up his alley. Now that Miss Davis has condescended to play a broad comedy role, we trust the Warners will permit her to have her fling in this type of role at least once a year."

Edgar Prue, BROOKLYN CITIZEN

"Bette is splendid as the heiress, though not as much at home among absurdities as Cagney is. She seems a little too tense about the whole business. But Cagney is perfect. What an actor he is: There isn't a false note in anything he does. At times he finds it a bit tough to keep the plot moving, but even then he is as convincing and persuasive as ever."

William Boehnel, NEW YORK WORLD-TELEGRAM

NOTES

The only notes about this so-so comedy come from Bette Davis, in her autobiography "The Lonely Life," and no one could have said it better: "Next I made a picture with Jimmy Cagney. It was called a comedy. It had been decided that my work as a tragedian should be temporarily halted for a change of pace. Jimmy, who had made the gangster artistic—Jimmy, who was one of the fine actors on mine or any lot—Jimmy, with whom I'd always wanted to work in something fine, spent most of his time in the picture removing cactus quills from my behind. This was supposedly hilarious. We romped about the desert and I kept falling into cactus. We both reached bottom with this one."

CAPTAINS OF THE CLOUDS

A Warner Bros. — First National Picture
In Technicolor

—1942—

CAST

Brian MacLean: JAMES CAGNEY; *Johnny Dutton:* DENNIS MORGAN; *Emily Foster:* BRENDA MARSHALL; *Tiny Murphy:* ALAN HALE; *Blimp Lebec:* GEORGE TOBIAS; *Scrounger Harris:* REGINALD GARDINER; *Air Marshal W. A. Bishop:* HIMSELF; *Commanding Officer:* REGINALD DENNY; *Prentiss:* RUSSELL ARMS; *Group Captain:* PAUL CAVANAGH; *Store-Teeth Morrison:* CLEM BEVANS; *Foster:* J. M. KERRIGAN; *Doctor Neville:* J. FARRELL MAC DONALD; *Fyffo:* PATRICK O'MOORE; *Carmichael:* MORTON LOWRY; *Chief Instructor:* O. CATHCART-JONES; *President of Court-Martial:* FREDERIC WORLOCK; *Officer:* ROLAND DREW; *Blonde:* LUCIA CARROLL; *Playboy:* GEORGE MEEKER; *Popcorn Kearns:* BENNY BAKER; *Kingsley:* HARDIE ALBRIGHT; *Mason:* ROY WALKER; *Nolan:* CHARLES HALTON; *Provost Marshall:* LOUIS JEAN HEYDT; *Student Pilots:* BYRON BARR (GIG YOUNG), MICHAEL AMES (TOD ANDREWS); *Willie:* WILLIE FUNG; *Blake:* CARL HARBORD; *Indians:* JAMES STEVENS, BILL WILKERSON, FRANK LACKTEEN; *Dog Man:* EDWARD MC NAMARA; *Bellboy:* CHARLES SMITH; *Clerk:* EMMETT VOGAN; *Woman:* WINIFRED HARRIS; *Churchill's Voice:* MILES MANDER; *Drill Sergeant:* PAT FLAHERTY; *Bartender:* TOM DUGAN; *Mechanic:* GEORGE OFFERMAN, JR.; *Orderly:* GAVIN MUIR; *Duty Officer:* LARRY WILLIAMS;

With George Tobias, John Hartley, Alan Hale, Reginald Gardiner, Patrick O'Moore and Tony Hughes

With Alan Hale and Dennis Morgan

and JOHN HARTLEY, JOHN KELLOGG, CHARLES IRWIN, BILLY WAYNE, RAFAEL STORM, JOHN GALLAUDET, BARRY BERNARD, GEORGE OVEY, WALTER BROOKS, RAY MONTGOMERY, HERBERT GUNN, DONALD DILLAWAY, JAMES BUSH

CREDITS

Director: MICHAEL CURTIZ; *Producer:* HAL B. WALLIS; *Associate Producer:* WILLIAM CAGNEY; *Scenarists:* ARTHUR T. HORMAN, RICHARD MACAULAY, NORMAN REILLY RAINE; *Based on a story by:* ARTHUR T. HORMAN, ROLAND GILLETT; *Photographers:* SOL POLITO, WILFRED M. CLINE; *Aerial Photographers:* ELMER DYER, CHARLES MARSHALL, WINTON C. HOCH; *Art Director:* TED SMITH; *Editor:* GEORGE AMY; *Dialogue Director:* HUGH MAC MULLAN; *Sound Recorder:* C. A. RIGGS; *Musical Score:* MAX STEINER; *Musical Director:* LEO F. FORBSTEIN; *Costumer:* HOWARD SHOUP; *Makeup Artist:* PERC WESTMORE; *Special Effects:* BYRON HASKIN, REX WIMPY; *Technicolor Consultant:* NATALIE KALMUS; *Technicolor Associate:* HENRI JAFFA; *Warners Chief Pilot:* FRANK CLARKE; *Technical Adviser:* SQUADRON LEADER O. CATHCART-JONES; *Song "Captains of the Clouds" by:* HAROLD ARLEN, JOHNNY MERCER

SYNOPSIS

In a semi-documentary account of how Canadians were being trained for Air Corps service, Brian MacLean is one of a group of north-woods bush pilots. MacLean, who steals jobs away from his competitors—and occasionally their girls—rebels at first against the stiff discipline required of a trainer in the RCAF. His struggle is that of a pilot who flies by instinct fighting against the modern pilot who flies by instruments.

When he graduates, he gets the important assignment of piloting a squadron of new, unarmed, American bombers which are being ferried to England over the Atlantic by the RCAF. Before reaching the other side, however, they encounter Nazi raiders.

CRITICS' CIRCLE

"*Captains of the Clouds* is virtually a documentary of Canada's large part in the British Commonwealth Air Training Plan. . . . Although Cagney is much better than his thankless role, the real heroes of *Captains* are Director Michael Curtiz and his five cameramen, who caught the matchless greens and browns of Canada's infinite north-country."

TIME

"Timely, topical, and strongly patriotic in theme, it zooms along at a zestful, attention—arresting pace. Cagney holds attention throughout as the nervy, adventurous and happy-go-lucky flying expert. It's a spotlight performance for Cagney in every foot of film."

VARIETY

". . . is pure tribute to the unchanging forcefulness of James Cagney. But no one can match James Cagney, except, oddly, a stoutish man who is not a professional actor at all. Air Marshal Billy Bishop, Canada's greatest flying ace in the last war, makes a speech to the air cadets who are about to receive their wings. It has a ring of iron to it, although the manner is not forced."

Archer Winston, NEW YORK POST

"This one literally roars with excitement. The flying scenes are breath-taking and will leave you limp with suspense. The color is excellent, the direction fast and the acting first-rate. Cagney is tops in this sort of role, and his Brian MacLean is one of his best performances."

William Boehnel, NEW YORK WORLD-TELEGRAM

"Even Cagney isn't enough to bolster the story's credibility throughout. His characterization packs a good deal more vitality and conviction than the authors provided."

NEWSWEEK

"Mr. Cagney is his usual swaggering self in a none too attractive role . . . but the scenes of R.C.A.F. training are impressive and dignified."

Bosley Crowther, THE NEW YORK TIMES

NOTES

Produced during the summer of 1941, *Captains of the Clouds* was Cagney's first Technicolor picture. As in many of his previous films, this was in praise of the Royal Canadian Air Force. The magnificent aerial photography was a joy to behold. Max Steiner composed a suitable musical score, and director Michael Curtiz pulled the whole show together into one tight unit.

Cagney as a hard-boiled bush pilot gave a competent performance, but the real star was the photography. Canada's own Air Marshal and World War I Ace, William Avery (Billy) Bishop, had a role in the picture—awarding wings to 1,000 RCAF cadets. It was an impressive scene. Sol Polito, one of Warners finest photographers, was nominated for an Academy Award.

With Brenda Marshall

YANKEE DOODLE DANDY

A Warner Bros. – First National Picture

—1942—

CAST

George M. Cohan: JAMES CAGNEY; *Mary:* JOAN LESLIE; *Jerry Cohan:* WALTER HUSTON; *Sam Harris:* RICHARD WHORF; *Dietz:* GEORGE TOBIAS; *Fay Templeton:* IRENE MANNING; *Nellie Cohan:* ROSEMARY DE CAMP; *Josie Cohan:* JEANNE CAGNEY; *Schwab:* S. Z. SAKALL; *Erlanger:* GEORGE BARBIER; *Manager:* WALTER CAT- LETT; *Nora Bayes:* FRANCES LANGFORD; *Ed Albee:* MINOR WATSON; *Eddie Foy:* EDDIE FOY, JR.; *Harold Goff:* CHESTER CLUTE; *George M. Cohan (Age 13):* DOUGLAS CROFT; *Josie (Age 12):* PATSY LEE PARSONS; *Franklin D. Roosevelt:* CAPTAIN JACK YOUNG; *Receptionist:* AUDREY LONG; *Madame Bartholdi:* ODETTE

MYRTIL; *White House Butler:* CLINTON ROSEMOND; *Stage Manager in Providence:* SPENCER CHARTERS; *Sister Act:* DOROTHY KELLY, MARIJO JAMES; *George M. Cohan (Age 7):* HENRY BLAIR; *Josie Cohan (Age 6):* JO ANN MARLOW; *Stage Manager:* THOMAS JACKSON; *Fanny:* PHYLLIS KENNEDY; *White House Guard:* PAT FLAHERTY; *Magician:* LEON BELASCO; *Star Boarder:* SYD SAYLOR; *Stage Manager, N.Y.:* WILLIAM B. DAVIDSON; *Dr. Lewellyn:* HARRY HAYDEN; *Dr. Anderson:* FRANCIS PIERLOT; *Teenagers:* CHARLES SMITH, JOYCE REYNOLDS, DICK CHANDLEE, JOYCE HORNE; *Sergeant:* FRANK FAYLEN; *Theodore Roosevelt:* WALLIS CLARK; *Betsy Ross:* GEORGIA CARROLL; *Sally:* JOAN WINFIELD; *Union Army Veterans:* DICK WESSEL, JAMES FLAVIN; *Schultz in* PECK'S BAD BOY: SAILOR VINCENT; *Irish Cop in* PECK'S BAD BOY: FRED KELSEY; *Hotel Clerks:* GEORGE MEEKER, FRANK MAYO; *Actor, Railroad Station:* TOM DUGAN; *Telegraph Operator:* CREIGHTON HALE; *Wise Guy:* MURRAY ALPER; *Army Clerk:* GARRY OWEN; *Nurse:* RUTH ROBINSON; *Reporters:* EDDIE ACUFF, WALTER BROOKE, BILL EDWARDS, WILLIAM HOPPER; *1st Critic:* WILLIAM FORREST; *2nd Critic:* ED KEANE; *Girl:* DOLORES MORAN; *Chorus Girls "LITTLE JOHNNY JONES":* POPPY WILDE, LORRAINE GETTMAN (LESLIE BROOKS)

CUT FROM FINAL PRINT:

Actors: VERA LEWIS, JIM TONEY, CHARLES DRAKE; *Receptionist:* ANN DORAN; *Porter:* NAPOLEON SIMPSON; *Call Boy:* BUDDY (LON) MC CALLISTER; *Housekeeper:* LEAH BAIRD

CREDITS

Director: MICHAEL CURTIZ; *Producer:* JACK L. WARNER; *Executive Producer:* HAL B. WALLIS; *Associate Producer:* WILLIAM CAGNEY; *Scenarists:* ROBERT BUCKNER, EDMUND JOSEPH; *Based on an original story by:* ROBERT BUCKNER; *Dialogue Director:* HUGH MAC MULLAN; *Photographer:* JAMES WONG HOWE; *Art Director:* CARL JULES WEYL; *Montages by:* DON SIEGEL; *Editor:* GEORGE AMY; *Sound Recorder:* EVERETT A. BROWN; *Musical Adaptation:* HEINZ ROEMHELD; *Musical Director:* LEO F. FORBSTEIN; *Orchestrator:* RAY HEINDORF; *Choreographers:* LEROY PRINZ, SEYMOUR FELIX; *Costumer:* MILO ANDERSON; *Makeup Artist:* PERC WESTMORE; *Mr. Cagney's Dances Staged by:* JOHN BOYLE; *Technical Adviser:* WILLIAM COLLIER, SR.; *Songs:* "I Was Born in Virginia," "The Warmest Baby in the Bunch," "Give My Regards to Broadway," "Mary's a Grand Old Name," "So Long Mary," "Yankee Doodle Boy,"

With Joan Leslie

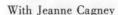

With Jeanne Cagney

With Richard Whorf, George Barbier and Irene Manning

With S. Z. Sakall and Richard Whorf

With Captain Jack Young

170

"Over There," "Harrigan," "Forty-Five Minutes from Broadway," "You're a Grand Old Flag," by: GEORGE M. COHAN; *New Song: "All Aboard for Old Broadway" by:* JACK SCHOLL, M. K. JEROME

SYNOPSIS

Vaudevillians Jerry and Nellie Cohan are visited by an agent who offers them an engagement, but their young son, George Michael, is so boastful that he loses them the job; George later falls in love with Mary, a stage-struck girl, and takes her with him when he tries to sell a musical show he has written. He fails, but, in the process, meets a young showman named Sam Harris and they form a partnership.

Cohan talks established star Fay Templeton into starring in his new show. Years later, after achieving greatness in the American theatre world, he retires, but is asked to return to help his old friend Sam. For his patriotic songs and actions, he is decorated by the President of the United States.

CRITICS' CIRCLE

"James Cagney plays the Cohan role, and it's unquestionably Mr. Cagney's most brilliant bit of make-believe. He gets over that characterization by suggestion rather than by out-and-out imitation, and a typical gesture here, a well-remembered mannerism there, and, at all times, a buoyant vitality, and it's a performance that has both authority and charm."

Rose Pelswick, NEW YORK JOURNAL-AMERICAN

"Essentially the film is an account of George M. Cohan's brilliant career as a vaudeville hoofer, dramatist, actor, song-writer and flag-waver, but at the same time it is a captivating record of a whole theatrical epoch. With James Cagney playing Cohan as only Cagney could have done, the new Hollywood Theater offering is a stunning show.

"Most of the magic . . . is conjured up by the consummate Cagney portrayal. He even looks a bit like Cohan at times and he has the great man's routines down cold. The point is that he adds his own individual reflections to the part, as should certainly be done in any dramatic impersonation of a celebrated figure. He has given many memorable and varied screen performances in the past, but this is nothing short of a brilliant tour-de-force of make-believe."

Howard Barnes, NEW YORK HERALD TRIBUNE

With Frances Langford

"*Yankee Doodle Dandy* is possibly the most genial screen biography ever made. Few films have bestowed such loving care on any hero as this one does on beaming, buoyant, wry-mouthed George M. Cohan. Canny Showman Cohan knew what he was doing when he insisted that Irish Jimmy Cagney was the one cinemactor who could play him. Smart, alert, hard-headed, Cagney is as typically American as Cohan himself. Like Cohan, he has a transparent personal honesty, a basic audience appeal. Like Cohan, he was once a hoofer.

"With these attributes, Cagney manages to suggest George M. Cohan without carbon copying the classic trouper. He has the Cohan trick of nodding and winking to express approval, the outthrust jaw, stiff-legged stride, bantam dance routines, side-of-the mouth singing, the air of likable conceit. For the rest, he remains plain Jimmy Cagney. It is a remarkable performance, possibly Cagney's best, and it makes *Yankee Doodle* a dandy."

TIME

"To begin with there is Jimmy Cagney as the great song and dance man, flag waver, dramatist, producer.

171

With Jeanne Cagney, Joan Leslie, Walter Huston and Rosemary DeCamp

Jimmy has never been better and that's saying something. Brash, sentimental, flip, serious, he plays the part with such joy and relish that not even the great George M. Cohan could have done better. It is a performance of which both Mr. Cagney and Mr. Cohan may well be proud."

William Boehnel, NEW YORK WORLD-TELEGRAM

"The picture *Yankee Doodle Dandy* is a triumph not only for it's superb timeliness but also for its portrait of a man and its vitality as a period piece. . . . Two wonderful performances keep the picture boiling. Walter Huston makes a marvelous elder Cohan. But front and center is James Cagney whose personal dynamism is a letter-perfect conception of the George M. Cohan the public has known. The gestures and the dances ring the bell of recognition at salient points. But it is the inner spirit that captures the imagination."

Archer Winston, NEW YORK POST

"James Cagney's portrayal of George M. Cohan in the Warners' delightful film biography, *Yankee Doodle Dandy*, is as bold and respectable a piece of acting as any one could wish. But the truly remarkable nature of Mr. Cagney's accomplishment turns not so much on a literal imitation of Mr. Cohan as it does on a shrewd and meticulous creation of a lusty, spontaneous character. Indeed, Mr. Cagney's Mr. Cohan is not so much an image of George M. as it is an exhilarating portrait of a spirited trouper and a warmly emotional man."

Bosley Crowther, THE NEW YORK TIMES

"To the part of Cohan, Warner Bros. assigned kinetic Jimmy Cagney who used to be a Broadway hoofer himself. Aside from being blond, brash and Irish, he does not resemble Cohan, but more important, Cagney has enough talent of his own to make you believe in Cohan's success. Cagney's performance may win him a 1942 Academy Award."

LIFE

"Fortunately, Cagney is present to provide the astonishingly versatile and driving impersonation of George M. Cohan that cannot help but swing this musical into the top popularity brackets."

NEWSWEEK

"James Cagney is a 'natural' for the Cohan role and he turns in a magnificent performance. He has faithfully copied Mr. Cohan's style of dancing, his stage work and other idiosyncrasies. Mr. Cagney also has a few sentimental scenes which he acts with genuine sincerity."

Kelcey Allen, WOMEN'S WEAR DAILY

"James Cagney is less happy as Mr. Cohan. Mr. Cagney is Irish; but his is the sharp-faced, shrewd Irish type. He lacks the winning sweetness of the Cohan personality. Except for the difference in personalities, Mr. Cagney does excellent work in the starring role. He dances well. He sings a little. He gets over the comedy and even the pathos. It is not Cohan; but it's entertaining."

Eileen Creelman, NEW YORK SUN

NOTES

George M. Cohan, after several years' negotiations with different studios, finally sold his life story rights (for $50,000) to Warners, retaining the right to approve casting as well as the screenplay. Warners, realizing that the time was ripe for such a patriotic, flag-waving biography of the celebrated song-and-dance man, spared no expense.

Cohan wrote and produced 40 plays and helped finance 125 others. He composed more than 500 songs and musical numbers, so there was plenty to choose from for this film. The choices could not have been bettered. Cagney was in his element as George M. and delivered a finely etched portrayal of the man and the entertainer.

The production was superb in every respect, and the cast was flawless down to the last member of the chorus. *Yankee Doodle Dandy* received eight Academy Award nominations and produced three winners. The non-winning nominations were: Picture, Supporting Actor (Huston), Original Story (Buckner), Director (Curtiz) and Editing (Amy). The winners were Actor (Cagney), Sound (Nathan Levinson, the department head, won the award) and Scoring of a Musical (Heindorf and Roemheld).

The Broadway opening sold first-night tickets for war bonds. The cheapest seats sold for $25. The eighty-eight best seats went for $25,000 each. The total take, $5,750,000, was donated to the U. S. Treasury Department.

With Eddie Foy, Jr.

JOHNNY COME LATELY

A William Cagney Picture
Released Through United Artists

—1943—

CAST

Tom Richards: JAMES CAGNEY; *Vinnie McLeod:* GRACE GEORGE; *Gashouse Mary:* MARJORIE MAIN; *Jane:* MARJORIE LORD; *Aida:* HATTIE MC DANIEL; *W. W. Dougherty:* EDWARD MC NAMARA; *Pete Dougherty:* BILL HENRY; *Bill Swain:* ROBERT BARRAT; *Willie Ferguson:* GEORGE CLEVELAND; *Myrtle Ferguson:* MARGARET HAMILTON; *Dudley Hirsh:* NORMAN WILLIS; *Blaker:* LUCIEN LITTLEFIELD; *Winterbottom:* EDWIN STANLEY; *Chief of Police:* IRVING BACON; *First Cop:* TOM DUGAN; *Second Cop:* CHARLES IRWIN; *Third Cop:* JOHN SHEEHAN; *Butler:* CLARENCE MUSE; *First Tramp:* JOHN MILLER; *Second Tramp:* ARTHUR HUNNICUTT; *Tramp in Box Car:* VICTOR KILIAN; *Bouncer:* WEE WILLIE DAVIS; *Old Timer:* HENRY HALL

CREDITS

Director: WILLIAM K. HOWARD; *Producer:* WILLIAM CAGNEY; *Scenarist:* JOHN VAN DRUTEN; *Based on the novel* MC LEOD'S FOLLY *by:* LOUIS BROMFIELD; *Photographer:* THEODORE SPARKUHL; *Art Director:* JACK OKEY; *Set Decorator:* JULIA HERON; *Editor:* GEORGE ARTHUR; *Sound Recorder:* BENJAMIN WINKLER; *Musical Director:* LEIGH HARLINE; *Assistant Director:* LOWELL FARRELL

SYNOPSIS

Travelling newspaperman Tom Richards is jailed for vagrancy in a small town, but is paroled to lady newspaper publisher Vinnie McLeod. Convinced to help expose the town's corrupt politicians, Richards enlists the aid of Gashouse Mary, who won't talk until injus-

176

tice arouses her. During a fast and furious election, a group of the leading reformers is hustled off to jail by the minions of the town's political boss.

Finally aroused, Gashouse Mary shows Richards how the town grafters raise money for an Orphan's Fund, then use the money to keep crooked henchmen in office. He produces a streamlined exposé edition of Mrs. McLeod's paper, which the opposition tries desperately to squash.

CRITICS' CIRCLE

"Cagney and Miss George provide some pleasant moments in a script that moves leisurely through its turn-of-the-century sets and plot complications. . . . Cagney gets a chance to do a bit of fighting during the course of the piece, but for the most part he's presented as the wanderer with the heart of gold and, despite some obstacles of scripting and direction, checks in a competent performance."

Rose Pelswick, NEW YORK JOURNAL-AMERICAN

"It is not dreadful—Cagney is still the unique Cagney —but it is far below his standard. To put it bluntly, it is an old-fashioned story told in a very old-fashioned manner.

"Please, Mr. Cagney for the benefit of the public, yourself and Warners, go back where you made pictures like *Yankee Doodle Dandy*."

Archer Winston, NEW YORK POST

"Grace George seems effortlessly to have learned what so many transplanted Broadway actors ache over— how to project her touching elegance in a medium new to her. James Cagney, who in his time had to plant fists or a grapefruit on young ladies' faces and shoes on young ladies' behinds, here develops his tenderest relationships with middle-aged ladies (the Misses George, Main and Hattie McDaniel), and each of them is worth a dozen average love scenes. . . .These pleasures would have been all but impossible to manufacture in any of the large studios, for they are given their warmth and life by the pleasure that the Cagneys' large cast and the whole production outfit obviously took in doing a job as they wanted to do it. Bit players who have tried creditably for years to walk in shoes that pinched them show themselves in this picture as the very competent actors they always were: there has seldom been as good a cinematic gallery of U. S. small-town types."

TIME

With George Cleveland and Grace George

With Marjorie Lord, Margaret Hamilton, George Cleveland and Grace George

With Marjorie Main

"It is a disappointing film in that there is too little action in the story to suit the ebullient personality of the star. . . . This isn't to imply that Jimmy Cagney doesn't give a good performance in the role of an itinerant newspaperman; on the contrary, his impression of Tom Richards is an interesting and impressive one and his selection of Grace George was an inspiration."

Kate Cameron, New York DAILY NEWS

On the set with producer William Cagney

With Grace George and Edward McNamara

With Hattie McDaniel

"Mr. Cagney must have picked this part for himself. Less striking than those he had at Warner Brothers, it is an amiable, fairly amusing characterization, much in the mood of the film itself."

Eileen Creelman, NEW YORK SUN

"Cagney's performance, however, combined with William Howard's direction, offset scripting flaws. Production is studded with excellent comedy character bits which, combined with Cagney, give the yarn a terrible lift."

VARIETY

"*Johnny Come Lately* is almost the kind of business that might result if Jimmy Cagney, the immortal Hollywood movie star, had returned to play the lead in the annual production of his old high school's Masque and Film Club.

"*Johnny Come Lately* is so palpably amateurish in production and direction, so hopelessly stagey, uneven and teamless in performance and so utterly pointless that it is bound to cause raised eyebrows wherever it is shown."

John T. McManus, PM

"Jim Cagney brings the full force of his dynamic swagger to this fluffball of a role, and the results are effective. This is a long step below the full-length characterization of any of his other recent pictures, so let's just say Johnny is played as well as any sad flimsy hero ever has been."

Alton Cook, NEW YORK WORLD-TELEGRAM

NOTES

This was the first film made by William Cagney Productions, an Independent Producing Company with James Cagney as Vice President. John Van Druten's scenario was based on Louis Bromfield's novel "McLeod's Folly"—the old chestnut revolving around the fearless crusader who gives the town their comeuppance.

It was rather a tame property for Cagney to choose, but perhaps he had grown weary of the action-and-grind films with which his name had long been associated. His performance was a competent one, indeed, but the film's important event was the casting of Grace George as Vinnie McLeod. Miss George had been a top star on the American stage for forty years. This was her first—and only—film. Leigh Harline received an Academy Award nomination for his scoring of this picture.

BLOOD ON THE SUN

A William Cagney Production
Released Through United Artists

—1945—

CAST

Nick Condon: JAMES CAGNEY; *Iris Hilliard:* SYLVIA SIDNEY; *Ollie Miller:* WALLACE FORD; *Edith Miller:* ROSEMARY DE CAMP; *Colonel Tojo:* ROBERT ARMSTRONG; *Premiere Tanaka:* JOHN EMERY; *Hijikata:* LEONARD STRONG; *Prince Tatsugi:* FRANK PUGLIA; *Captain Oshima:* JACK HALLORAN; *Kajioka:* HUGH HO; *Yomamoto:* PHILIP AHN; *Hayoshi:* JOSEPH KIM; *Yamada:* MARVIN MILLER; *Joseph Cassell:* RHYS WILLIAMS; *Arthur Bickett:* PORTER HALL; *Charley Sprague:* JAMES BELL; *Amah:* GRACE LEM; *Chinese Servant:* OY CHAN; *Hotel Manager:* GEORGE PARIS; *Johnny Clarke:* HUGH BEAUMONT; *American Newspapermen in Tokyo:* GREGORY GAY, ARTHUR LOFT, EMMETT VOGAN, CHARLIE WAYNE

With Sylvia Sidney and Frank Puglia

179

With Jack Halloran

With Jack Halloran, Joseph Kim and Porter Hall

CREDITS

Director: FRANK LLOYD; *Producer:* WILLIAM CAGNEY; *Assistant to Producer:* GEORGE ARTHUR; *Scenarist:* LESTER COLE; *Based on a story by:* GARRETT FORT; *Additional Scenes by:* NATHANIEL CURTIS; *Photographer:* THEODORE SPARKUHL; *Art Director:* WIARD IHNEN; *Set Director:* A. ROLAND FIELDS; *Production Manager:* DANIEL KEEFE; *Editors:* TRUMAN K. WOOD, WALTER HANNEMAN; *Sound Recorder:* RICHARD DE WESSE; *Musical Score:* MIKLOS ROZSA; *Costumer:* ROBERT MARTIEN; *Makeup Artists:* ERN WESTMORE, JOSEF NORIN; *Assistant Director:* HARVEY DWIGHT; *Technical Adviser:* ALICE BARLOW

SYNOPSIS

Nick Condon, the American editor of a Tokyo newspaper, is incensed by the brutal murders of his good friends, a reporter and his wife. He then tries to get the secret Tanaka Plan of world conquest, formulated by Japanese militarists, out of Japan. His task is a formidable one, and the opposition is heavy.

In his one-man campaign, he is framed by the Japanese police, makes the romantic acquaintance of Iris Hilliard, a half-Chinese beauty whose access to high places stirs his suspicions, unmasks the crookedness of a fellow journalist, and helps drive Tanaka to hari-kari.

CRITICS' CIRCLE

"*Blood on the Sun*, a story about a Hoover-era American editor who learned of Baron Tanaka's plan for world conquest and tried to get the document out of Japan, is mainly apocryphal. But as melodrama it is as hard, tidy and enjoyable as the work of its star James Cagney, the dean of the sort of movie in which action and good sense collaborate instead of colliding.

"In its stretches of muted menace and its well-designed explosions of violence, *Blood on the Sun* has much of the clean, sharp-nerved charm which used to distinguish the adventure romances of the late great Douglas Fairbanks, Sr. A shade less inspired than Fairbanks as an athlete, Cagney is an even better actor. He cannot even put a telephone receiver back on its hook without giving the action special spark and life."

TIME

"The stars of this picture are given plenty of opportunity to display their histrionics. Cagney is the same rough and tumble character he's always been. . . . Miss Sidney, back after a too-long hiatus from Hollywood, is gowned gorgeously and photographs ditto."

VARIETY

"It is the most violent workout Mr. Cagney has had since *Public Enemy*, and it ought to be fine for those who admire a good, ninety-minute massacre."

NEW YORKER

NOTES

With this film, Cagney Productions gave the public an actioner—with Jimmy as a hot-shot American reporter in the Tokyo of the twenties. It was packed with action and romance under the direction of Frank Lloyd, for whom Jimmy once worked as an "extra" (in M-G-M's *Mutiny on the Bounty*) during one of his frequent layoff periods from Warners. Sylvia Sidney returned to the screen after a long absence in this film, which was filmed entirely on the Goldwyn lot.

With Sylvia Sidney

For authenticity in playing his role, Jimmy took Judo lessons with an ex-L. A. cop named Jack Halloran. He was as nimble as ever and, as usual, convincing in his role.

With Rhys Williams and Sylvia Sidney

181

13 RUE MADELEINE

A 20th Century-Fox Picture

—1946—

CAST

Bob Sharkey: JAMES CAGNEY; *Suzanne de Bouchard:* ANNABELLA; *Bill O'Connell:* RICHARD CONTE; *Jeff Lassiter:* FRANK LATIMORE; *Charles Gibson:* WALTER ABEL; *Pappy Simpson:* MELVILLE COOPER; *Mayor Galimard:* SAM JAFFE; *Duclois:* MARCEL ROUSSEAU; *Psychiatrist:* RICHARD GORDON; *Emile:* EVERETT G. MARSHALL; *Madame Thillot:* BLANCHE YURKA; *Karl:* PETER VON ZERNECK; *Hans Feinkl:* ALFRED LINDER; *Hotel Clerk:* BEN LOW; *R.A.F. Officer:* JAMES CRAVEN; *Joseph:* ROLAND BELANGER; *Burglary Instructor:* HORACE MAC MAHON; *Briefing Officer:* ALEXANDER KIRKLAND; *La Roche:* DONALD RANDOLPH; *Peasant Lady:* JUDITH LOWRY; *Dispatcher:* RED BUTTONS; *German Staff Officer:* OTTO SIMANEK; *Psychiatrist:* WALTER GREAZA; *Van Duyval:* ROLAND WINTERS; *Tailor:* HAROLD YOUNG; *Chief Operator:* SALLY MC-MARROW; *Flyers:* COBY NEAL, KARL MALDEN; *French Peasant:* JEAN DEL VAL; *Narrator:* REED HADLEY

With Sam Jaffe

CREDITS

Director: HENRY HATHAWAY; *Producer:* LOUIS DE ROCHEMONT; *Original Screenplay by:* JOHN MONKS, JR., SY BARTLETT; *Photographer:* NORBERT BRODINE; *Art Directors:* JAMES BASEVI, MAURICE RANSFORD; *Set Decorator:* THOMAS LITTLE; *Editor:* HARMON JONES; *Sound Recorders:* W. D. FLICK, HARRY M. LEONARD; *Musical Score:* ALFRED NEWMAN; *Musical Director:* DAVID BUTTOLPH; *Orchestral Arrangements:* EDWARD POWELL, SIDNEY CUTNER, LEO SHUKEN; *Costumer:* RENE HUBERT; *Makeup Artist:* BEN NYE; *Special Photographic Effects:* FRED SERSEN; *Assistant Director:* ABE STEINBERG

SYNOPSIS

This is a semi-documentary tale of the careers of four American espionage agents from induction to fulfillment of their mission overseas. The agents featured are: Bob Sharkey, a world-traveler and adventurer; Suzanne de Bouchard, a Frenchwoman; Jeff Lassiter, a high-school teacher; and Bill O'Connell, an American university graduate who has lived abroad.

The major portion of the mission assigned to the quartet is to locate a German rocket-bomb launching site in France so that the Air Corps can bomb it before D-Day. To make things more intriguing, one of their own group is a German agent.

CRITICS' CIRCLE

"Far and away the roughest, toughest spy chase yet gleaned from the bulging files of the OSS is 20th Century-Fox's *13 Rue Madeleine*. Surpassing its predecessors, *Cloak and Dagger* and *OSS*, the film gets its name from the address of a Gestapo headquarters, much of its realistic wallop by paralleling actual OSS training."

TIME

"Himmler's operatives in the picture, in fact, are so extravagantly simple-minded that at one point they accept James Cagney, the hero of the piece, as a representative of the Vichy government. This demands a great deal more credulity than is generally found even in circles where shoes are a phenomenon, for Mr. Cagney has an air and accent more suited to Stillman's Gymnasium than to the tired coteries of collaborationist governments. Mr. Cagney is much more plausible in the early part of the film when he is shown putting

With Annabella

With Richard Conte

With Richard Conte, Annabella and Frank Latimore

183

O.S.S. apprentices through their paces with the red-blooded manliness of a football coach."

John McCarten, NEW YORKER

NOTES

Producer Louis de Rochemont made the first *March of Time* in 1934 and produced that excellent series for almost a decade. Utilizing his know-how as a documentary-maker, he and scenarist John Monks, Jr., met with great success in 1945 with *The House on 92nd Street. 13 Rue Madeleine*, a superb follow-up spy yarn, used the same off-screen documentary exposition.

Cagney and a fine cast, which included Annabella, Richard Conte and Frank Latimore, were mere pawns in the hands of director Henry Hathaway, but the results were most satisfactory. This film was a success and gave Cagney additional funds with which to continue his own productions.

Location work at Cardinal O'Connell Hall at Boston College—formerly the Louis K. Liggett estate—was picked because of its English Tudor architecture. Other scenes were shot in Quebec and many New England locales.

With Blanche Yurka

THE TIME OF YOUR LIFE

A William Cagney—United Artists Picture

—1948—

CAST

Joe: JAMES CAGNEY; *Nick:* WILLIAM BENDIX; *Tom:* WAYNE MORRIS; *Kitty Duval:* JEANNE CAGNEY; *Policeman:* BRODERICK CRAWFORD; *McCarthy:* WARD BOND; *Kit Carson:* JAMES BARTON; *Harry:* PAUL DRAPER; *Mary L:* GALE PAGE; *Dudley:* JAMES LYDON; *Willie:* RICHARD ERDMAN; *Arab:* PEDRO DE CORDOBA; *Wesley:* REGINALD BEANE; *Blick:* TOM POWERS; *A Drunk:* JOHN "SKINS" MILLER; *Society Lady:* NATALIE SCHAFER; *Society Gentleman:* HOWARD FREEMAN; *Blind Date:* RENIE RIANO; *Newsboy:* LANNY REES; *Girl in Love:* NANETTE PARKS; *Nick's Mother:* GRAZIA MARCISO; *"Killer":* CLAIRE CARLETON; *Sidekick:* GLADYS BLAKE; *Nick's Daughter:* MARLENE AAMES; *Cook:* MOY MING; *Bookie:* DONALD KERR; *B Girl:* ANN CAMERON; *Sailor:* FLOYD WALTERS; *Salvation Army Man:* EDDIE BORDEN; *Salvation Army Woman:* RENA CASE

CREDITS

Director: H. C. POTTER; *Producer:* WILLIAM CAGNEY; *Scenarist:* NATHANIEL CURTIS; *Based on the play by:* WILLIAM SAROYAN; *Photographer:* JAMES WONG HOWE; *Art Director:* WIARD IHNEN; *Production Manager:* KAN KEEFE; *Assistant Production Manager:* EDWARD CAGNEY; *Unit Production Manager:* JOHN W. KIRSTEN; *Set Decorator:* A. ROLAND FIELDS; *Editors:* WALTER HANNEMANN, TRUMAN K. WOOD; *Sound Recorder:* EARL SITAR; *Musical Score:* CARMEN DRAGON; *Piano Compositions:* REGINALD BEANE; *Costumer:* COURTNEY HASLAM; *Talent Department:* IRVING KUMIN; *Makeup Artist:* OTIS MALCOLM; *Hair Stylist:* SCOTTY RACKIN; *Still Photographer:* MADISON S. LACY; *Assistant Director:* HARVEY DWIGHT

SYNOPSIS

A group of eccentric, lovable people, habitués of a San Francisco waterfront bar, spend a great deal of time philosophizing about life. Joe, the leading character, believes in encouraging everybody in their intoxicating dreams. He freeloads from Kitty Duval, a street walker, and cons Nick, the bartender, into giving a part-time job to Harry, a vagabond dancer. Living for his dream world, he also encourages an old man named Kit Carson to spin his exciting yarns about the wild west.

With Gale Page

With James Barton, Howard Freeman and Natalie Schafer

With Jeanne Cagney

"It took a lot of courage for the Cagney brothers, William and James, to make a film of William Saroyan's capricious stage play, *The Time of Your Life*. For with all its genial disposition and its capacity for attracting prize awards, the play lacked dramatic foundation, all the way down the line. Mr. Cagney is physically solid and spiritually luminous as a gent who has the kindly and sympathetic feelings toward the world's wistful dreamers of dreams. And Miss Cagney is grave and affecting as the slightly damaged goods who kids herself with the pretense that she was once a burlesque queen. Likewise, James Barton is magnificent as the bunko artist of the West and William Bendix, who appeared in the stage play back in 1939, tends a fine bar."

Bosley Crowther, THE NEW YORK TIMES

"*The Time of Your Life* is William Saroyan's rosy look-in on a San Francisco saloon and, in the late Charles Butterworth's enduring phrase, its habitués and sons-of-habitués. The performance—notably those of James Barton, Reginald Beane and James Cagney—are as deft a compromise between stage and screen as you are likely to see. Nevertheless, a good deal which would be as taut and resonant as a drumhead on the stage is relatively dull and slack on the screen. On the other hand, those who made the picture have given it something very rare. It's obvious that they love the play and their work in it, and their affection and enjoyment are highly contagious. They have done so handsomely by Saroyan that in the long run everything depends on how much of Saroyan you can take."

TIME

"So the Cagney version of *The Time of Your Life* must be appraised as a collection of great moments set into a string of lulls. Nothing fancy has been attempted in the way of camera technique. Cagney and his director, H. C. Potter, simply assembled a set of good actors and let them cut loose on their odd Saroyan characters."

Alton Cook, NEW YORK WORLD-TELEGRAM

"Since *The Time of Your Life* has more talk than action—and some of the talk is stupid—it is occasionally dull. But most of the time it is exhilarating comedy, full of kindness and proving conclusively that people, especially Saroyan people, have more fun than anybody. With some likeable performances added to all this by James Cagney as Joe, William Bendix as Nick

With Jimmy Lydon, Richard Erdman and James Barton

and James Barton as a ratchety old windbag, people who see *The Time of Your Life* should have considerable fun too."

LIFE

"The film has many fine moments, but not enough to bring to life the wonderful people of Mr. Saroyan's imagination. James Barton is excellent as the old Indian fighter Kit Carson; William Bendix is a fine choice as bartender Nick; and Jeanne Cagney, Wayne Morris and Paul Draper do very well by their roles. Mr. Cagney does his best with the central role of the philosophic Joe. But he was Mr. Saroyan's weakest figure in the play, and he remains so to harass Mr. Cagney on screen."

CUE

NOTES

William Saroyan turned down several big studio offers for *The Time of Your Life* and it paid off. His strange fantasy was beautifully captured by Cagney and his well-chosen cast under the inspired direction of H. C. Potter. The original Saroyan ending was filmed but, when previewed, audiences were bewildered. A conventional fadeout was used, which managed to retain some of the beauty of the original.

When the film opened, Saroyan sent a letter to William Cagney Productions which said, in part, "Early one morning two or three weeks ago I stood in line at the United Artist Theater and bought a ticket to the first showing of *The Time of Your Life* in San Francisco. I did this because, as you know, I wrote the play and wanted to find out as quickly as possible if my kind of writing could be made to mean anything at all in a movie.

"The people came into the theater and sat down and finally the lights dimmed and the movie started. It wasn't more than three minutes until I had forgotten that I had written the play. I was too busy enjoying it to care who wrote it. Before I knew it the film was over, and as far as I was able to tell everybody in the theater was sorry it was over. That bar was just naturally a very good place to visit.

"All of which is by way of telling you I think you have made one of the most original and entertaining movies I have seen. Furthermore, I have no intention of pretending that it's my fault that you have made such a film, for I think the truth of the matter is this: that you and your associates have expertly edited and translated into the medium of the motion picture a most difficult and almost unmanageable body of material.

"I send you congratulations, profound thanks and all good wishes."

Yours truly, (signed) Bill Saroyan.

With Wayne Morris and Jeanne Cagney

With Broderick Crawford and Ward Bond

WHITE HEAT

A Warner Bros. — First National Picture

—1949—

CAST

Cody Jarrett: JAMES CAGNEY; *Verna Jarrett:* VIRGINIA MAYO; *Hank Fallon:* EDMOND O'BRIEN; *Ma Jarrett:* MARGARET WYCHERLY; *"Big Ed" Somers:* STEVE COCHRAN; *Philip Evans:* JOHN ARCHER; *Cotton Valetti:* WALLY CASSELL; *Het Kohler:* MICKEY KNOX; *The Trader:* FRED CLARK; *The Reader:* G. PAT COLLINS; *Roy Parker:* PAUL GUILFOYLE; *Happy Taylor:* FRED COBY; *Zuckie Hommell:* FORD RAINEY; *Tommy Ryley:* ROBERT OSTERLOH; *Bo Creel:* IAN MAC DONALD; *Chief of Police:* MARSHALL BRADFORD; *Ernie Trent:* RAY MONTGOMERY; *Police Surgeon:* GEORGE TAYLOR; *Willie Rolf:* MILTON PARSONS; *Cashier:* CLAUDIA BARRETT; *Popcorn Vendor:* BUDDY GORMAN; *Jim Donovan:* DE FORREST LAWRENCE; *Ted Clark:* GARRETT CRAIG; *Judge:* GEORGE SPAULDING; *Clerk:* SHERRY HALL; *Guards:* HARRY STRANG, JACK WORTH; *Russell Hughes:* SID MELTON; *Margaret Baxter:* FERN EGGEN; *Nat Lefeld:* EDDIE FOSTER; *Tower Guard:* LEE PHELPS

With Virginia Mayo

CREDITS

Director: RAOUL WALSH; *Producer:* LOUIS F. EDELMAN; *Scenarists:* IVAN GOFF, BEN ROBERTS; *Based on a story by:* VIRGINIA KELLOGG; *Script Supervisor:* IRVA MAE ROSS; *Photographer:* SID HICKOK; *Operating Cameraman:* MIKE JOYCE; *Art Director:* FRED M. MACLEAN; *Editor:* OWEN MARKS; *Sound Recorder:* LESLIE HEWITT; *Musical Score:* MAX STEINER; *Orchestrator:* MURRAY CUTNER; *Hair Stylist:* GERTRUDE WHEELER; *Costumer:* LEAH RHODES; *Makeup Artist:* PERC WESTMORE, EDDIE ALLEN; *Special Effects:* ROY DAVIDSON, H. F. KOENEKAMP; *Assistant Director:* RUSSELL SAUNDERS; *Grip:* RUDY MASHMEYER; *Gaffer:* PAUL BURNETT; *Still Man:* FRANK BJEERING

SYNOPSIS

Cody Jarrett, a homicidal, paranoiac mamma's boy, is the leader of a gang of train robbers and hijackers.

T-Men are hot on his trail, but cannot get really close. They then plant Hank Fallon, a "roper" (detective who works from the inside), to be a cellmate with Cody, who has turned State's evidence in a minor holdup case to hide out in prison for protection.

Although he is continually going berserk from inherent insanity, Cody and his new friend, Hank, execute a successful jailbreak. The next job is the holdup of a chemical plant's payroll office. Hank gets word to T-Men and the gang is killed off, one by one. Cody's own doom is sealed atop a gasoline tank.

CRITICS' CIRCLE

"The Warners have pulled all the stops in making this picture the acme of the gangster-prison film. They have crammed it with criminal complications—some of them old, some of them glittering new—pictured to technical perfection in a crisp documentary style. And Mr. Cagney has played it in a brilliantly graphic way, matching the pictorial vigor of his famous *Public Enemy* job.

"And Mr. Cagney's performance is not the only one in this film. Director Raoul Walsh has gathered vivid acting from his whole cast. Miss Mayo, in fact, is excellent as the gangster's disloyal spouse—brassy, voluptuous and stupid to just the right degree. Edmond O'Brien does a slick job . . . Steve Cochran is ugly as an outlaw, John Archer is stout . . . and Margaret Wycherly is darkly invidious as the gangster's beloved old 'ma.' "

Bosley Crowther, THE NEW YORK TIMES

"*White Heat* is in the hurtling tabloid tradition of the gangster movies of the '30s, but its matter-of-fact violence is a new, postwar style. Brilliantly directed by Raoul (*Roaring Twenties*) Walsh, an old master of cinema hoodlumism, it returns a more subtle James Cagney to the kind of thug role that made him famous. The leading character, a scientific hijacker, is completely abnormal, but Cagney plays him in a stodgy workingman style that makes him as believable as the most ordinary man."

TIME

"To let the kids see Cagney as he was in happier days, Warner Brothers has produced a wild and exciting mixture of mayhem and madness, called *White Heat*, in which Cagney plays a bestial killer named Cody Jarrett. Hollywood has, however, grown more sophisticated since the old days, and Cody is presented not merely as a gangster but, in the studio's words, as

With Edmond O'Brien and Virginia Mayo

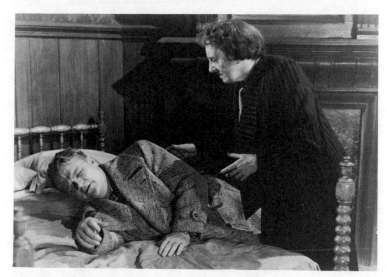

With Margaret Wycherly

With Edmond O'Brien

'a homicidal paranoiac with a mother fixation.' Neither the psychiatry nor the complicated plot bothers audiences which have seen the film. They screech with joy when the hero appears pummeling society with both hands and both feet, a tigerish snarl on his lips. The old Jimmy is back again."

LIFE

"For two hours in *White Heat* you are subjected to an unending procession of what is probably the most gruesome aggregation of brutalities ever presented upon the motion picture screen under the guise of entertainment. James Cagney, heavier in voice, body and jowl, plays a homicidal paranoiac with a mother fixation—a crazy killer who mixes train robbery with murder, bestiality with sadism and tops the whole unsavory mess with a slobbering, shuddering series of epileptic fits the like of which I hope I may never again see in the fearful darkness of a movie theatre."

CUE

With Margaret Wycherly

With Virginia Mayo

NOTES

Warners got Jimmy Cagney back with this one and presented him to a new generation of moviegoers as he had begun in the early thirties—but even more violent. The old style crime melodrama was further broadened by the addition of a mother fixation and a few epileptic fits to keep you on the edge of your seat.

White Heat was based on an original story by Virginia Kellogg, who received an Academy Award nomination for it. She followed this film up with the sensational *Caged* under John Cromwell's direction, starring Eleanor Parker.

Under Raoul Walsh's brilliant direction, Cagney rolled everything he ever knew or did into one gigantic portrayal—his Cody Jarrett has to be seen to be believed. Everyone in his support was perfectly matched; especially good were Margaret Wycherly as Ma, Virginia Mayo as his moll, and Edmond O'Brien as the agent. Cagney's last scene—atop a gas tank—was filmed in Torrance, California. It is a great cinematic moment!

THE WEST POINT STORY

A Warner Bros. – First National Picture

—1950—

CAST

Elwin Bixby: JAMES CAGNEY; *Eve Dillon:* VIRGINIA MAYO; *Jan Wilson:* DORIS DAY; *Tom Fletcher:* GORDON MAC RAE; *Hal Courtland:* GENE NELSON; *Bull Gilbert:* ALAN HALE, JR.; *Harry Eberhart:* ROLAND WINTERS; *Bixby's "Wife":* RAYMOND ROE; *Lieutenant Colonel Martin:* WILTON GRAFF; *Jocelyn:* JEROME COWAN; *Commandant:* FRANK FERGUSON; *Acrobat:* RUSS SAUNDERS; *Officer-in-Charge:* JACK KELLY; *Hoofer:* GLEN TURNBULL; *Piano Player:* WALTER RUICK; *Senator:* LUTE CROCKETT; *Cadets:* JAMES DOBSON, JOEL MARSTON, BOB HAYDEN, DE WIT BISHOP

CREDITS

Director: ROY DEL RUTH; *Producer:* LOUIS F. EDELMAN; *Production Manager:* AL ALLEBORN; *Scenarists:* JOHN MONKS, JR., CHARLES HOFFMAN, IRVING WALLACE; *Script Supervisor:* JEAN BAKER; *Based on a story by:* IRVING WALLACE; *Photographer:* SID HICKOX; *Operating Cameraman:* MIKE JOYCE; *Art Director:* CHARLES H. CLARKE; *Hair Stylist:* GERTRUDE WHEELER; *Set Decorator:* ARMOR E. MARLOWE; *Editor:* OWEN MARKS; *Gaffer:* PAUL BURNETT; *Sound Recorder:* FRANCIS J. SCHEID; *Musical Director:* RAY HEINDORF; *Dance Director:* LEROY PRINZ; *Staged by:* EDDIE PRINZ, AL WHITE; *Mr. Cagney's dances created by:* JOHNNY BOYLE, JR.; *Vocal Arrangements:* HUGH MARTIN; *Orchestrator:* FRANK PERKINS; *Makeup Artist:* OTIS MALCOLM; *Costumes:* MILO ANDERSON, MARJORIE BEST; *Special Effects:* EDWIN DUPAR; *Assistant Director:* MEL DELLER; *Grip:* DUDE NASCHMEYER; *Still Man:* MAC JULIAN; *Songs* "Ten Thousand Sheep," "By the Kissing Rock," "You Love Me," "Military Polka," "Long Before I Knew You," "It Could Only Happen in Brooklyn," "Brooklyn" *by:* JULIE STYNE, SAMMY CAHN; *Musical Number "The Corps"* Ensembled; *Vocaled by:* GORDON MAC RAE

191

With Virginia Mayo and Doris Day

With Virginia Mayo and Gordon MacRae

With Virginia Mayo

SYNOPSIS

Brash Broadway musical director Elwin Bixby, down on his luck, accepts an assignment from producer Harry Eberhart to stage the annual West Point show, "100th Night." Tom Fletcher, a cadet, has written the show's book and tunes, and his producer uncle wants it—and the young man—for a Broadway staging. The producer hopes to persuade Cadet Fletcher to resign from the Academy and tackle Broadway.

Ex-GI Bixby razzes the cadets so energetically that they force him to become a plebe so the corps can keep him on a leash. He persuades his assistant, Eve Dillon, with whom he is in love, to appear in the show, as well as movie star Jan Wilson. All these machinations are, of course, calculated to make Fletcher choose theatre over a military career.

CRITICS' CIRCLE

"If everything about *The West Point Story* were anywhere near as good as Jimmy Cagney is in it, this Warner musical show would be the top musical of the year. For the estimable Mr. Cagney is in rare good form in this film, singing, dancing and wisecracking in his most electrifying style and putting on a show of braggadocio that makes one tingle with gleeful delight.

"The measure of Mr. Cagney's impact upon the whole tenuous show is patently indicated when he is not on the screen. For then the thing sags in woeful fashion, the romance becomes absurd and the patriotic chest-thumping becomes so much chorus-boy parade."

Bosley Crowther, THE NEW YORK TIMES

"It's been eight years since James Cagney tackled a musical assignment and he sparkplugs the fun and frolic among a group of players who press him hard for top honors. . . . The Cagney character is a delight, particularly his bombastic, temperamental storming, his hoofing and cocky personality whether making love or directing a stage show."

VARIETY

"*The West Point Story* crossbreeds two thin Hollywood strains: the backstage musical and the plot that glorifies the U.S. Military Academy. The result is a little monster of a flag-waving, hip-wagging movie combining the misshapen features of both. In a fine burst of freakishness, the Warners have even stuffed overage (46) James Cagney, into the uniform of a West Point plebe.

"Through it all, breathing hard and never able to obey the cadets' admonitions to 'suck in that gut,' Cagney struts, mugs and rampages with the embarrassing insistence of a pugnacious drunk whom no one quite dares to lead to the door. For its best moments, *The West Point Story* depends on talented dancer Gene Nelson and the pleasant voices of Gordon MacRae and Doris Day in some tuneful Julie Styne-Sammy Cahn songs. As Cagney's girl friend, who all but joins the corps herself, Virginia Mayo fills her tights admirably."

TIME

NOTES

Warners had big hopes for this musical—Jimmy's first since *Yankee Doodle Dandy*—but they couldn't have been more off base. This belabored musical-comedy wasted the talents of its cast and was a bore from start to finish. Even the songs, by Julie Styne and Sammy Cahn, were disappointing. Cagney sang "It Could Only Happen in Brooklyn" and "Brooklyn" and, with Doris Day, Virginia Mayo and Gordon MacRae, sang "Military Polka." Despite everything, Ray Heindorf received an Academy Award nomination for his scoring of this picture.

With William Neff, Virginia Mayo, Roland Winters and Gene Nelson

With Doris Day

KISS TOMORROW GOODBYE

A William Cagney Production
A Warner Bros. – First National Picture

—1950—

CAST

Ralph Cotter: JAMES CAGNEY; *Holiday:* BARBARA PAY-TÓN; *Inspector Weber:* WARD BOND; *Mandon:* LUTHER ADLER; *Margaret Dobson:* HELENA CARTER; *Jinx:* STEVE BRODIE; *Vic Mason:* RHYS WILLIAMS; *Reece:* BARTON MAC LANE; *Ezra Dobson:* HERBERT HEYES; *Doc Green:* FRANK REICHER; *Tolgate:* JOHN LITEL; *District Attorney:* DAN RISS; *Cobbett:* JOHN HALLORAN; *Byers:* WILLIAM FRAWLEY; *Detective Gray:* ROBERT KARNES; *Detective Fowler:* KENNETH TOBEY; *Carleton:* NEVILLE BRAND; *Ralph's Brother:* WILLIAM CAGNEY; *Judge:* GEORGE SPAULDING; *Bailiff:* MARK STRONG; *Satterfield:* MATT MC HUGH; *Julia:* GEORGIA CAINE; *Driver:* KING DONOVAN; *Doctor:* FRANK WILCOX; *Butler:* GORDON RICHARDS

With Barbara Payton

CREDITS

Director: GORDON DOUGLAS; *Producer:* WILLIAM CAG-NEY; *Scenarist:* HARRY BROWN; *Based on the novel "Kiss Tomorrow Goodbye" by* HORACE MC COY; *Photographer:* PEVERELL MARLEY; *Art Director:* WIARD IHNEN; *Set Decorator:* JOE KISH; *Editors:* TRUMAN K. WOOD, WALTER HANNEMANN; *Sound Recorder:* WILLIAM LYNCH; *Musical Score:* CARMEN DRAGON; *Make-up Artist:* OTIS MALCOLM; *Special Effects:* PAUL EAGLER; *Assistant Director:* WILLIAM KISSELL

SYNOPSIS

Ralph Cotter pulls a successful jailbreak and later kills his partner. He then beats his ex-partner's sister, Holi-

day, into romantic submission. After he stages a daring daylight robbery of a market, two crooked cops try to shake him down. Turning the tables, he frames them with a hidden recorder and uses them for his own criminal gains.

CRITICS' CIRCLE

"All the snarling, mangling, triple-crossing and exterminating on the screen . . . adds up to one thing—James Cagney is back in town and right in the same old crime groove. . . . Mr. Cagney is taking up where he left off in last season's *White Heat*. Not nearly as rewardingly, however . . . a poor man's copy of *The Asphalt Jungle*. . . . As the moll, a superbly curved young lady named Barbara Payton performs as though she's trying to spit a tooth—one of the few Mr. Cagney leaves her."

H. H. T., THE NEW YORK TIMES

"Cagney is up to his usual tricks in *Kiss Tomorrow Goodbye*, habits like smiling when he is most dangerous, speaking softly to enemies and harshly to friends, and striking fast, preferably with the barrel of a pistol, when the time comes for action. His villainy is almost sentimental; it is nostalgic rather than inventive, the mixture as before without an ingredient changed."

Otis Guernsey, Jr., NEW YORK HERALD TRIBUNE

With Ward Bond

With Barton MacLane, Barbara Payton and Ward Bond

With Barbara Payton

"*Kiss Tomorrow Goodbye* sends Hollywood's aging (46) tough guy James Cagney off on another gay whirl of crime. Cast as the same strutting, wise-cracking thug he played so often in the '30s (now, in a fleeting nod to movie progress, labeled a paranoiac), Cagney kills six men, breaks out of a chain gang, pulls off a couple of daring heists, blackmails a bribe-taking cop (Ward Bond) and viciously swats a blonde doll (Barbara Payton) with a rolled-up towel."

TIME

NOTES

The studio went overboard with this crime melodrama. It reeked of violence for violence's sake, but that was merely a cover-up for a faulty script. Cagney was still fascinating to watch, especially when he beat the hell out of Barbara Payton. The only other cast member to equal his performance was Luther Adler, as a shifty shyster lawyer.

Kiss Tomorrow Goodbye was banned in Ohio, because it was considered "a sordid, sadistic presentation of brutality and an extreme presentation of crime with explicit steps in commission." How right they were.

William Cagney, who produced, also appeared as his brother's brother.

COME FILL THE CUP

A Warner Bros. – First National Picture

—1951—

CAST

Lew Marsh: JAMES CAGNEY; *Paula Copeland:* PHYLLIS THAXTER; *John Ives:* RAYMOND MASSEY; *Charley Dolan:* JAMES GLEASON; *Boyd Copeland:* GIG YOUNG; *Dolly Copeland:* SELENA ROYLE; *Julian Cuscaden:* LARRY KEATING; *Maria Diego:* CHARLITA; *Lennie Carr:* SHELDON LEONARD; *Ike Bashaw:* DOUGLAS SPENCER; *Don Bell:* JOHN KELLOGG; *Hal Ortman:* WILLIAM BAKEWELL; *Travis Ashbourne, 2nd:* JOHN ALVIN; *Kip Zunches:* KING DONOVAN; *Homicide Captain:* JAMES FLAVIN; *Welder:* TORBEN MEYER; *Ora:* NORMA JEAN MACIAS; *Lila:* ELIZABETH FLOURNOY; *Bobby:* HENRY BLAIR

CREDITS

Director: GORDON DOUGLAS; *Producer:* HENRY BLANKE; *Scenarists:* IVAN GOFF, BEN ROBERTS; *Based on a novel by:* HARLAN WARE; *Photographer:* ROBERT BURKS; *Operating Cameraman:* WILLIAM SCHEERR; *Art Director:* LEO F. KUTER; *Set Decorator:* WILLIAM L. KUEHL; *Hair Stylist:* TILLIE STARRETT; *Editor:* ALAN CROSLAND, JR.; *Sound Recorder:* STANLEY JONES; *Musical Director:* RAY HEINDORF; *Costumer:* LEAH RHODES; *Makeup Artist:* GORDON BAU; *Stills Man:* MAC JULIAN; *Assistant Director:* FRANK MATTISON

SYNOPSIS

Ace newspaperman Lew Marsh becomes an alcoholic, drinking himself right out of a job. He also loses Paula, the girl who wants to marry him. A narrow brush with death under the wheels of a truck and a night in the drunk tank convince Marsh to stop drinking. With the help of Charley Dolan, a reformed lush, he painfully succeeds, but never loses that craving for one drink that would put him at the bottom again.

Marsh rises to city editor and is ultimately enlisted by his publisher, John Ives, to reform his drunken nephew Boyd, now the husband of Marsh's old girl. Boyd, who is involved with gangsters, proves hard to reform, and before he succeeds, he causes the death of Marsh's friend Charley.

CRITICS' CIRCLE

"The vigor on the part of Mr. Cagney is, indeed, the most compensating thing about this melodramatic dissertation on newspaper work and strong drink. . . . Mr. Cagney puts on such a show that he almost disguises the pretensions and the melodramatics of the yarn. In his cups he is positively staggering and, when sober, he stimulates the lust of an ex-drunk for liquor so shrewdly that he makes your throat feel dry. To be

196

With Gig Young

sure, his professional comprehension of a newspaperman is slightly wry, but even in this much-libeled business he gives an aggressive show."

Bosley Crowther, THE NEW YORK TIMES

"For the first third of the film, sharp dialogue, a good Cagney performance and the dramatized lore of alcoholism give *Come Fill The Cup* some of the kick of *The Lost Weekend*. But the rest is watered down with flat melodramatics. . . . The film's crude mixture of social problem and underworld formula is epitomized in the climax: a plug-ugly points a gun at Cagney and orders him to take a slug of bourbon."

TIME

"Here you have a double feature: two dramas rolled into one; and either normally would be strong enough to hold up as a sound full-length dramatic feature. Although they don't always jell too smoothly, they do manage to create a generally interesting multi-drama. . . . As always, Cagney gives a hard and competent performance."

CUE

"While it is frequently convincing in portraying the troubles the hard stuff inflicts on men with no defense against it, its virtues are almost hopelessly marinated in good Hollywood oil. The plot is preposterous . . . but in case you think it's too silly to cope with, I ought to point out that Mr. Cagney is a very solid actor, and that most of his assistants here—Phyllis Thaxter, James Gleason and Gig Young, in particular —are all right, too."

THE NEW YORKER

With Phyllis Thaxter

With Selena Royle, Raymond Massey and Gig Young

With Gig Young

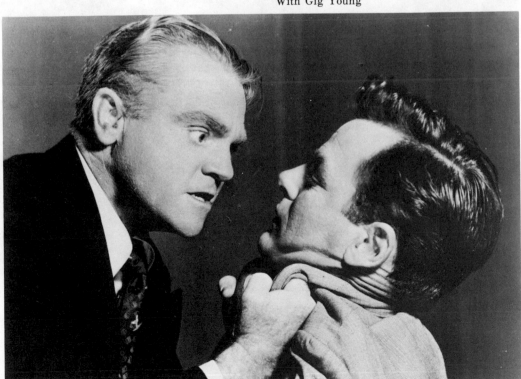

197

Gordon Douglas, who had directed *Kiss Tomorrow Goodbye*, did a fine job with this film, for he had a much better script to work with. That does not mean, however, that the script was without faults. Ivan Goff and Ben Roberts provided a fine scenario in the first half, but then went Hollywood in the cop-out of all time. They almost had an important picture on their hands, matching the caliber of *The Lost Weekend*, but muffed it.

Cagney was splendid throughout, even when the script offered him little to do. The supporting cast, especially James Gleason and Gig Young (who received an Academy Award nomination for Best Supporting Actor), was excellent. It is interesting to note that Gig Young—under his real name, Byron Barr—had appeared in a small part in Jimmy's *Captains of the Clouds* in 1942.

With Phyllis Thaxter and Gig Young

With James Gleason

STARLIFT

A Warner Bros. Picture

—1951—

CAST

Themselves: DORIS DAY, GORDON MAC RAE, VIRGINIA MAYO, GENE NELSON, RUTH ROMAN; *Nell Wayne:* JANICE RULE; *Sergeant Mike Nolan:* DICK WESSON; *Corporal Rick Williams:* RON HAGERTHY; *Colonel Callan;* RICHARD WEBB; *Chaplain:* HAYDEN RORKE; *Steve Rogers:* HOWARD ST. JOHN; *Mrs. Callan:* ANN DORAN; *Turner:* TOMMY FARRELL; *George Norris:* JOHN MAXWELL; *Bob Wayne:* DON BEDDOE; *Sue Wayne:* MARY ADAMS; *Dr. Williams:* BIGELOWE SAYRE; *Mrs. Williams:* ELEANOR AUDLEY; *Theatre Manager:* PAT HENRY; *Chief Usher:* GORDON POLK; *Piano Player:* ROBERT HAMMACK; *Captain Nelson:* RAY MONTGOMERY; *Co-Pilot:* BILL NEFF; *Ground Officer:* STAN HOLBROOK; *Flight Nurse:* JILL RICHARDS; *Litter Case:* JOE TURKEL; *Virginia Boy:* RUSH WILLIAMS; *Pete:* BRIAN MC KAY; *Will:* JACK LARSON; *Nebraska Boy:* LYLE CLARK; *Nurses:* DOROTHY KENNEDY, JEAN DEAN, DOLORES CASTLE; *Boy With Cane:* WILLIAM HUNT; *Army Nurse:* ELIZABETH FLOURNOY; *Driver:* WALTER BRENNAN, JR.; *Lieutenants:* ROBERT KARNES, JOHN HEDLOE; *Boy With Camera:* STEVE GREGORY; *Morgan:* RICHARD MONOHAN; *Soldiers in Bed:* JOE RECHT, HERB LATIMER; *Doctor:* DICK RYAN; *Crew Chief:* BILL HUDSON; *Miss Parson's Assistant:* SARAH SPENCER; *Non-Com:* JAMES BROWN; *Waitress:* EZELLE POULE; *and the following Guest Stars:* JAMES CAGNEY, GARY COOPER, VIRGINIA GIBSON, PHIL HARRIS, FRANK LOVEJOY, LUCILLE NORMAN, LOUELLA PARSONS, RANDOLPH SCOTT, JANE WYMAN, PATRICE WYMORE

With Dick Wesson, Ron Hagerthy, Doris Day and Ruth Roman

CREDITS

Director: ROY DEL RUTH; *Producer:* ROBERT ARTHUR; *Scenarists:* JOHN KLORER, KARL KAMB; *Based on a story by:* JOHN KLORER; *Photographer:* TED MC CORD; *Art Director:* CHARLES H. CLARKE; *Set Decorator:* G. W. BERNTSEN; *Editor:* WILLIAM ZIEGLER; *Sound Recorder:* FRANCIS J. SCHEID; *Musical Director:* RAY HEINDORF; *Costumer:* LEAH RHODES; *Makeup Artist:* GORDON BAU; *Hair Stylist:* GERTRUDE WHEELER; *Choreographer:* LE ROY PRINZ; *Assistant Director:* MEL DELLAR; *Technical Advisers:* MAJOR JAMES G. SMITH, USAF, M.A.T.S., MAJOR GEORGE E. ANDREWS, USAF, S.A.C.; *Songs "S'wonderful" by:* IRA GERSHWIN; *"Liza" by:* GEORGE GERSHWIN; *"You Do Something To Me," "What Is This Thing Called Love?" by:* COLE PORTER; *"You're Gonna Lose Your Gal" by:* JOE YOUNG, JIMMY MONACO; *"You Ought To Be In Pictures" by:* EDWARD HEYMAN, DAND SUESSE; *"It's Magic" by:* SAMMY CAHN, JULIE STYNE; *"Good Green Acres of Home" by:* IRVING KAHAL, SAMMY FAIN; *"I May Be Wrong, But I Think You're Wonderful" by:* HARRY RUSKIN, HENRY SULLIVAN; *"Look Out, Stranger, I'm A Texas Ranger" by:* RUBY RALESIN, PHIL HARRIS; *"Noche Carib" by:* PERCY FAITH

SYNOPSIS

Romance blossoms between Hollywood star Nell Wayne and Air Force Corporal Rich Williams, who is from her home town, when a number of film stars visit Travis Air Force Base. The stars, including James Cagney, Gary Cooper, Jane Wyman, Randolph Scott, Gordon MacRae, and many others, present a show of songs and comic sketches for the servicemen.

CRITICS' CIRCLE

"*Starlift* was Hollywood's ill-starred project of ferrying troupes of movie performers to Travis Air Base, north of San Francisco, to entertain replacements bound for Korea and wounded veterans on their way back to U. S. Hospitals. The film trots out Warner's full stable of stars—Doris Day, Ruth Roman, Gordon MacRae, Virginia Mayo, Gene Nelson, James Cagney, Gary Cooper, Phil Harris, Jane Wyman, Frank Lovejoy, et al.

"But *Starlift* is guilty of its worst breach of good taste when it takes a low bow for Hollywood's patriotic gesture, makes the project seem exclusively Warner's, includes in its cast some stars who never troubled to fly up to Travis Air Base. And the $1,000,000 *Starlift* is entertaining U.S. theaters just a month after Hollywood's Operation Starlift shut down, after running out of the $5,000 that Hollywood chipped in for its expenses."

TIME

NOTES

Jimmy, along with ten other Warners stars, did what is known in the trade as "box-office duty" by appearing in this piffle. It was not worth his time or talent.

WHAT PRICE GLORY ?

A 20th Century-Fox Picture
In Technicolor

—1952—

CAST

Captain Flagg: JAMES CAGNEY; *Charmaine:* CORINNE CALVET; *Sergeant Quirt:* DAN DAILEY; *Corporal Kiper:* WILLIAM DEMAREST; *Lieutenant Aldrich:* CRAIG HILL; *Lewisohn:* ROBERT WAGNER; *Nicole Bouchard:* MARISA PAVAN; *Lieutenant Moore:* CASEY ADAMS; *General Cokely:* JAMES GLEASON; *Lipinsky:* WALLY VERNON; *Cognac Pete:* HENRY LETONDAL; *Lieutenant Schmidt:* FRED LIBBY; *Mulcahy:* RAY HYKE; *Gowdy:* PAUL FIX; *Young Soldier:* JAMES LILBURN; *Morgan:* HENRY MORGAN; *Gilbert:* DAN BORZAGE; *Holsen:* BILL HENRY; *Company Cook:* HENRY "BOMBER" KULKOVICH; *Ferguson:* JACK PENNICK; *Nun:* ANN CODEE; *Lieutenant Cunningham:* STANLEY JOHNSON; *Captain Davis:* TOM TYLER; *Sister Clotilde:* OLGA ANDRE; *Priest:* BARRY NORTON; *The Great Uncle:* LUIS ALBERNI; *Mayor:* TORBEN MEYER; *English Colonel:* ALFRED ZEISLER; *English Lieutenant:* GEORGE BRUGGEMAN; *Lieutenant Bennett:* SCOTT FORBES; *Lieutenant Austin:* SEAN MC CLORY; *Captain Wickham:* CHARLES FITZSIMMONS; *Bouchard:* LOUIS MERCIER; *M. P.:* MICKEY SIMPSON

CREDITS

Director: JOHN FORD; *Producer:* SOL C. SIEGEL; *Scenarists:* PHOEBE EPHRON, HENRY EPHRON; *Based on the play by:* MAXWELL ANDERSON, LAURENCE STALLINGS; *Photographer:* JOSEPH MAC DONALD; *Art Director:* LYLE R. WHEELER; *Set Decorators:* GEORGE W. DAVIS, THOMAS LITTLE, STUART A. REISS; *Editor:* DOROTHY SPENCER; *Sound Recorders:* WINSTON LEVERETT, ROGER HEMAN; *Musical Score:* ALFRED NEWMAN; *Orchestrator:* EDWARD POWELL; *Technicolor Consultant:* LEONARD DOSS; *Songs "My Love, My Life" by:* JAY LIVINGSTON, RAY EVANS; *"Oui, Oui, Marie" Sung by:* CORINNE CALVET

SYNOPSIS

During World War I, Marine Captain Flagg and his top sergeant, Quirt, are faced with taking a company of old men and boys from a little French village into the front-line trenches. In the off-duty hours, they vie for the affections of Charmaine, the innkeeper's daughter.

CRITICS' CIRCLE

"What reason lay behind this revision of a great theatrical classic are beyond my own understanding. All the meat, all of the body, all of the point and substance of *What Price Glory?* seems to have been drained from its present distillation.

"Both Mr. Cagney and Mr. Dailey have themselves a field day under these circumstances, screaming, shrieking and roaring at each other all over the place. Mr. Cagney himself appears rather more beefy and, with a noticeable paunch, somewhat out of breath in all this exertion, but Mr. Dailey makes up for it in his long, lean, gangling physique and his own strenuous efforts to make as much noise as his co-star. The sight of a sawed-off, slightly pot-bellied Jimmy Cagney squaring off for a fist fight with the beanpole Dailey is an indication of the sort of effects Mr. Ford has staged to milk as much farce out of *What Price Glory?* as he possibly could."

Leo Mishkin, NEW YORK MORNING TELEGRAPH

"The total result is deplorable, which is shocking when you see the name of John Ford as director. . . . All those soldiers are either 'characters' or chorus boys. The essential impact is that of musical comedy."

Archer Winston, NEW YORK POST

"It has been more than a quarter of a century since *What Price Glory?* first was transferred to the screen, but the passage of time has not worked wonders with this World War I drama. . . . To judge by appearances, James Cagney is a somewhat corpulent Captain Flagg, a leader who would be hard put to stand the gaff of continuously guzzling cognac, chasing the enemy and the luscious and lively Charmaine, as well as swinging at Sergeant Quirt in every reel. But he is a raspy-voiced, un-shaven gyrene, who gives the role a broad reading, and that apparently is satisfactory. Dan Dailey is a cocky top kick whose performance is equally broad, and, physically, Corinne Calvet leaves no doubt in the mind of a viewer what all the fighting is about."

A. W., THE NEW YORK TIMES

With Robert Wagner

With Corinne Calvet

With Dan Dailey

"*What Price Glory?* is a soft-boiled movie version of the hard-boiled Maxwell Anderson–Laurence Stallings war play of 1924. The original drama is one of the all time greats of the American stage.

"This adaptation adds Technicolor, songs and slapdash comedy routines to the original. It subtracts much of the play's bawdy vitality and grim view of war. As the rambunctious Flagg and Quirt, paunchy James Cagney and rangy Dan Dailey work hard snarling at each other out of the sides of their mouths, but most of the time they seem merely about to break into a song and dance routine."

TIME

"James Cagney, a corpulent Captain Flagg and looks like he'll bust out of his britches any minute, and Dan Dailey, the braggart Sergeant Quirt, enact the top male roles as rivals for gals and glory with amusing emphasis on frenetics. Both are inclined to mumble or shout their dialog, but the physical business that goes with the lines make them understandable."

VARIETY

"The new film version of *What Price Glory?* is a well watered rewriting of the monumental Maxwell Anderson–Laurence Stallings play of three decades ago. The salty vigor of the dialogue and the savage cruelties of war are omitted from this new film. The battle scenes are conducted in settings that might have been designed for musical comedy. One even is played in a pink pastel shade of lighting.

"The characters smack of the musical comedy tradition, too. These impetuous young heroes can hardly wait to dart out to certain death. The ironic implications originally intended in the title are exactly reversed.

"James Cagney and Dan Dailey have lowered their acting standards in keeping with the new spirit of the vehicle."

Alton C. Cook, NEW YORK WORLD-TELEGRAM
AND SUN

"Ineffectual humor and drama could have been omitted and, if James Cagney had to play Captain Flagg, director John Ford could have done us and Cagney a favor by curbing his tendencies to ham it."

Wanda Hale, New York DAILY NEWS

NOTES

This was John Ford's second-rate remake of Raoul Walsh's first-rate 1926 production, which starred Vic-

tor MacLaglen, Dolores Del Rio and Edmund Lowe. Ford concentrated only on a physical effect through rough-and-tough dialogue, rather than examining or accenting the grimness and futility of combat. It was a mish-mash of old chestnuts.

Barry Norton, who played a priest in this film version, also appeared as a disturbed soldier whom Dolores Del Rio consoles in the original silent.

The only thing that kept this picture afloat was the dynamic frenzy with which Cagney and Dan Dailey approached their parts. To see these two in action was almost worth the price of admission.

With Corinne Calvet and Dan Dailey

With Dan Dailey, William Demarest and Corinne Calvet

A LION IS IN THE STREETS

A William Cagney Production
Distributed by Warner Bros. Pictures Inc.
In Technicolor

—1953—

CAST

Hank Martin: JAMES CAGNEY; *Verity Wade:* BARBARA HALE; *Flamingo:* ANNE FRANCIS; *Jules Bolduc:* WARNER ANDERSON; *Jeb Brown:* JOHN MC INTYRE; *Jennie Brown:* JEANNE CAGNEY; *Spurge:* LON CHANEY, JR.; *Rector:* FRANK MC HUGH; *Robert J. Castelberry:* LARRY KEATING; *Guy Polli:* ONSLOW STEVENS; *Mr. Beach:* JAMES MILLICAN; *Tim Beck:* MICKEY SIMPSON; *Lula May:* SARA HADEN; *Singing Woman:* ELLEN CORBY; *Prosecutor:* ROLAND WINTERS; *Smith:* BURT MUSTIN; *Sophy:* IRENE TEDROW; *Townswoman:* SARAH SELBY

CREDITS

Director: RAOUL WALSH; *Producer:* WILLIAM CAGNEY; *Scenarist:* LUTHER DAVIS; *Based on the novel by:* ADRIA LOCKE LANGLEY; *Photographer:* HARRY STRADLING; *Production Designer:* WIARD IHNEN; *Set Decorator:* FRED M. MAC LEAN; *Editor:* GEORGE AMY; *Sound Recorder:* JOHN KEAN; *Musical Score:* FRANZ WAXMAN; *Makeup Artist:* OTIS MALCOLM; *Special Effects:* ROSCOE CLINE; *Assistant Director:* WILLIAM KISSEL; *Technicolor Color Consultant:* MONROE W. BURBANK; *Story Editor:* EDWARD CAGNEY

SYNOPSIS

An itinerant swamp peddler, Hank Martin, who meets and marries grade-school teacher Verity Wade from up North, is romantically pursued by the tempestuous Flamingo. He makes his early reputation by leading a

With Anne Francis

With Jeanne Cagney

With Frank McHugh

With Anne Francis and Barbara Hale

crusade to rectify the plight of poor sharecroppers, during which he suddenly learns that he has power to bend people to his will by whatever means he can—cajolery, argument, Bible-thumping and sheer presence of his personality. He opens a small office and is soon catapulted into the race for governorship.

CRITICS' CIRCLE

"This picture . . . is a headlong and dynamic drama about a back-country champion of the poor who permits his political ambitions to pull him down a perilously crooked road. It offers the aggressive Mr. Cagney in one of his most colorful and meaningful roles. His fellow is breezy and brassy, he is everybody's friend and from him there flows a forceful torrent of direct and pungent gab. He is clever, perceptive and pugnacious, loaded with confidence and bluff; yet ready to back up his bluffing or challenge that of another man. But inside this firm and ruddy apple there gnaws an ugly, evil worm, and Mr. Cagney artfully reveals it as the picture goes along. It is the worm of personal ambition, of insincerity and deceit. Before the picture is over, the worm has chewed a big hole in the fruit."

Bosley Crowther, THE NEW YORK TIMES

"Raoul Walsh's direction keeps the film moving briskly and Cagney dominates the film in the grand manner of the 1930's, when he was Hollywood's top tough-guy star. Though his looks and sounds are more Broadway than Deep South, he is thoroughly persuasive as a fast-talking politico equally able to bamboozle a backwoods crowd or to make a deal with the big-city gangsters."

TIME

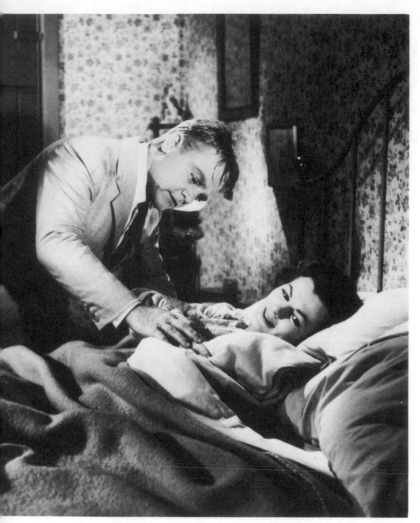

"(Cagney's) portrayal has an occasional strength, but mostly is a stylized performance done with an inconsistent Southern dialect that rarely holds through a complete line of dialog. . . . Luther Davis scripted the Langley novel and some of the choppy feet to the footage may be more chargeable to editing than writing. The film has excellent Technicolor lensing by Harry Stradling."

VARIETY

NOTES

The Cagney brothers originally took a ten-year lease on Adria Locke Langley's 1945 best-seller (undoubtedly based on Louisiana's Huey Long) with the intent to produce it for their own company. William Cagney was still the producer, but the company was Warner Bros. Jeanne Cagney was outstanding in a character part and Edward Cagney became the film's story editor.

With all those Cagneys behind him, Jimmy had to be good. And good he was. His Hank Martin captured the very soul of the backwoods politician whose ambitions rose with every bit of cajolery and Bible-thumping rhetoric. It is one of his very best performances. Barbara Hale also did her best work as Verity Wade, while Anne Francis was properly sassy as a creature called Flamingo.

Raoul Walsh directed from Luther Davis' scenario. Harry Stradling's superb Technicolor photography captured the very essence of the deep South.

With Barbara Hale

With Mickey Simpson and Barbara Hale

206

RUN FOR COVER

A Paramount Picture in Technicolor
and VistaVision

—1955—

CAST

Mat Dow: JAMES CAGNEY; *Helga Swenson:* VIVECA LINDFORS; *Davey Bishop:* JOHN DEREK; *Mr. Swenson:* JEAN HERSHOLT; *Gentry:* GRANT WITHERS; *Larsen:* JACK LAMBERT; *Morgan:* ERNEST BORGNINE; *Sheriff:* RAY TEAL; *Scotty:* IRVING BACON; *Paulsen:* TREVOR BARDETTE; *Mayor Walsh:* JOHN MILJAN; *Doc Ridgeway:* GUS SCHILLING; *Bank Manager:* EMERSON TREACY; *Harvey:* DENVER PYLE; *Townsman:* HENRY WILLS

CREDITS

Director: NICHOLAS RAY; *Producer:* WILLIAM H. PINE; *Scenarist:* WILLIAM C. THOMAS; *Based on a story by:* HARRIET FRANK, JR., IRVING RAVETCH; *Photographer:* DANIEL FAPP; *Art Directors:* HAL PEREIRA, HENRY BUMSTEAD; *Set Decorators:* SAM COMER, FRANK MCKELVY; *Editor:* HOWARD SMITH; *Sound Recorders:* GENE MERRITT, JOHN COPE; *Musical Director:* HOWARD JACKSON; *Costumer:* EDITH HEAD; *Makeup Artist:* WALLY WESTMORE; *Special Effects:* JOHN P. FULTON; *Special Photographic Effects:* FARCIOT EDOUART; *Assistant Director:* FRANCISCO DAY; *Technicolor Color Consultant:* RICHARD MUELLER; *Song:* "Run For Cover" by HOWARD JACKSON, JACK BROOKS

SYNOPSIS

Released from a six-year prison term for a crime he did not commit, Matt Dow goes West, where he meets twenty-year old Davey Bishop. Riding along, they innocently become involved in a train robbery and are later ambushed by a posse. Davey's leg is smashed and the youngster is taken to the Swenson farm, where Helga nurses him and falls in love with Matt.

The townspeople offer Matt the job of sheriff and he appoints Davey, who is now a cripple, as his deputy. Davey's bitterness over his injury pulls the two men apart, and soon they are on opposite sides in a conflict involving the notorious Gentry gang and a band of Indians.

CRITICS' CIRCLE

"The memorable hard-headed sheriff that Gary Cooper played in *High Noon* appears to have been the model for the one James Cagney portrays in Paramount's *Run For Cover*. . . . [however] there is little in *Run For Cover* to compare with the lean, leathery pictorial poetry and the stunning social comment of *High Noon*. For this William Pine–William Thomas Western, directed by Nicholas Ray, is sheer horse opera without freshness or feeling and with practically nothing to say.

"Mr. Cagney's performance, as usual, is cocky and colorful without a great deal of substance or strenuous sincerity."

Bosley Crowther, THE NEW YORK TIMES

"An off-beat Westerner, *Run For Cover* spends more time and thought than most horse operas in sounding out plot and characters. The result is vigorous entertainment strikingly photographed. . . . It's [the story] smoothly and believably spun out, with Cagney doing a bang-up job in his first boots-and-saddler role in years."

Rose Pelswick, NEW YORK JOURNAL-AMERICAN

With Viveca Lindfors

With John Derek

208

NOTES

This was Cagney's first Western since *The Oklahoma Kid* and, once again, he had a fine script. Nicholas Ray directed with one eye on action and the other on characterization and the results paid off. Daniel Fapp's fine Technicolor photography (shot in the VistaVision process) also was an asset.

Cagney was beginning to show his age now, but his energy and vitality were the same as always. John Derek was effective as his young nemesis, while Viveca Lindfors was, unfortunately, merely beautiful. It is interesting to note that Grant Withers, whom Cagney had *supported* in his first film (*Sinner's Holiday*) and his third film (*Other Men's Women*), was in his support as Gentry.

On the set with John Derek and Viveca Lindfors

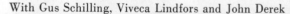

With Gus Schilling, Viveca Lindfors and John Derek

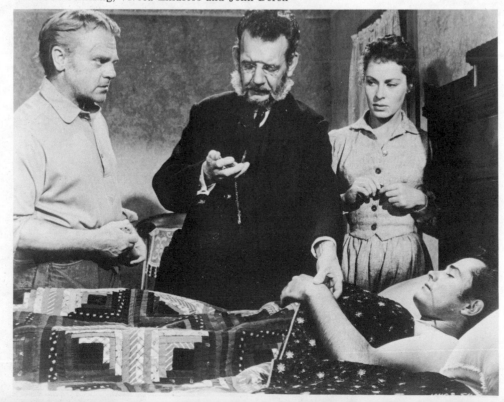

LOVE ME OR LEAVE ME

A Metro-Goldwyn-Mayer Picture
in CinemaScope and Eastman Color

—1955—

CAST

Ruth Etting: DORIS DAY; *Martin "The Gimp" Snyder:* JAMES CAGNEY; *Johnny Alderman:* CAMERON MITCHELL; *Bernard V. Loomis:* ROBERT KEITH; *Frobisher:* TOM TULLY; *Georgie:* HARRY BELLAVER; *Paul Hunter:* RICHARD GAINES; *Fred Taylor:* PETER LEEDS; *Eddie Fulton:* CLAUDE STROUD; *Jingle Girl:* AUDREY YOUNG; *Greg Trent:* JOHN HARDING; *Dancer:* DOROTHY ABBOTT; *Bouncer:* PHIL SCHUMACHER; *Second Bouncer:* OTTO REICHOW; *Bouncer:* HENRY KULKY; *Orry:* JAY ADLER; *Irate Customer:* MAURITZ HUGO; *Hostess:* VEDA ANN BORG; *Claire:* CLAIRE CARLETON; *Stage Manager:* BENNY BURT; *Mr. Brelston, Radio Station Manager:* ROBERT B. CARSON; *Assistant Director:* JAMES DRURY; *Dance Director:* RICHARD SIMMONS; *Assistant Director:* MICHAEL KOSTRICK; *First Reporter:* ROY ENGEL; *Second Reporter:* JOHN DAMLER; *Woman:* GENEVIEVE AUMONT; *Propman:* ROY ENGEL; *Stagehands:* DALE VAN SICKEL, JOHNNY DAY; *Chorus Girls:* LARRI THOMAS, PATTI NESTOR, WINONA SMITH, SHIRLEY WILSON; *Doorman:* ROBERT MALCOLM; *Waiter:* ROBERT STEPHENSON; *Drapery Man:* PAUL MC GUIRE; *Guard:* BARRY REGAN; *Photographers:* JIMMY CROSS, HENRY RANDOLPH; *Chauffeur:* CHET BRANDENBERG

CREDITS

Director: CHARLES VIDOR; *Producer:* JOE PASTERNAK; *Scenarists:* DANIEL FUCHS, ISOBEL LENNART; *Based on original story by:* DANIEL FUCHS; *Photographer:*

With Doris Day

ARTHUR E. ARLING; *Art Directors:* CEDRIC GIBBONS, URIE MC CLEARY; *Editor:* RALPH E. WINTERS; *Musical Director:* GEORGE STOLL; *Miss Day's Music:* PERCY FAITH; *Sound Recorder:* WESLEY C. MILLER; *Choreographer:* ALEX ROMERO; *Costumer:* HELEN ROSE; *Musical Adviser:* IRVING AARONSON; *Special Effects:* WARREN NEWCOMBE; *Songs:* "Stay on the Right Side, Sister" *by:* TED KOEHLER, RUBE BLOOM; "You Made Me Love You" *by:* JOE MC CARTHY, JAMES MONACO; "Everybody Loves My Baby" *by:* JACK PALMER, SPENCER WILLIAMS; "Sam, the Old Accordian Man" *by:* WALTER DONALDSON; "At Sundown" *by:* WALTER DONALDSON; "It All Depends on You" *by:* B. G. DE SYLVA, LEW BROWN, RAY HENDERSON; "Love Me or Leave Me" *by:* GUS KAHN, WALTER DONALDSON; "Mean to Me" *by:* ROY TURK, FRED AHLERT; "Ten Cents a Dance" *by:* RICHARD RODGERS, LORENZ HART; "Shaking the Blues Away" *by:* IRVING BERLIN; *New Songs:* "Never Look Back" *by:* CHILTON PRICE; "I'll Never Stop Loving You" *by:* NICHOLAS BRODZKY, SAMMY CAHN

With Doris Day and Harry Bellaver

With Doris Day

SYNOPSIS

Nebraska farm girl Ruth Etting is singing in an obscure Chicago nightclub when she encounters racketeering laundryman Martin "The Gimp" Snyder. In Svengali-like fashion, Snyder soon proves what he can do for Ruthie's career in show biz and her salary zooms from $25 to $2,500 per week. He forces her into marriage and, although it drives her to alcoholic despair, their hot-and-cold relationship spans seventeen years. When she finally confronts him with a divorce, Marty shoots her accompaniest, Johnny Alderman.

CRITICS' CIRCLE

"Best of all for everybody, it has Doris Day to play the role of the blonde and bewitching Miss Etting and it has James Cagney to play The Gimp. We would say that the latter advantage is by far the most propitious to the film, for it is Mr. Cagney's verve and virtuosity that makes the character sufferable. It is his skill at giving the hard-boiled 'muscler' a certain vividness and gutter gallantry that make it possible not only to stand him but to like him a little bit for nigh two hours.

"But one must admit that Mr. Cagney and Miss Day do their jobs extremely well and make an uncommonly interesting and dramatic couple for a musical film. And, of course, it is hard to think of anyone better

211

With Doris Day and Roy Engel

With Doris Day

With Doris Day

With Doris Day and Harry Bellaver

qualified to do the job of singing Miss Etting's old numbers than the lovely and lyrical Miss Day."

Bosley Crowther, THE NEW YORK TIMES

"*Love Me or Leave Me* is a Hollywood paradox: a CinemaScope musical that has the bite of authenticity. In telling the story of Ruth Etting, the famed torch singer of the '20s, the film rings true just by following the broad outline of her career as it was carried in the tabloid headlines of the day. As Snyder, James Cagney has his best role in years and serves it well, mounting to successive levels of exasperation with as much ease and artistry as Bix Beiderbecke ever displayed in reaching the high note on his cornet. Those who remember the sexy serenity with which Ruth Etting handled such numbers as the title song, 'Everybody Loves My Baby,' 'At Sundown,' and 'It All Depends On You,' may find Doris Day's characterization of the star both too pallid and too girl-next-door. Doris tries hard, but, like the film costumes that are supposed to represent the F. Scott Fitzgerald era, she just isn't the real thing."

TIME

"Doris Day, as Ruth, does well in an unusual role, particularly with such Etting favorites as 'Ten Cents a Dance,' 'Mean To Me' and the title song. But the film's biggest boost comes from Jimmy Cagney who makes the Gimp into a ruthless yet understandable villain and achieves the greatest success so far in his movie comeback."

LIFE

"Their relationship is dramatized with such explosive realism that audiences are never sure how the picture will end—a novelty for biographical movies. Under director Charles Vidor, Doris Day and James Cagney give dazzling performances as the mismated pair."

LOOK

"In the early reels of the film, Mr. Cagney does a neat job of caricaturing the sort of hoodlum he used to specialize in a couple of decades ago, but eventually the script compels him to become a real villain and then *Love Me or Leave Me* gets quite monotonous.

"As Miss Day, plumply disconsolate, pursues her weary way through the script, she is completely overshadowed by Mr. Cagney; so, for that matter, is practically everyone else in the cast. Cameron Mitchell, as the piano player, and Robert Keith, as the theatrical agent, occasionally manage to get into the act, though, and the dialogue is at times sprightly."

John McCarten, THE NEW YORKER

"James Cagney and Doris Day are brilliant as Miss Etting and Snyder. Mr. Cagney's performance of the lame racketeer is a sort of retrospective from his rogues' portrait gallery. Yet with customary skill, he manages never to lose sight of the fact that Snyder's behavior, however monstrous, is increasingly motivated by an obsessive determination to help the singer realize her ambitions. . . . Miss Day's expert singing of old popular songs (in Percy Faith's first-rate arrangements) provides a nostalgic treat."

J. B., THE CHRISTIAN SCIENCE MONITOR

" 'The Gimp,' so ably played by James Cagney. His presentation of the clubfooted Chicago Hoodlum and muscle-man is the Cagney of the Warner Bros. gangster pictures of the early 1930s—hard-bitten, cruel, sadistic and unrelenting."

VARIETY

"It has plenty of songs of the jazz age to gratify the nostalgically-inclined; it has a story to grip those who don't care a Coolidge dollar about the music of yesteryear, and it has a performance by James Cagney that will be remembered for a long time.

"Cagney has created a fascinating portrait of the Gimp. In every mannerism—heavy limp, coarse speech, taunting sarcasm, flashes of rage—he moulds an obnoxious character who tramples over everybody in his lust for power. It's a high tribute to Cagney that he makes this twisted man steadily interesting for two hours.

"Doris Day graduates out of her world of peppy collegiate revels with this picture, and the change is all to the good. She gives a mature performance."

William K. Zinsser, NEW YORK HERALD TRIBUNE

NOTES

Just as *Run for Cover* was Cagney's first film in the VistaVision process, *Love Me or Leave Me* was his first film in CinemaScope. Metro-Goldwyn-Mayer's good sense in obtaining the joint permission of Ruth Etting, Martin Snyder and Johnny Alderman broke those rose-colored glasses most Hollywood musical biographies are shot through. Thus resulted one of the finest, most realistic, musical dramas to hit the screen.

Cagney was again perfectly cast as "The Gimp" and handled his game leg well throughout his performance. In this candid and unvarnished atmosphere, Doris Day also worked better and, together, they spelled "terrific."

The musical numbers were well selected and two new songs were added. Oddly enough, two songs most associated with Ruth Etting were left out. "Shine On, Harvest Moon" (her theme song on radio) and "Back in Your Own Back Yard."

The film received six Academy Award nominations: Actor (Cagney's third), Motion Picture Story (Fuchs), Screenplay (Mr. Fuchs and Isobel Lennart), Sound (Wesley C. Miller), Scoring of a Musical (Percy Faith and George Stoll), and Song ("I'll Never Stop Loving You," Brodszky and Cahn). Mr. Fuchs won an Oscar for his Original Motion Picture Story. Miss Day didn't even win a nomination and should have.

With Cameron Mitchell

With John Harding, Robert Keith and Peter Leeds

MISTER ROBERTS

A Warner Bros. Picture
An Orange Production
In CinemaScope & WarnerColor

—1955—

CAST

Lieutenant (J.G.) Roberts: HENRY FONDA; *Captain:* JAMES CAGNEY; *Ensign Frank Thurlowe Pulver:* JACK LEMMON; *Doc:* WILLIAM POWELL; *C.P.O. Dowdy:* WARD BOND; *Lieutenant Ann Girard:* BETSY PALMER; *Mannion:* PHIL CAREY; *Reber:* NICK ADAMS; *Stefanowski:* HARRY CAREY, JR.; *Dolan:* KEN CURTIS; *Gerhart:* FRANK ALETTER; *Lidstrom:* FRITZ FORD; *Mason:* BUCK KARTALIAN; *Lieutenant Billings:* WILLIAM HENRY; *Olson:* WILLIAM HUDSON; *Schlemmer:* STUBBY KRUGER; *Cookie:* HARRY TENBROOK; *Rodrigues:* PERRY LOPEZ; *Insignia:* ROBERT ROARK; *Bookser:* PAT WAYNE; *Wiley:* TIGE ANDREWS; *Kennedy:* JIM MOLONEY; *Gilbert:* DENNY NILES; *Johnson:* FRANCIS CONNER; *Cochran:* SHUG FISHER; *Jonesy:* DANNY BORZAGE; *Taylor:* JIM MURPHY; *Nurses:* KATHLEEN O'MALLEY, MAURA MURPHY, MIMI DOYLE, JEANNE MURRAY-VANDER-BILT, LONNIE PIERCE; *Shore Patrol Officer:* MARTIN MILNER; *Shore Patrolman:* GREGORY WALCOTT; *M.P.:* JAMES FLAVIN; *Marine Sergeant:* JACK PENNICK; *Native Chief:* DUKE KAHANAMOKO; *Chinese Girl Who Kisses Bookser:* CAROLYN TONG; *French Colonial Officer:* GEORGE BRANGIER; *Naval Officer:* CLARENCE E. FRANK

CREDITS

Directors: JOHN FORD, MERVYN LE ROY; *Producer:* LELAND HAYWARD; *Scenarists:* FRANK NUGENT, JOSHUA LOGAN; *From the play by:* JOSHUA LOGAN, THOMAS HEGGEN; *Based on the novel by:* THOMAS HEGGEN; *Photographer:* WINTON C. HOCH; *Art Director:* ART LOEL; *Set Decorator:* WILLIAM L. KUEHL; *Editor:* JACK MURRAY; *Production Manager:* NORMAN COOK; *Sound*

Recorder: EARL N. CRAIN; *Musical Score:* FRANZ WAX-
MAN; *Orchestrator:* LEONID RAAB; *Makeup Artist:*
GORDON BAU; *Assistant Director:* WINGATE SMITH;
Technical Advisers: ADMIRAL JOHN DALE PRICE, USN,
COMMANDER MERLE MAC BAIN, USN

With Jack Lemmon, Henry Fonda and William Powell

SYNOPSIS

The scene presents life aboard a small Naval cargo
vessel in the back waters of the Pacific—between the
islands of Tedium and Ennui. Lt. (J.G.) Roberts acts
as the buffer between the lunatic captain and the ship's
long-suffering crew. Roberts functions efficiently in his
job, but his heart is with the men fighting the real
battle. After many run-ins with the Captain, Roberts
is granted his transfer to a combat area.

CRITICS' CIRCLE

"*Mister Roberts* should be one of the biggest money-
makers of the year. The acting, direction (by John
Ford and Mervyn Le Roy) and writing have all the
high surface polish and potent inward efficiency of a
1955 car fresh from the assembly line. Fonda, enlarg-
ing on his stage performance, has caught every nuance
appropriate to the nation's big brother; William
Powell, as the ship's doctor, is endlessly kind, bene-
ficent and wise; Jack Lemmon proves once more that
he is easily the most engaging of Hollywood's new
comedians, and James Cagney makes his jack-in-the-
box appearances with all of the peppery rancor of a
Mr. Punch. The best evidence of the film's accomplishment is that *Mister Roberts* seldom drags during its
more than two hours' running time."

TIME

"The superb photography, in CinemaScope and color,
the smoothly paced direction (by John Ford and
Mervyn Le Roy), and a perfect cast, contribute toward
making this *Mister Roberts* the No. 1 comedy of 1955.
Fonda's performance is as fresh as the night he made
his debut on stage; and it is today probably better.
William Powell as 'Doc' reminds us once more how
much the screen needs him back again. Jack Lemmon
as the wobble-brained young Ensign Pulver is hilarious—undoubtedly the best thing he's done in films to
date. And James Cagney, as the bull-headed, mean-
minded old merchant marine, is a gem of choleric
characterization."

Jesse Zunser, CUE

With Jack Lemmon

With Henry Fonda

On the set with director John Ford (seated) and
Henry Fonda

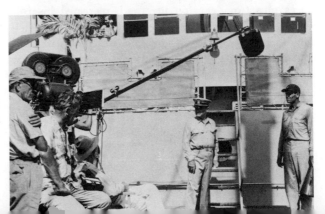

"James Cagney is simply great as the captain of the ship, a 'little' man in size and soul who makes life aboard even more tedious and unbearable for the men under him. Audiences everywhere will enter whole-heartedly into the sailors' conspiracy against Cagney and enjoy thoroughly the comedy that results."

VARIETY

"In the role of the captain, James Cagney comes up with another remarkable portrait. This cranky auto-crat, sputtering with rage when Roberts crosses his narrow mind with logic, excoriating the crew in a New England accent so flat that it grates the nerves of every-one on his miserable ship, is a memorable specimen in a memorable film."

William K. Zinsser, NEW YORK HERALD TRIBUNE

"Above all, they [the directors] have been exception-ally fortunate in having Henry Fonda on hand to re-peat the title role he created on stage! This is not merely a duplication. He is a towering figure whose dignity, self-sacrifice, and understanding command not only the respect of his men but also that of a viewer.

"James Cagney's portrait of the captain is straight-forward but he does emerge as a destructive tyrant. Jack Lemmon makes a properly amorous and ebullient Ensign Pulver and William Powell's characterization of the tired, bored but wise ship's doctor is a model of restraint.

"In this case, the screen has reached out for fine source material and enhanced it."

A. H. Weiler, THE NEW YORK TIMES

"There was one good surprise in the screen version of *Mister Roberts:* James Cagney's performance as the pettily tyrannical captain. Cagney put a spin of his own on the part and played the bullying bantam with plus qualities that made one realize anew he is a more versatile actor than people think."

Henry Hart, FILMS IN REVIEW

NOTES

Mister Roberts was a best seller in 1946, became a hit play in 1948 and enjoyed many years on the road. Henry Fonda, who played 1121 Broadway perform-ances plus two years on the road, recreated his role for the movie version. It was an effortless piece of act-ing. Cagney blended humor into the otherwise one-dimensional part of the captain. William Powell was

216

amusing as Doc, while Jack Lemmon began a whole career out of his role as Ensign Pulver.

John Ford took ill during his directorial chores and Mervyn Le Roy completed the picture for him. They were both credited for their contributions. It was filmed on the South Pacific island of Midway and aboard the U.S.S. *Hewell*, a 172-foot, 250-ton Navy cargo ship. The entire cast and crew then moved to Hawaii—near the U.S. Marine Air Station at Kaneoke Bay—for final shooting.

Mister Roberts was nominated for Best Picture, Best Supporting Actor (Jack Lemmon) and Sound Recording. Lemmon won. Trying to capitalize on a good thing, this property later became a dull and labored television series in the early 60s.

On the set with co-director Mervyn LeRoy and pro-ducer Leland Hayward

THE SEVEN LITTLE FOYS

A Paramount Picture
In VistaVision and Technicolor

—1955—

CAST

Eddie Foy: BOB HOPE; *Madeleine Morando:* MILLY VITALE; *Barney Green:* GEORGE TOBIAS; *Clara:* ANGELA CLARKE; *Judge:* HERBERT HEYES; *Stage Manager:* RICHARD SHANNON; *Brynie:* BILLY GRAY; *Charley:* LEE ERICKSON; *Richard Foy:* PAUL DE ROLF; *Mary Foy:* LYDIA REED; *Madeleine Foy:* LINDA BENNETT; *Eddie, Jr.:* JIMMY BAIRD; *George M. Cohan:* JAMES CAGNEY; *Irving:* TOMMY DURAN; *Father O'Casey:* LESTER MATTHEWS; *Elephant Act:* JOE EVANS, GEORGE BOYCE; *Santa Claus:* OLIVER BLAKE; *Driscoll:* MILTON FROME; *Harrison:* KING DONOVAN; *Stage Doorman:* JIMMY CONLIN; *Soubrette:* MARIAN CARR; *Stage Doorman At Iroquois:* HARRY CHESHIRE; *Italian Ballerina Mistress:* RENATA VANNI; *Dance Specialty Double:* BETTY UITTI; *Priest:* NOEL DRAYTON; *Theatre Manager:* JACK PEPPER; *Tutor:* DABBS GREER; *Customs Inspector:* BILLY NELSON; *Second Priest:* JOE FLYNN; *Brynie (5 Years):* JERRY MATHERS; *Presbyterian Minister:* LEWIS MARTIN

CREDITS

Director: MELVILLE SHAVELSON; *Producer:* JACK ROSE; *Original screenplay by:* MELVILLE SHAVELSON, JACK ROSE; *Photographer:* JOHN F. WARREN; *Art Directors:* HAL PEREIRA, JOHN GOODMAN; *Editor:* ELLSWORTH HOAGLAND; *Musical Director:* JOSEPH J. LILLEY; *Narrator:* EDDIE FOY, JR.; *Choreography:* NICK CASTLE; *Technical Adviser:* CHARLEY FOY

SYNOPSIS

Vaudevillian Eddie Foy wants his wife and seven children to love the stage as much as he does. When his wife dies, Foy, faced with problems of bringing up the brood, decides to make the kids a part of his act—an act they soon begin to steal. Later in his life, the Friars Club honors Foy with a dinner, at which he and his old pal, George M. Cohan, do a dance routine to the delight of its members.

With Bob Hope

Rehearsing with Bob Hope

"The Seven Little Foys has a story as relentlessly cute as an elephant in pinafores. Out of this unlikely material emerges a better-than-average VistaVision musical mostly because of the near-maniacal energy of Bob Hope, whose timing was never better as he splutters gags like an endless string of comic firecrackers. Italy's Milly Vitale is decorative as the long-suffering wife, and the children are always on hand to trigger a succession of mildly daring jokes about childbirth. "

TIME

"Perhaps the best sequence occurs without the seven little Foys but with George M. Cohan, in the person of James Cagney. At a Friars Club dinner Cohan and Foy amiably exchange insults until they have talked themselves into an impromptu dancing contest. Messrs. Hope and Cagney handle the repartee will casual expertness, and their footwork on a table top is unexpectedly fancy."

Rod Nordell, THE CHRISTIAN SCIENCE MONITOR

"High point is a Friar's testimonial dinner to Foy in which James Cagney, as George M. Cohan, exchanges kidding insults-on-the-square with Hope, then both swing into a lovely, graceful soft-shoe challenge routine to the tune of Cohan's 'Mary.' The sequence captures all the hard-shelled sentimentality of the old pros, emerging as a warming tribute to Foy and Cohan from two latter-day pros, Hope and Cagney."

SATURDAY REVIEW

NOTES

Jimmy played a "guest star" bit as George M. Cohan as a special favor to his friend Bob Hope in this film, and it turned out to be the highlight of the picture. He and Hope rehearsed for two weeks for the few minutes Cagney appeared on the screen.

Melville Shavelson and Jack Rose received an Academy Award nomination for their story and screenplay.

TRIBUTE TO A BAD MAN

A Metro-Goldwyn-Mayer Picture
in CinemaScope and Eastman Color

—1956—

CAST

Jeremy Rodock: JAMES CAGNEY; *Steve Miller:* DON DUBBINS; *McNulty:* STEPHEN MC NALLY; *Jocasta Constantine:* IRENE PAPAS; *Lars Peterson:* VIC MORROW; *Barjak:* JAMES GRIFFITH; *Hearn:* ONSLOW STEVENS; *L. A. Peterson:* JAMES BELL; *Mrs. L. A. Peterson:* JEANETTE NOLAN; *Baldy:* CHUBBY JOHNSON; *Abe:* ROYAL DANO; *Fat Jones:* LEE VAN CLEEF; *Cooky:* PETER CHONG; *Shorty:* JAMES MC CALLION; *Red:* CLINT SHARP; *Tom:* CARL PITTI; *First Buyer:* TONY HUGHES; *Second Buyer:* ROY ENGEL; *Cowboys:* BUD OSBORNE, JOHN HALLORAN, TOM LONDON, DENNIS MOORE, BUDDY ROOSEVELT, BILLY DIX

CREDITS

Director: ROBERT WISE; *Producer:* SAM ZIMBALIST; *Scenarist:* MICHAEL BLANKFORT; *Based on a short story by:* JACK SCHAEFER; *Photographer:* ROBERT SURTEES; *Art Directors:* CEDRIC GIBBONS, PAUL BROESSE; *Set Directors:* EDWIN B. WILLIS, FRED MAC LEAN; *Editor:* RALPH E. WINTERS; *Sound Recorder:* DR. WESLEY C. MILLER; *Musical Score:* MIKLOS ROZSA; *Costumer:* WALTER PLUNKETT; *Hair Stylist:* SYDNEY GUILAROFF; *Makeup Artist:* WILLIAM TUTTLE; *Assistant Director:* ARVID GRIFFEN; *Color Consultant:* CHARLES K. HAGEDON

SYNOPSIS

In the lawless frontier of the 1870s, hard-bitten pioneer horse rancher Jeremy Rodock is extremely protective of his vast land holdings in the Colorado Rockies. He catches and hangs rustlers and forces horse thieves to march barefoot over rocky terrain.

Into this wild country rides Steve Miller, a young grocery clerk from Pennsylvania, who stays to grow

219

With Don Dubbins, James Griffith, Vic Morrow and
Stephen McNally

With Irene Papas

up under Rodock's tutelage. Steve seeks the affection
of Jocasta, a woman Rodock has befriended, but learns
that the woman really loves the older man. Through
their relationship, the "bad man" learns that justice
should be tempered with mercy and reveals a warm
heart that few suspected he had.

CRITICS' CIRCLE

"The title is somewhat of a misnomer. The man portrayed so well by Cagney is a hard-bitten pioneer who
must enforce his own law on the limitless range he
controls. . . . Pictorially, the Sam Zimbalist production
is a sight to behold, using the location sites for full
visual worth."

VARIETY

"Any way you look at it, the old master, James Cagney,
really is at home in *Tribute to a Bad Man*. He's got

'handling fever' and his word is law. The eyes narrow,
the nose wrinkles, the mouth twists arrogantly, the
forefinger coolly grips the trigger and the voice, oozing
venom, says 'Do-o-on't move.' And nobody moves.

"*Tribute to a Bad Man* in CinemaScope and color,
is pictorially striking, thanks to cameraman Robert
Surtees. The script sags now and then but Metro has
surrounded the old pro with a talented junior varsity.
But when the smoke clears, it's all Mr. Cagney."

M. E., THE NEW YORK TIMES

" 'A wrangler is a nobody on a horse . . . with bad
teeth, broken bones, a double hernia and lice.' The
self-description sits James Cagney, the bad man of the
title, like Cagney sits a horse. The actor is now 52, but
what a hoss-bustin', man-killin', skirt-rippin', jug-
totin' buckaroo he can still believably pretend to be.
He runs horses on his range, hangs rustlers from his
trees, and keeps the home fires burning with a plenty

220

With Irene Papas and Don Dubbins

hot number (Irene Papas) who smokes wicked little
black cigars between the acts."

TIME

NOTES

M-G-M had begun filming *Tribute to a Bad Man* with
Spencer Tracy on location in the early fifties, but argu-
ments over the script and conditions at the location
site resulted in Tracy's being fired. He was fortunate
to be out of this weak pioneer story, which can boast
only the beautiful color photography of Robert Sturtees
and a sweeping musical score by Miklos Rozsa.

Cagney did his best to pump life into the character
of Jeremy Rodock, but the odds were against him.
Nevertheless any effort on Cagney's part is fascinating
to witness. Greek actress Irene Papas—in her first
Hollywood film—was completely wasted.

THESE WILDER YEARS

A Metro-Goldwyn-Mayer Picture

—1956—

CAST

Steve Bradford: JAMES CAGNEY; *Ann Dempster:* BARBARA STANWYCK; *James Rayburn:* WALTER PIDGEON; *Suzie Keller:* BETTY LOU KEIM; *Mark:* DON DUBBINS; *Mr. Spottsford:* EDWARD ANDREWS; *Judge:* BASIL RUYSDAEL; *Roy Oliphant:* GRANDON RHODES; *Old Cab Driver:* WILL WRIGHT; *Dr. Miller:* LEWIS MARTIN; *Aunt Martha:* DOROTHY ADAMS; *Hardware Clerk:* DEAN JONES; *Traffic Cop:* HERB VIGRAN; *Miss Finch:* RUTH LEE; *Gateman:* MATT MOORE; *Chauffeur:* JACK KENNY; *Doorman:* HARRY TYLER; *Stenographer:* LUANA LEE; *Board of Directors:* WILLIAM FORREST, JOHN MAXWELL, EMMETT VOGAN, CHARLES EVANS; *Football Player:* TOM LAUGHLIN; *Bellhop:* BOB ALDEN; *Boy in Pool Room:* MICHAEL LANDON; *Ad Lib Boy:* JIMMY OGG; *Spottsford's Secretary:* ELIZABETH FLOURNOY; *Farmer:* RUSSELL SIMPSON; *Prim Lady:* KATHLEEN MULQUEEN; *Hotel Clerk:* RUSS WHITNEY; *Proprietress:* LILLIAN POWELL

CREDITS

Director: ROY ROWLAND; *Producer:* JULES SCHERMER; *Scenarist:* FRANK FENTON; *Based on a story by:* RALPH WHEELWRIGHT; *Photographer:* GEORGE J. FOLSEY; *Art Directors:* CEDRIC GIBBONS, PRESTON AMES; *Set Decorators:* EDWIN B. WILLIS, EDWARD G. BOYLE; *Editor:* BEN LEWIS; *Sound Recorder:* DR. WESLEY C. MILLER; *Musical Score:* JEFF ALEXANDER; *Miss Stanwyck's Costumes:* HELEN ROSE; *Makeup Artist:* WILLIAM TUTTLE; *Hair Stylist:* SYDNEY GUILAROFF; *Assistant Director:* AL JENNINGS

SYNOPSIS

Multi-millionaire Steve Bradford, now middle-aged, sets out to find the son he fathered, but whose paternity he had denied. He meets opposition from Ann Dempster, head of the adoption home who placed his child with

With Barbara Stanwyck

foster parents, and Miss Dempster defies him all the way to court.

During the heated legal battle, Bradford chances upon sixteen-year old Suzie Keller, an unwed mother, who has a little baby. In an unselfish act, he decides to adopt the unwed mother, whose position resembles that of his girl friend of twenty years earlier.

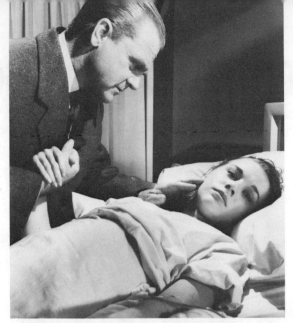

With Betty Lou Keim

CRITICS' CIRCLE

"A slight scent of radio soap opera hovers over *These Wilder Years*, a mild Metro-Goldwyn-Mayer drama. And, of all people, hard-boiled James Cagney finds himself in the focal role that gives off the strongest aroma of sentimentality.

"The intent of this little drama is lofty enough, as one can see, and Mr. Cagney and Miss Stanwyck go at it with becoming restraint and goodwill. But the story is hackneyed and slushy and Roy Rowland's direction is so slow and pictorially uninteresting that the picture is mawkish and dull."

Bosley Crowther, THE NEW YORK TIMES

"*These Wilder Years* is a glum little tale about unwed mothers and unhappy tycoons. The three leading players (Cagney, Stanwyck and Keim) are all competently troubled and Walter Pidgeon, as the lawyer, does little else but drink martinis."

NEW YORK WORLD-TELEGRAM

With Walter Pidgeon

NOTES

This was originally scheduled as a film for Debbie Reynolds, called *All Our Tomorrows*, but by the time it was ready, Miss Reynolds was busy elsewhere, so Barbara Stanwyck and Cagney were secured. It was at first called *Somewhere I'll Find Him*, but, later, became *These Wilder Years* in hopes of appealing to a wider audience. It didn't.

Stanwyck and Cagney both were convincing in their roles, but the script was a bit sugary. Between "takes," the old pros practiced dance steps together: the Charleston, the tango, Black Bottom, maxixe and others. It's a shame they didn't put one of their routines into the film—it might have helped.

Cagney and Stanwyck had almost appeared together in William A. Wellman's *Night Nurse* back in 1931, but *The Public Enemy* outweighed the event and Cagney was replaced by Clark Gable.

With Barbara Stanwyck

On the set with director Roy Rowland and Don Dubbins

MAN OF A THOUSAND FACES

A Universal—International Picture
in CinemaScope

—1957—

As Chaney in *The Hunchback of Notre Dame*

CAST

Lon Chaney: JAMES CAGNEY; *Cleva Creighton Chaney:* DOROTHY MALONE; *Hazel Bennett:* JANE GREER; *Gert:* MARJORIE RAMBEAU; *Clarence Locan:* JIM BACKUS; *Irving Thalberg:* ROBERT J. EVANS; *Mrs. Chaney:* CELIA LOVSKY; *Carrie Chaney:* JEANNE CAGNEY; *Dr. J. Wilson Shields:* JACK ALBERTSON; *Pa Chaney:* NOLAN LEARY; *Creighton Chaney (At 21):* ROGER SMITH, *Creighton Chaney (At 13):* ROBERT LYDEN, *Creighton Chaney (At 8):* RICKIE SORENSEN, *Creighton Chaney (At 4):* DENNIS RUSH; *Carl Hastings:* SIMON SCOTT; *Clarence Kolb:* HIMSELF; *Max Dill:* DANNY BECK; *George Loane Tucker:* PHIL VAN ZANDT; *Comedy Waiters:* HANK MANN, SNUB POLLARD

CREDITS

Director: JOSEPH PEVNEY; *Producer:* ROBERT ARTHUR; *Scenarists:* R. WRIGHT CAMPBELL, IVAN GOFF, BEN ROBERTS; *Based on a story by:* RALPH WHEELWRIGHT; *Photographer:* RUSSELL METTY; *Art Directors:* ALEXANDER GOLITZEN, ERIC ORBOM; *Sound Recorders:* LESLIE I. CAREY, ROBERT PRITCHARD; *Editor:* TED J. KENT; *Musical Score:* FRANK SKINNER; *Orchestrator:* JOSEPH GERSHENSON; *Costumer:* BILL THOMAS; *Makeup Artists:* BUD WESTMORE, JACK KEVAN; *Special Effects:* CLIFFORD STINE; *Assistant Director:* PHIL BOWLES

SYNOPSIS

Lon Chaney, the son of deaf-mute parents, becomes a vaudeville entertainer, marries his partner Cleva Creighton, and has a son Creighton. An ensuing marital scandal forces him to look for work in another media and, in 1913, he begins as an extra in Hollywood movies.

His early struggles with disguises of all types ultimately make him a star. A second marriage is a success, but ghosts of the first always haunt him. At the peak of his career as the silent screen's greatest star of horror films, he dies of cancer of the throat.

CRITICS' CIRCLE

"Thanks to a dandy performance by James Cagney in the role of the great silent-film star, Lon Chaney, there is drama and personality in *Man of a Thousand Faces*. It may not be Chaney exactly that Mr. Cagney gives us in this film, but it is a person of reasonable resemblance and comparable complexity.

"Being Mr. Cagney, it is difficult for him to remove all the familiar Cagney cockiness and pugnacity from the role. Even so, there is an abundance of tenderness, sensitivity and pride in his creation of the driven actor. This is the heart of the film.

"Mr. Cagney also manages to do a superlative job of taking on the make-up that allows him to simulate Chaney as two of his most famous 'monsters'—those in *The Phantom of the Opera* and *The Hunchback of Notre Dame*. Joseph Pevney's direction has a curious affection for clichés, but Mr. Cagney rises above it. He etches a personality."

Bosley Crowther, THE NEW YORK TIMES

"Universal, the studio that first found Lon Chaney popping up in practically any male bit role it was casting, has done justice to the once-famed star it detected. James Cagney plays the role with sensitivity and understanding.

"In private life Chaney, son of deaf-mutes, was aloof and withdrawn. In 1930 he died of cancer. Now in *Man of a Thousand Faces*, Universal has made his movie biography. Months of work helped actor James Cagney re-create the make-up and monsters Chaney had created. But, more important, in giving a superb performance as the unmade-up Chaney, Cagney turns the film into a tender salute to a fine artist and troubled man."

LIFE

"Cagney gives an outstanding performance in the title role. [He] submerges his own personality completely into that of the man whom he portrays. The result is a characterization that rates among his best."

Rose Pelswick, NEW YORK JOURNAL-AMERICAN

"As Chaney, Cagney gives one of his most notable performances. He has immersed himself so completely in the role that it is difficult to spot any Cagney mannerism."

VARIETY

"As a fascinating and reasonably authentic portrait of Chaney, Cagney's contribution to *Man of a Thousand Faces* is magnificent and surely worthy of Oscar consideration."

E. S. H., WOMANS WEAR DAILY

"The boys at Universal have come along with a biography of Lon Chaney, called *Man of a Thousand Faces*, and someone on the lot had the wit to put James Cagney in the leading role. This, in three words, saves the picture. On the surface, Cagney is just about the most unlikely actor in Hollywood, or anywhere else, to portray the late (1883–1930) Lon Chaney, the master of makeup, and the man who scared, and perhaps even scarred, an entire generation now settling into middle age. Chaney was an actor of commanding talents. He was dark and forbidding, a monument to a troubled youth and a troubled life. In the past, Cagney, whatever his background, has usually managed to present himself on the screen as a person of charm, bravado and devil-may-care. In *Man of a Thousand Faces*, Cagney pulls off a minor miracle, projecting himself into the turmoiled life of Chaney and making it believable.

". . . A part like this is just about paradise for an actor of Cagney's skill. . . . Celia Lovsky, as Chaney's deaf-mute mother, brings a tremendous dignity and warmth to her role, and although her communications are conducted entirely with rapid motions of her fingers, she got through to me, all right."

THE NEW YORKER

"In *Man of a Thousand Faces* we are granted far more than just another cinematic success story. It is also a fascinating account of an earlier era in Hollywood, recreated with a degree of verisimilitude altogether too rare in films of this genre. . . .

"To all of this the performance of James Cagney in the title role adds immeasurably. Physically Cagney is far from ideal for the part. He is smaller, heavier and somewhat older than Chaney was at the time of his

With Jane Greer, Dennis Rush, Danny Beck and Clarence Kolb

With Dorothy Malone and Jane Greer

With Dorothy Malone, Celia Lovsky, Jeanne Cagney and Nolan Neary

With Robert J. Evans

With Marjorie Rambeau

With Jane Greer and Roger Smith

As Chaney in *The Phantom of the Opera*

death, while Cagney's own features are so familiar that it is difficult to superimpose Chaney's upon them. But Cagney has obviously studied his man. His step is buoyant, like Chaney's. He moves nervously, expresses himself through grimace and gesture as Chaney, the son of deaf-mute parents, had done. And in the recreated scenes from *The Miracle Man, Hunchback of Notre Dame* and *Phantom of the Opera*, he seems to have undergone some of the same terrible punishment that Chaney knew."

SATURDAY REVIEW

NOTES

This is one of the best biographies to come out of Hollywood about one of its own. Cagney was superb as Lon Chaney, the great silent screen actor who died in 1930 of cancer of the throat. The entire production was handled with the utmost taste and dignity and facts about his films were accurate. Some facts about his personal life, however, had been altered for dramatic effect. Chaney's credo "Unless I suffer, how can I make the public believe me?" also served Cagney

well. The makeup effects, created by Bud Westmore and Jack Kevan, were marvelous recreations of Chaney's originals, whose secrets died with him.

Dorothy Malone did her finest screen work as Cleva Creighton Chaney and Jane Greer was sympathetic as the second Mrs. Chaney. Robert Evans was "discovered" by Norma Shearer in Palm Springs to play Irving Thalberg. Of the supporting cast, Celia Lovsky was outstanding in a few brief scenes as Chaney's mother.

R. Wright Campbell, Ivan Goff and Ben Roberts received an Academy nomination for their screenplay, but Cagney was slighted in the Best Actor race. His telling portrayal warranted a nomination, as did Miss Lovsky's supporting role. This film was selected by the Department of Health, Education, and Welfare, to be captioned for the deaf.

A rare still of Cagney as Chaney in *West of Zanzibar*; it was used exclusively in a montage sequence.

On the set with James Stewart and Orson Welles

On the set with producer Robert Arthur and director Joseph Pevney

228

SHORT CUT TO HELL

A Paramount Picture

— 1957 —

CAST

Kyle: ROBERT IVERS; *Glory Hamilton;* GEORGANN JOHNSON; *Stan:* WILLIAM BISHOP; *Bahrwell:* JACQUES AUBUCHON; *Adams:* PETER BALDWIN; *Daisy:* YVETTE VICKERS; *Nichols:* MURVYN VYE; *Los Angeles Police Captain:* MILTON FROME; *Waitress:* JACQUELINE BEER; *Girl:* GAIL LAND; *Los Angeles Policeman:* DENNIS MCMULLEN; *Hotel Manager:* WILLIAM NEWELL; *Adam's Secretary:* SARAH SELBY; *Inspector Ross:* MIKE ROSS; *Conductor:* DOUGLAS SPENCER; *Piano Player:* DANNY LEWIS; *A. T.:* RICHARD HALE; *Mr. Henry:* DOUGLAS EVANS; *Patrolman:* HUGH LAWRENCE; *Patrolman:* JOE BASSETT; *Used-Car–Lot Manager:* WILLIAM PULLEN; *Trainman:* RUSSELL TRENT; *Ticket Seller:* JOE FORTE; *Ext. Road Driver:* ROSCOE ATES; *Guard:* JOHN HALLORAN

CREDITS

Director: JAMES CAGNEY; *Producer:* A. C. LYLES; *Scenarists:* TED BERKMAN, RAPHAEL BLAU; *Based on a screenplay by:* W. R. BURNETT; *From the novel* This Gun for Hire *by:* GRAHAM GREENE; *Photographer:* HASKELL BOGGS; *Art Directors:* HAL PEREIRA, ROLAND ANDERSON; *Set Decorators:* SAM COMER, FRANK MCKELVY; *Editor:* TOM MC ADOO; *Sound Recorders:* LYLE FIGLAND, WINSTON LEVERETT; *Musical Score:* IRVIN TALBOT; *Costumer:* EDITH HEAD; *Makeup Artist:* WALLY WESTMORE; *Special Photographic Effects:* JOHN P. FULTON; *Hair Stylist:* NELLIE MANLEY; *Assistant Director:* RICHARD CAFFEY

On the set with visitor Chester Morris

SYNOPSIS

Kyle, a young professional killer, searches for the man who has paid him off in marked money for two murders. He picks up Glory, a girl friend of the detective in charge of investigating the murders, and forcibly keeps her with him during the police hunt.

CRITICS' CIRCLE

"The picture has its moments, and the plot is still fresh and Greene enough. Director James Cagney, in his first appearance behind the camera, manages to beauty-spot a few of the bare places with some characteristic Cagney touches."

TIME

"Updated version of the 1942 *This Gun for Hire* comes off as a crackling melodrama. Marking James Cagney's first pitch as a director and A. C. Lyle's initial full producer chore, film packs enough gusty action to see it satisfactorily through program situations.

"Cagney socks over his helming in expected style from one who has specialized in hardboiled characters, and gives parts plenty of meaning."

VARIETY

"The new film marks the debut of Jimmy Cagney as director. There are some crisp flashes of his talent in which he permits the camera to do the talking, instead of the actors. Jimmy also appears in a brief prologue to introduce his new players."

Frank Quinn, New York DAILY NEWS

NOTES

Jimmy Cagney not only made his directorial debut with this conventional re-make of *This Gun for Hire*, but also appeared in a brief prologue. His deal with producer A. C. Lyles called for minimum salary but a percentage of the profits, if there were any.

NEVER STEAL ANYTHING SMALL

A Universal–International Picture
in CinemaScope and Eastman Color

—1958—

CAST

Jake MacIllaney: JAMES CAGNEY; *Linda Cabot:* SHIRLEY JONES; *Dan Cabot:* ROGER SMITH; *Winnipeg:* CARA WILLIAMS; *Pinelli:* NEHEMIAH PERSOFF; *Words Cannon:* ROYAL DANO; *Lieutenant Tevis:* ANTHONY CARUSO; *O. K. Merritt:* HORACE MAC MAHON; *Ginger:* VIRGINIA VINCENT; *Sleep-Out Charlie:* JACK ALBERTSON; *Lennie:* ROBERT J. WILKE; *Hymie:* HERBIE FAYE; *Ed:* BILLY M. GREENE; *Ward:* JOHN DUKE; *Osborne:* JACK ORRISON; *Doctor:* ROLAND WINTERS; *Model:* INGRID GOUDE; *Fats Ranney:* SANFORD SEEGAR; *Thomas:* ED (SKIPPER) MC NALLY; *Deputy Warden:* GREGG BARTON; *Policeman:* EDWIN PARKER; *Judge:* JAY JOSTYN; *1st Detective:* JOHN HALLORAN; *2nd Detective:* HARVEY PERRY; *Waitress:* PHYLLIS KENNEDY; *Coffee Vendor:* REBECCA SAND

CREDITS

Director: CHARLES LEDERER; *Producer:* AARON ROSENBERG; *Scenarist:* CHARLES LEDERER; Based on the play *Devil's Hornpipe* by: MAXWELL ANDERSON, ROUBEN MAMOULIAN; *Photographer:* HAROLD LIPSTEIN; *Unit Production Manager:* LEW LEARY; *Art Director:* ALEXANDER GOLITZEN; *Set Decorators:* RUSSELL A. GAUSMAN, OLLIE EMERT; *Editor:* RUSS SCHOENGARTH; *Sound Recorders:* LESLIE I. CAREY, ROBERT PRITCHARD; *Musical Score:* ALLIE WRUBEL; *Musical Supervision:* JOSEPH GERSHENSON; *Choreographer:* HERMES PAN; *Costumer:* BILL THOMAS; *Makeup Artist:* BUD WESTMORE; *Assistant Directors:* DAVE SILVER, RAY DE CAMP; *Songs:* "Never Steal Anything Small," "I'm Sorry, I Want a Ferrari," "I Haven't Got a Thing to Wear," "It Takes Love to Make a Home," "Helping Our Friends" *by:* ALLIE WRUBEL, MAXWELL ANDERSON

With Roger Smith, Shirley Jones and Anthony Caruso

With Shirley Jones and Roger Smith

With Shirley Jones

With Cara Williams

SYNOPSIS

Jake MacIllaney, a rough-hewn, self-taught stevedore, tries to get Linda, the girl he loves, away from her husband Dan, a young lawyer, by hanging a fake charge of corruption on him. Once Jake becomes the president of one local in the powerful longshoremen's union, there is no stopping him in his struggle to be president of United Stevedores. He makes liberal use of perjury and bribery, rigs elections, gets rid of witnesses and commits grand larceny.

CRITICS' CIRCLE

"There is no doubt that Mr. Cagney and his spirited aides make every effort to make *Never Steal Anything Small* entertaining. As the Machiavellian terror of the docks, Mr. Cagney gives a charming, bouncy and un-inhibited performance. If he makes no bones about the fact that he is older than he was twenty years ago, it is done with professional eclat and an absence of scenery-chewing. He gambols through the role with relish and, in addition to the title tune, warbles 'Sorry, I Want a Ferrari' with Cara Williams with enough verve to make this comedy item the film's cheeriest asset."

A. H. Weiler, THE NEW YORK TIMES

"Cagney is in fighting trim for his part, and the script by Charles Lederer, who also directed, gives him some fairly lively canvas to bounce around on. The songs are not much, but Cagney carries them off nicely in a hollered-out, newsboy alto that makes Shirley (*Oklahoma!*) Jones, the girl he doesn't get, sound like Renata Tebaldi. But not even the pleasure of catching Cagney at close to his best can entirely appease the sense that this is really an amoral little movie. Not even the greediest hands in labor's till have ever publicly demanded what this picture demands: the right to steal."

TIME

"Mr. Cagney attempts to make a lovable, comic, and even sentimental character out of a waterfront hoodlum. . . . Miss Jones and Mr. Cagney sing a few songs, none of any merit, and Mr. Cagney obliges at one point with a dance routine."

John McCarten, THE NEW YORKER

"The mood is spritely thanks to the frequent presence of James Cagney, who alternates as a tough gangster and a frolicsome travesty of that same specialty. . . . The events put him more in the spirit of *Yankee*

Doodle Dandy than *Public Enemy*. It is full of reminders that if Cagney had not been such a notable, swaggering gangster type, he would have been our favorite song and dance boy."

Alton C. Cook, NEW YORK WORLD-TELEGRAM

NOTES

Based upon the unproduced 1952 musical *The Devil's Hornpipe* by Maxwell Anderson and Rouben Mamoulian, this little spoof of union politics received a class-A budget from Universal-International (complete with CinemaScope and Eastman Color) that it did not warrant.

Producer Aaron Rosenberg and director-scenarist Charles Lederer were banking a lot on the Cagney name, but some things are just impossible. The script, the songs and the acting were second-rate from start to finish.

With Virginia Vincent

On the set with Cara Williams

233

SHAKE HANDS WITH THE DEVIL

A Pennebaker Production
Released through United Artists

—1959—

CAST

Sean Lenihan: JAMES CAGNEY; *Kerry O'Shea:* DON MURRAY; *Jennifer Curtis:* DANA WYNTER; *Kitty:* GLYNIS JOHNS; *General:* MICHAEL REDGRAVE; *Lady Fitzhugh:* SYBIL THORNDIKE; *Chris:* CYRIL CUSACK; *McGrath:* JOHN BRESLIN; *Cassidy:* HARRY BROGAN; *Sergeant:* ROBERT BROWN; *Mary Madigan:* MARIANNE BENET; *The Judge:* LEWIS CARSON; *Mike O'Callaghan:* JOHN CAIRNEY; *Clancy:* HARRY CORBETT; *Mrs. Madigan:* EILEEN CROWE; *Captain (Black & Tans):* ALAN CUTHBERTSON; *Willie Cafferty:* DONAL DONNELLY; *Tommy Connor:* WILFRED DAWNING; *Eileen O'Leary:* EITHNE DUNNE; *Doyle:* PAUL FARRELL; *Terence O'Brien:* RICHARD HARRIS; *Sergeant Jenkins:* WILLIAM HARTNELL; *British General:* JOHN LE MESURIER; *Michael O'Leary:* NIALL MAC GINNIS; *Donovan:* PATRICK MCALINNEY; *Paddy Nolan:* RAY MC ANALLY; *Sir Arnold Fielding:* CLIVE MORTON; *Liam O'Sullivan:* NOEL PURCELL; *Captain (Black & Tans):* PETER REYNOLDS; *Colonel Smithson:* CHRISTOPHER RHODES; *Sergeant (Black & Tans):* RONALD WALSH; *Captain Fleming:* ALAN WHITE

CREDITS

Director: MICHAEL ANDERSON; *Producer:* MICHAEL ANDERSON; *Executive Producers:* GEORGE GLASS, WALTER SELTZER; *Scenarists:* IVAN GOFF, BEN ROBERTS; *Adapta-*

tion: MARIAN THOMPSON; *Based on the novel by:* REARDON CONNER; *Photographer:* ERWIN HILLIER; *Production Designer:* TOM MORAHAN; *Production Supervisor:* WILLIAM J. KIRBY; *Set Decorator:* JOSIE MACAVIN; *Editor:* GORDON PILKINGTON; *Sound Recorder:* WILLIAM BULKLEY; *Musical Score:* WILLIAM ALWYN; *Music played by:* SINFONIA OF LONDON; *Music conducted by:* MUIR MATHIESON; *Wardrobe Supervisor:* TONY SFORZINI; *Ladies Costumer:* IRENE GILBERT; *Second Unit Photographer:* ERIC BESCHE; *Dubbing Editor:* RONALD COPPLEMAN; *Assistant Director:* CHRIS SUTTON; *Hair Stylist:* JOAN WHITE; *Special Military Adviser:* LIEUTENANT COLONEL WILLIAM O'KELLY; *Casting Director:* ROBERT LENNARD

SYNOPSIS

Kerry O'Shea, an American of Irish parentage who is attending Dublin's Royal College of Surgeons, finds himself innocently involved in the 1921 struggle for "home rule." When he is pursued by the Black and Tans, he is spirited away by one of his professors, Sean Lenihan, who, it turns out, is also a commandant of the underground rebel forces, the IRA. Although he disapproves of violence, O'Shea is convinced that he should join the rebellion against England and soon finds himself torn between his love for Jennifer Curtis and his duty to the cause.

CRITICS' CIRCLE

"It is perhaps the most successful amalgamation of exciting action and deep-thinking moral conflict since Carol Reed's *The Third Man.* . . . The acting can hardly be faulted."

PICTUREGOER

"*Shake Hands with the Devil* turns a heap of expensive ingredients—James Cagney, Don Murray, Michael Redgrave, Dame Sybil Thorndike, Dana Wynter, Glynis Johns—into an everyday Irish stew. . . . Best bit: a dockside rumble in which Cagney, jazzy as ever with his side arms, sputters some real far-out riffs on his revolver. Worst fault: the inconsistency of speech. Four of the featured players speak the king's English. Two of them talk plain American. Only the bit-players, picked up from the Abbey Theater and other Dublin companies, ever seem to have honestly laid lip to the Blarney stone."

TIME

With Donal Donnelly, Cyril Cusack, Glynis Johns and John Breslin

With Dana Wynter

"One of the fastest, toughest and most picturesque dramas about the Irish Revolution. . . . Watching Cagney, Mr. Murray and such rabid anti-British colleagues as Glynis Johns, Michael Redgrave, Sybil Thorndike and Cyril Cusack bravely tangle with the enemy occupiers of Dublin in the Twenties, a customer might wonder about the English viewpoint.

"However, Mr. Cagney's portrait of an aging, hard-headed warrior is a ferocious but tragic one, like the conflict itself, as seen here."

Howard Thompson, THE NEW YORK TIMES

"On the side of violence as the surgeon is James Cagney, still no great shakes as an actor but coming out extremely well in this one despite being handicapped by a not well-defined character."

Kenneth Johnson, TORONTO GLOBE & MAIL

With Michael Redgrave

With John Breslin and Don Murray

"The principals, paced by Cagney, are interesting and sometimes moving. But they seem posed against the Irish background, rather than part of it. Perhaps because they are required to posture in situations not authentic, the supporting cast looms larger than it should."

VARIETY

"If you shrink from the thought of another Irish story about 'the troubles' then let me say straight away that *Shake Hands with the Devil* avoids most of the usual whimsical characters and stock situations. . . . Much of the acting is excellent. James Cagney as the rebel leader, with his face of pouched granite: a misogynist taking a suspicious, compensatory satisfaction in the execution of summary, violent justice; Don Murray as an Irish-American medical student finely portraying the dilemma of a divided conscience. *Shake Hands with the Devil* is a good adventure yarn which through fastidious production and a driving integrity, often reaches distinction."

THE TIMES (London)

"Cagney gives the role everything he's got, so that he injects a fiery note into the picture which, on the whole, has enough pace and passion to electrify anyone."

Justin Gilbert, New York DAILY MIRROR

NOTES

"Those who shake hands with the devil often find they have difficulty getting their hands back" was used as the theme of this picture, depicting the 1921 struggle of the I.R.A to free the Irish people from English domination. It was filmed at the Ardmore Studios in Bray, Ireland, along the beautiful Irish countryside. The 1934 novel by Rearden Conner had the hero resolve his conflict between love and his comrades by selling them to the Tans.

Shake Hands with the Devil was well directed by Michael Anderson, who made perfect use of a tightly knit script. The production values were excellent. The international cast did splendid work and were supported by many fine Irish actors of the famous Abbey Theatre.

This is one of Jimmy Cagney's best pictures of the latter period, and contains a marvelously controlled, yet electrical portrayal of a top surgeon who is involved in the underground movement for the sheer sake of violence.

With Dana Wynter and Don Murray

THE GALLANT HOURS

A Cagney-Montgomery Production
Released Through United Artists

—1960—

CAST

Fleet Admiral William F. Halsey Jr.: JAMES CAGNEY;
Lieutenant Commander Andy Lowe: DENNIS WEAVER;
Captain Harry Black: WARD COSTELLO; *Lieutenant
Commander Roy Webb:* RICHARD JAECKEL; *Captain
Frank Enright:* LES TREMAYNE; *Major General Roy
Geiger:* ROBERT BURTON; *Major General Archie Van-
dergrift:* RAYMOND BAILEY; *Vice Admiral Robert
Ghormley:* CARL BENTON REID; *Captain Horace Keys:*
WALTER SANDE; *Captain Bill Bailey:* KARL SWENSON;
Commander Mike Pulaski: VAUGHAN TAYLOR; *Captain
Joc Foss:* HARRY LANDERS; *Father Gchring:* RICHARD
CARLYLE; *Manuel:* LEON LONTOC; *Admiral Isoroku
Hamamoto:* JAMES T. GOTO; *Rear Admiral Jiro Kobe:*
JAMES YAGI; *Lieutenant Harrison Ludlum:* JOHN MC-
KEE; *Major General Harmon:* JOHN ZAREMBA; *Colonel
Evans Carlson:* CARLETON YOUNG; *Captain Tom Lam-
phier:* WILLIAM SCHALLERT; *Admiral Callaghan:* NEL-
SON LEIGH; *Admiral Scott:* SYDNEY SMITH; *Admiral
Murray:* HERBERT LYLTON; *Admiral Chester Nimitz:*
SELMER JACKSON; *Admiral Ernest J. King:* TYLER
MC VEY; *Red Cross Girl:* MAGGIE MAGENNIO; *with,*
James Cagney, Jr., Robert Montgomery, Jr.

CREDITS

Director: ROBERT MONTGOMERY; *Producer:* ROBERT
MONTGOMERY; *Original Screenplay by:* BEIRNE LAY,
JR., FRANK D. GILROY; *Photographer:* JOE MAC DONALD;
Production Manager: GENE BRYANT; *Art Director:*
WIARD IHMAN; *Set Decorator:* FRANK MC KELVEY; *Edi-
tor:* FREDERICK Y. SMITH; *Musical Score:* ROGER
WAGNER; *Sung by:* ROGER WAGNER CHORALE; *Music
Editor:* ALFRED PERRY; *Costumer:* JACK MARTELL;

As Fleet Admiral William F. ("Bull") Halsey, Jr.

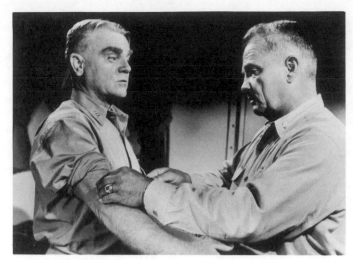

With Karl Swenson

With Raymond Bailey and Dennis Weaver

On the set with Admiral William F. ("Bull") Halsey, Jr., and Robert Montgomery

Makeup Artist: LORAND COSAND; *Special Effects:* FINN ULBACK; *Assistant Director:* JOSEPH C. BEHM; *Narrator of Japanese Sequences:* ART GILMORE; *Casting Director:* LEONARD MURRAY; *Technical Supervisor:* CAPTAIN IDRIS B. MONAHAN, USN (RET.); *Technical Consultant:* CAPTAIN JOSEPH U. LADEMAN, USN (RET.); *Japanese Navel Technical Adviser:* JAMES T. GOTO

SYNOPSIS

In this authoritative, semi-documentary study of a five-week period (October 18 to December 1, 1942) in the Pacific, Admiral "Bull" Halsey's battle becomes almost a personal one between himself and Japanese Admiral Hamamoto. What emerges is a conflict between men, rather than between nations.

The gallant hours in the life of Admiral Halsey begin when he assumes command of the American naval forces in the South Pacific and last until the smashing of the Japanese counter assault on Guadalcanal.

CRITICS' CIRCLE

"*The Gallant Hours* is Robert Montgomery's film tribute to the late Fleet Admiral William F. Halsey, with James Cagney, who bears a close resemblance to the admiral, playing the role of the officer. As a tribute it is eloquent enough and, although a few dramatic liberties may have been taken with historical fact, the film likewise comprises a rather authoritative, sometimes almost documentary, study of the functioning of high command.

"Although [the absence of battle sequences] may be disappointing to an audience, the truth is that it helps keep the picture focussed tightly on its essential point, Cagney's dignified but energetic portrait of Halsey and the solitary drama of command decision."

Paul V. Beckley, NEW YORK HERALD TRIBUNE

"No actual naval battle action is depicted in Robert Montgomery's *The Gallant Hours* . . . but there is so much superb comprehension of the ordeal an admiral goes through when he sends his ships into action, and so much sense of the endless strain of command, that there is a powerful lot more than the mere turmoil of graphic action in this film.

"Even though Mr. Montgomery has bravely put it upon the screen in a calm, unhurried fashion that belies the usual slambang of war, and may very well irritate the patron who is looking for more explosive things, it comes out in his adroit direction as drama of intense restraint and power. But it is Mr. Cagney's performance, controlled to the last detail, that gives life and strong, heroic stature to the principal figure in the film.

"There is no braggadocio in it, no straining for bold or sharp effects. It is one of the quietest, most reflective, subtlest jobs that Mr. Cagney has ever done. From it there emerges an awareness of a clever, firm, but truly humble, man who tackles a task with resolution, learns as much about it as he can, plays hunches and makes his decisions with courageous finality and then awaits the fatal outcomes with philosophical, but vastly painful, calm."

Bosley Crowther, THE NEW YORK TIMES

"*The Gallant Hours* is a dignified, dramatic documentary, relating a focal fragmentary incident in the auspicious career of Fleet Admiral William F. Halsey, with James Cagney distinguishing himself in the starring role. Montgomery, a Navy officer himself, has introduced no offside romance; has tolerated no comic jesting. Altogether, the 115-minute drama is played in low pitch. This and Cagney's dedicated performance—his every gesture and mannerism in keeping— are to the credit of all concerned. *The Gallant Hours* is not for the sensation seeker."

Irene Thirer, NEW YORK POST

"James Cagney gives an able portrait of the admiral, emphasizing the gruff, outspoken manner that was the dominant trait of his personality. Cagney also makes clear that this crusty exterior was a mask for a kindly man with a reasonable attitude toward considering objections to his decisions.

"The eccentric approach to battle drama obviously was deliberately chosen by Cagney and his producer-director, Robert Montgomery. But the dependence entirely on dialogue without action gives the picture anything but brisk pace and keeps its dramatic climax to a minimum. It is a painstaking study of a man rather than of his glorious deeds."

Alton Cook, NEW YORK WORLD-TELEGRAM AND SUN

"*The Gallant Hours* has James Cagney as the U.S. Admiral Halsey at the time of the fighting over Guadalcanal, and is much better than some of our bristling patriots suggest. Plenty of narration, which I usually disapprove of, but this is intelligently done and gives the film a documentary interest. Would you rather have a lot of splashes and bangs and model shots?"

Richard Mallett, PUNCH

"But for all its well-intentioned honesty of purpose the film would be a protracted endurance test for the mere civilian were it not for the performance of James Cagney as the Admiral; a profound compassionate study of a man in supreme authority and the gruelling strain imposed by this on an imaginative conscience.

But how did Robert Montgomery, the producer-director, ever allow a male voice choir to moon incessantly over the sound-track ludicrously opposed to the factual atmosphere?"

THE TIMES (London)

"An accurate, incisive portrayal of Halsey is created by James Cagney. The veteran actor has managed not only a correct physical suggestion of the admiral, but has successfully subordinated his own electric personality in striving for, and achieving, far more than a mere surface delineation of the character. It is a fine performance."

VARIETY

NOTES

This was a tribute, pure and simple, to one of the great militarists of the twentieth century. It stressed the loneliness of high command and the inner tension and strength that must be inside such a man during war. Director Robert Montgomery deliberately played down the physical gore of fighting and wrestled with the quiet side of such a conflict.

Cagney gave a highly individual impersonation of the Admiral. His usual energetic personality gave way to the calm seriousness of the man he was portraying. It is a fine performance.

William F. ("Bull") Halsey, 76, the subject of the story, visited Cagney on the set of *The Gallant Hours*. Said Cagney: "This film is a labor of love and gratitude to a man who, when the chips were down, performed for us. After one big scene I walked over to him and asked him if it went the way he thought it should. He said, 'You would know that better than I would. You're the pros.'"

Cagney's son Jimmy and Montgomery's son Bob were extras in this film as was Montgomery himself.

On the set with James T. Goto

ONE, TWO, THREE

A Mirisch Company, Inc. Production
in association with
Pyramid Productions, A.G.
released through United Artists in
Panavision

—1961—

CAST

C. P. MacNamara: JAMES CAGNEY; *Otto Ludwig Piffl:* HORST BUCHHOLZ; *Scarlett:* PAMELA TIFFIN; *Mrs. Mac-Namara:* ARLENE FRANCIS; *Ingeborg:* LILO PULVER; *Hazeltine:* HOWARD ST. JOHN; *Schlemmer:* HANNS LOTHAR; *Peripetchikoff:* LEON ASKIN; *Mishkin:* PETER CAPELL; *Borodenko:* RALF WOLTER; *Fritz:* KARL LIEFFEN; *Dr. Bauer:* HENNING SCHLUTER; *Count Von Droste-Schattenburg:* HUBERT VON MEYERINCK; *Mrs. Hazeltine:* LOIS BOLTON; *Newspaperman:* TILE KIWE; *Zeidlitz:* KARL LUDWIG LINDT; *Military Police Sergeant:* RED BUTTONS; *Tommy MacNamara:* JOHN ALLEN; *Cindy MacNamara:* CHRISTINE ALLEN; *Bertha:* ROSE RENEE ROTH; *Military Police Corporal:* IVAN ARNOLD; *East German Police Corporal:* HELMUD SCHMID; *East German Interrogator:* OTTO FRIEBEL; *East German Police Sergeant:* WERNER BUTTLER; *Second Policeman:* KLAUS BECKER; *Third Policeman:* SIEGFRIED DORN-BUSCH; *Krause:* PAUL BOS; *Tailor:* MAX BUSCHBAUM; *Haberdasher:* JASPAR VON OERTZEN; *Stewardess:* INGA DE TORO; *Pierre:* JACQUES CHEVALIER; *Shoeman:* WERNER HASSENLAND

CREDITS

Director: BILLY WILDER; *Producer:* BILLY WILDER; *Associate Producers:* I. A. L. DIAMOND, DOANE HAR-RISON; *Scenarists:* BILLY WILDER, I. A. L. DIAMOND; *Based on a one-act play by:* FERENC MOLNAR; *Pho-*

tographer: DANIEL FAPP; *Art Director:* ALEXANDER TRAUNER; *Editor:* DANIEL MANDELL; *Sound Recorder:* BASIL FENTON-SMITH; *Musical Score:* ANDRE PREVIN; *Production Managers:* WILLIAM CALIHAN, WERNER FISCHER; *Second Unit Director:* ANDRE SMAGGHE; *Special Effects:* MILTON RICE; *Assistant Director:* TOM PEVSNER

SYNOPSIS

C. P. MacNamara, West Berlin's manager for Coca-Cola, has his hands full with the boss's scatter-brained daughter, who is visiting from Atlanta, when she falls in love with a Red from across the Berlin Wall. Mac-Namara is at that point in the middle of a deal with the Russians, who have just been unsuccessful with their Kremlin Cola.

MacNamara is not only responsible for the girl, he is also bucking for a better job. When little Scarlett defiantly marries the young communist, in just "one, two, three" MacNamara has the task of converting him from a shaggy beatnik into a suitable husband for her.

CRITICS' CIRCLE

"In spite of the over obviousness, . . . the generally shrill character of the picture and the fact that it has been a long time since we have been able to enjoy so wholeheartedly the frantic antics of Jimmy Cagney makes it one of the bright spots of the holiday season. As a matter of fact, everybody, but particularly Cagney, shouts incessantly throughout the film, and I must admit that nobody can shout a line better than Cagney. All in all it is a personable cast, directed by Wilder with furious energy, and we do need this kind of nonsense once in a while even though it may not be in this instance quite up to the level Wilder and Diamond set for themselves and for us in their earlier farce, *Some Like It Hot.*"

Paul V. Beckley, NEW YORK HERALD TRIBUNE

"He [Wilder] purposely neglects the high precision of hilarity that made *Some Like It Hot* a screwball classic and *The Apartment* a peerless comedy of officemanship. But in the rapid, brutal, whambam style of a man swatting flies with a pile driver, he has produced a sometimes bewildered, often wonderfully funny exercise in nonstop nuttiness."

TIME

"*One, Two, Three* provides a wonderfully entertaining demonstration of Billy Wilder's way with film, cutting, comedy, performers, and the middle-European mind, Teutonic or Slav, which he knows and satirizes so well. This is the story of a Coca Cola exec played by James Cagney as if he were starting all over again to become the hardest-hitting actor in show biz."

Archer Winston, NEW YORK POST

"Who ever would have thought that at his age, Jimmy Cagney would prove to be the funniest man in films? Well, the evidence is overwhelming in *One, Two, Three.* Cagney is a full-blown, full-time, fulfilled comedian."

Justin Gilbert, New York DAILY MIRROR

"Jimmy Cagney, playing the aggressive, fast-talking, bungling, middle-aged American businessman, is the best casting since Clark Gable played Rhett Butler. I am going to make a statement without fear of being contradicted: Cagney is the only actor in the world who could give this character, MacNamara, the zest, life and humor that he puts into the part."

Wanda Hale, New York DAILY NEWS

"There is nothing subtle about it, least of all about Mr. Cagney's role, which is that of the deus ex machina (or 'mein fuehrer,' as his wife refers to him). It is simply a matter of moving very fast and getting lots of things done, from sales pitching for Coca-Cola to an automobile chase through East Berlin.

"With all due respect for all the others, all of whom are very good . . . the burden is carried by Mr. Cagney, who is a good 50 per cent of the show. He has seldom worked so hard in any picture or had such a brow-beating ball."

Bosley Crowther, THE NEW YORK TIMES

"Although that human dynamo, James Cagney, plays with notable success the part of a comic human dynamo in *One, Two, Three*, the picture's basic strength as a farce is the result of the sort of cunning and experience that went into the making of *Some Like It Hot.*"

PUNCH

"James Cagney was hammered out of spring steel, and if he were tossed from the top of the Empire State Building he would starve to death long before he stopped bouncing. It is Mr. Cagney's astounding bounce, not a whit diminished by age, that makes *One, Two, Three* an extremely funny picture, in part because he is on camera nearly every moment of the time, and also because his energy seems to prompt an

242

With Lilo Pulver and Hanns Lothar

With Horst Buchholz
and Pamela Tiffin

With Arlene Francis and Pamela Tiffin

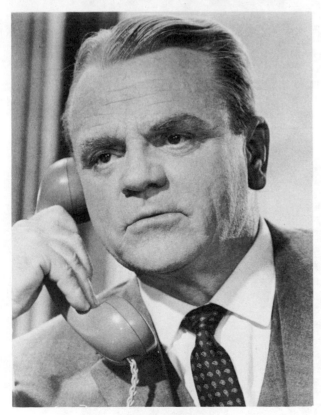

extra display of energy by everyone else in the cast, and because the screen personality that he invented long ago—that harsh, sassy, devious go-getter, at once charming and murderous-hearted on either side of the law—is able to dominate any setting."

THE NEW YORKER

"But Mr. Wilder's greatest inspiration . . . was casting Cagney as the Coca-Cola salesman. He plays it fortissimo all the way, as is right, and his vulgar vitality is just what is needed to keep the act from falling off the high wire. It often totters, but it stays on, which is all that is required."

ESQUIRE

"Cagney, I fear, has done Wilder an ill service. He shouts his way through the entire movie, bellowing and bowling over all opposition. After awhile I found myself flinching every time he gathered his breath. A man just can't keep that up without strain to the vital organs."

SATURDAY REVIEW

"The film as a whole, including the overwrought editing, takes its tone from the swift rasp of James Cagney, and the effect is not so much breathlessly funny as flustered. Its failing is really the old Broadway trouble: plenty of speed, but not much pace."

Penelope Gilliat, THE OBSERVER (London)

As C. P. MacNamara

With Pamela Tiffin and Horst Buchholz

"The cast selected for this satirical farce is a serviceable, not a distinguished, one. The key role—that of the hyperactive sales director—was entrusted to James Cagney, and he keeps things hopping in a believable and enjoyable way."

Henry Hart, FILMS IN REVIEW

NOTES

Billy Wilder offered Cagney a tremendous part as C. P. MacNamara, the Coca-Cola manager who had to convert a shaggy beatnik into a suitable husband in just "one, two, three." His performance was chock full of energy and gusto. In fact, as conceived, he never stopped shouting throughout.

Filmed entirely on location in West Berlin and at the Bavaria Studios in Munich during the summer of 1961, this was one of the funniest comedies of the sixties. Daniel L. Fapp's excitingly beautiful black-and-white photography was nominated for an Academy Award.

On the set with Lilo Pulver and director Billy Wilder

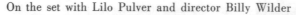

244

A THEATRE CHRONICLE

PITTER PATTER

Book by Will M. Hough
Lyrics and Music by William B. Friedlander
Adapted from *Caught in the Rain*
by William Collier and Grant Stewart
Dances and Ensembles staged by
David Bennett
At the Longacre Theatre
September 29, 1920

CAST

Bob Livingston: JOHN PRICE JONES; *Bryce Forrester:*
GEORGE EDWARD REED; *Violet Mason:* MILDRED KEATS;
Mrs. George Meriden: VIRGINIA CLEARY; *James Max-
well:* FREDERICK HALL; *Muriel Mason:* JANE RICHARD-
SON; *"Dick Crawford":* WILLIAM KENT*; *George*

* Replaced by ERNEST TRUEX

Thompson: CHARLES LEROY; *Howard Mason:* HUGH
CHILVERS; *Proprietor of Candy Shop:* GEORGE SPELVIN;
Butler: ARTHUR GREETER

THE GIRLS: Dawn Renard, Anne Foose, Billie Vernon,
Rae Fields, Hazel Rix, Aileen Grenier, Florence Davis,
Mabel Benelisha, Katherine Powers, Sunny Harrison,
Estelle Callen, Mildred Morgan, Florence Carroll,
Pearl Crossman, Violet Hazel, Grace Lee, Agnes Walsh
and Marie Boerl

THE BOYS: Messrs. Fields, Cagney, Le Voy, Grager,
Maclyn, Smith, Jackson, Jenkins and Mayo.

SONGS INCLUDED: "Somebody's Waiting for Me," "Pitter
Patter," "I Saved a Waltz for You," "Wedding Blues,"
"Bagdad on the Subway," "Send for Me," and "True
Love."

OUTSIDE LOOKING IN

By Maxwell Anderson
Based on Jim Tully's autobiography
Beggars of Life
Directed by Augustin Duncan
Settings designed by Cleon Throckmorton
At the Greenwich Village Playhouse, Inc.,
on Sept. 8, 1925
(Moved to the 39th Street Theatre
by December 1925)
(113 performances)

CAST

Shelly: WALLACE HOUSE; *Bill:* RAPHAEL BYRNES; *Rubin:*
SLIM MARTIN; *Mose:* HARRY BLAKEMORE; *Little Red:*
JAMES CAGNEY; *Edna:* BLYTH DALY; *Baldy:* REGINALD
BARLOW; *Hopper:* BARRY MACOLLUM; *Arkansas Snake:*
DAVID A. LEONARD; *Oklahoma Red:* CHARLES A. BICK-
FORD; *Deputy:* G. O. TAYLOR; *Chief of Police:* WALTER
DOWNING; *Railroad Detective:* MORRIS ARMOR; *Ukie:*
SYDNEY MACHAT; *Blind Sims:* RICHARD SULLIVAN;
Brakeman: GEORGE WESTLAKE; *Another Deputy:* FRED-
ERICK C. PACKARD, JR.; *Sheriff:* JOHN C. HICKEY

"Three or four fine performances stand clearly out of
the cast. Principally, there is Charles A. Bickford, a
vital and immense young man whom you may remember from *Zander the Great,* and whose playing here
of the part of Oklahoma Red is as much of a lark as it
is life. James Cagney does tidily as Little Red."

Gilbert W. Gabriel, NEW YORK SUN

"In a role with fewer temptations to be gaudy James
Cagney, as Little Red, is likewise complete."

NEW YORK HERALD TRIBUNE

Cagney, extreme left, with Blyth Daly and Charles Bickford in Maxwell Anderson's *Outside Looking In.*

"In that performance Reginald Barlow, James Cagney, Slim Martin and others are excellent, but the real achievement in direction was the finding of a tall, ruddy actor named Charles A. Bickford to play the rootless Oklahoma Red. He was a treasure trove."

NEW YORK WORLD

"Blythe Daly as the girl, the only one in the cast, had very little to do. Charles A. Bickford and Reginald Barlow offered the best performances, and the part of 'Little Red,' by James Cagney, was smooth."

NEW YORK GRAPHIC

BROADWAY

By Philip Dunning and George Abbott
Staged by the authors
Settings designed by Arthur P. Segal
Produced by Jed Harris
At the Broadhurst Theatre, New York City
(1926–27)

CAST

Nick Verdis: PAUL PORCASI; *Roy Lane:* LEE TRACY*; *Lil Rice:* CLARE WOODBURY; *Katie:* ELIZABETH NORTH; *Joe:* JOSEPH SPURIN CALLEIA; *Mazie Smith:* MILDRED

* Understudy: JAMES CAGNEY

246

WALL; *Ruby:* EDITH VAN CLEVE; *Pearl:* ELOISE STREAM; *Grace:* MOLLY RICHARDEL; *Ann:* CONSTANCE BROWN; *"Billie" Moore:* ELIZABETH ALLEN; *Steve Crandall:* ROBERT GLECKLER; *Dolph:* HENRY SHERWOOD; *"Porky" Thompson:* WILLIAM FORAN; *"Scar" Edwards:* ARTHUR VEES; *Dan McCorn:* THOMAS JACKSON; *Benny:* FRANK VERIGUN; *Larry:* MILLARD MITCHELL; *Mike:* ROY R. LLOYD**

** Replaced by JAMES CAGNEY in mid-1927

WOMEN GO ON FOREVER

By Daniel N. Rubin
Staged by John Cromwell
Settings designed by Louis Kennel
Produced by William A. Brady, Jr.,
and Dwight Deere Wiman
(in association with John Cromwell)
At the Forrest Theatre, New York City,
September 7, 1927
(117 performances)

CAST

Minnie: ELIZABETH TAYLOR; *Mary:* EDNA THROWER; *Billy:* SAM WREN; *Pearl:* CONSTANCE MC KAY; *Mrs. Daisy Bowman:* MARY BOLAND; *Mr. Givner:* FRANCIS PIERLOT; *Dr. Bevin:* WILLARD FOSTER; *Jake:* MORGAN WALLACE; *Pete:* OSGOOD PERKINS; *Harry:* DOUGLASS

With Mary Law in Daniel N. Rubin's
Women Go on Forever

MONTGOMERY; *Louie:* EDWIN KASPER; *Daly:* DAVID LANDAU; *Hulbert:* MYRON PAULSON; *Mabel:* MARY LAW; *Eddie:* JAMES CAGNEY; *Sven:* HANS SANDQUIST

"Mary Boland, out of farce and joyful over her chance to act, is forceful and brittle, keenly and coldly assertive as the Bowman woman."

Burns Mantle, New York DAILY NEWS

"It is played to the hilt by a good cast, wherein Mary Boland, as the raffish landlady, gives the best and the most temperate performance she has vouchsafed us in several unbridled seasons and wherein all the cast is good, notably, I think, Osgood Perkins and James Cagney."

Alexander Woollcott, THE MORNING WORLD

THE GRAND STREET FOLLIES OF 1928

(A TOPICAL REVUE OF THE SEASON)

Book and Lyrics by Agnes Morgan,
Marc Loebell & Max Ewing
Music by Max Ewing, Lily Hyland and
Serge Walter
Entire Production directed by
Agnes Morgan
Dances by James Cagney and
Michel Fokine
Music directed by Fred Fleming
Settings & Costumes designed by
Aline Bernstein
Produced by The Actor-Managers, Inc.
At the Booth Theatre, May 29, 1928
(144 performances)

CAST

DOROTHY SANDS, ALBERT CARROLL, MARC LOEBELL, PAULA TRUEMAN, GEORGE BRATT, JAMES CAGNEY, HAL BROGAN, VERA ALLEN, OTTO HULETT, LILY LUBELL, RUTH MC COONKLE, MAE NOBLE, FRANCES COWLES, JEAN CRITTENDEN, ROBERT WHITE, DELA FRANKAU, MICHAEL MC CORMACK, ROBERT GORHAM, BLAKE SCOTT, SOPHIA DELZA, HAROLD MINJIR, RICHARD FORD, MARY WILLIAMS, GEORGE ELIAS HOAG, LAURA EDMOND, JO-ANNA ROOS, GEORGE HOAG, GEORGE HELLER, MILTON LE ROY, HAROLD HECHT and JOHN RYNNE

"Among the other features of the revue worth noting were a comical burlesque of talking pictures, the Spanish dancing of Sophia Delza and the American dancing of James Cagney."

Stephen Rathbun, NEW YORK SUN

The sketches in which James Cagney appeared:

1) "MY SOUTHERN BELLE"—with Paula Trueman.

2) "FROM TANGO TO TAPS"—tap danced and tango-ed with Sophia Delza.

3) "JUST A LITTLE LOVE SONG"—he and Lily Lubell played a 1928 couple.

4) "A PARTY ON THE S.S. 'ILE DE FRANCE,' IN PORT"— as one of the Blues Dancers, with Jean Crittenden.

5) "BROADCASTING FROM STATION W.H.Y."—announcing the safety—clutch–suspenders hour.

6) "ROMEO AND JULIET" according to Max Reinhardt —Cagney was Harland Dixon as Tybalt.

7) "HEY, NONNY, NONNY"—finale.

With Sophia Delza in *The Grand Street Follies* of 1928.

THE GRAND STREET FOLLIES OF 1929

Book and Lyrics by Agnes Morgan
Music by Arthur Schwartz and Max Ewing
Additional numbers by William Irwin
and Serge Walter
Produced by The Actor-Managers, Inc.
(in association with Paul Moss)
Staged by Agnes Morgan
Dances by Dave Gould
At the Booth Theatre, New York
May 1, 1929
(53 performances)

CAST

ALBERT CARROLL, OTTO HULETT, MARC LOEBELL, DORO-
THY SANDS, PAULA TRUEMAN, EDLA FRANKAU, JAMES
CAGNEY, JUNIUS MATTHEWS, HAL BROGAN, BLAINE
CORDNER, GEORGE HELLER, MARY WILLIAMS, MAE
NOBLE, KATHLEEN KIDD, KATHERINE GAUTHIER

The sketches in which James Cagney appeared:

1) "THE GARDEN OF EDEN": *Adam*—James Cagney;
Eve—Edla Frankau; *The Serpent*—Paula Trueman

2) "THE SIEGE OF TROY" as produced by David Belasco: *Two Youths*—James Cagney and George
Heller

3) "CAESAR'S INVASION OF BRITAIN," as set to music
by Noel Coward: Force & Montana, the Dancing
Pixies—Mae Noble and James Cagney

4) "I NEED YOU SO," a Commedia dell' Arte Production: Harlequin—James Cagney

5) "PAUL REVERE'S RIDE," as produced by Jed Harris:
Hellett Loose (reporter from *The Front Page*)—
James Cagney

6) "A VICTORIAN VICTIM," produced by Civil Repertory
Theatre: Alla Nazimova—Dorothy Sands; A Dominant Male—James Cagney

7) "THE A.B.C. OF TRAFFIC": The Dancing Cop—
James Cagney

8) "GHOSTS AT THE WALDORF": Modern Jazzer—
James Cagney

248

MAGGIE THE MAGNIFICENT

By George Kelly
Staged by Mr. Kelly
Settings by Livingston Platt
Presented by Lauren & Rivers, Inc.
At the Cort Theatre, New York City
October 21, 1929
(32 performances)

CAST

Katie Giles: MARY FREY; *Etta:* JOAN BLONDELL; *Mar-
garet:* SHIRLEY WARDE; *Mrs. Reed:* MARION S. BARNEY;
Mrs. Buchannan: MARY CECIL; *Ward:* FRANK ROWAN;
Elwood: JAMES CAGNEY; *Mrs. Groves:* DORIS DAGMAR;
House Boy: RANKIN MANSFIELD; *Burnley:* J. P. WIL-
SON; *Stella:* FRANCES WOODBURY; *Mrs. Winters:* ELLEN
MORTIMER

"Your admiration need not be confined to the writing
of the play, for Mr. Kelly is his own director and he
has assembled a cast that plays with his own fidelity
. . . the scapegrace son played with clarity and spirit
by James Cagney, and the gum-chewing, posing, bra-
zen jade played by Joan Blondell."

J. Brooks Atkinson, THE NEW YORK TIMES

With Shirley Warde in George Kelly's *Maggie the
Magnificent*

PENNY ARCADE

By Marie Baumer
Directed by William Keighley
Settings by Cleon Throckmorton
Produced by Mr. Keighley and
W. P. Tanner
At the Fulton Theatre, New York City,
March 11, 1930
(24 performances)

CAST

Bum Rogers: ACKLAND POWELL; *George:* DON BEDDOE;
Mrs. Delano: VALERIE BERGERE; *Angel:* ERIC DRESSLER;
Happy: MILLARD F. MITCHELL; *Joe Delano:* PAUL
GUILFOYLE; *Mitch McKane:* FRANK ROWAN; *Sikes:*
GEORGE BARBIER; *Myrtle:* JOAN BLONDELL; *Harry Del-
ano:* JAMES CAGNEY; *Jenny Delano:* LENITA LANE;
Nolan: MARTIN MALLOY; *Dugan:* BEN PROBST; *Dick:*
HARRY GRESHAM; *Mabel:* DESIREE HARRIS; *Fred:* JULES
CERN; *Vivian:* ANNIE-LAURIE JAQUES; *Mr. James:* ED-
MUND NORRIS; *Rose:* LUCILE GILLESPIE; *Jim:* JOHN J.
CAMERON; *Anna:* ELEANOR ANDRUS; *Bob:* MARSHALL
HALE; *Jack:* WILLIAM WHITHEAD; *Johnson:* HARRY
BALCOM

"Eric Dressler, the guy that almost gets framed, he
sure can act, and this Jimmy Cagney what acts Sonny
and pulls some swell sob-stuff, and his maw, Valerie
Bergere—they certainly act natural, and this jane Joan
Blondell—they're some actors, on the level."

Robert Littell, NEW YORK WORLD

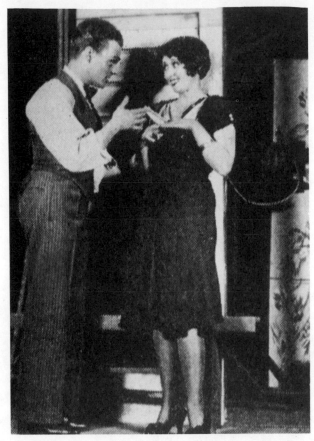

With Joan Blondell in Marie Baumer's *Penny Arcade*

"Chief among the good acting jobs were those of
James Cagney, Joan Blondell, Paul Guilfoyle and Eric
Dressler."

Philo Higley, NEW YORK TELEGRAPH